RENEWALS 458-4574
DATE DUE

GAYLORD			PRINTED IN U.S.A.

'Speaking Truth to Power'

'Speaking Truth to Power'
Religion, Caste, and the Subaltern Question in India

Edited by
Manu Bhagavan
and
Anne Feldhaus

OXFORD
UNIVERSITY PRESS

OXFORD
UNIVERSITY PRESS

YMCA Library Building, Jai Singh Road, New Delhi 110 001

Oxford University Press is a department of the University of Oxford.
It furthers the University's objective of excellence in research, scholarship,
and education by publishing worldwide in

Oxford New York
Auckland Cape Town Dar es Salaam Hong Kong Karachi
Kuala Lumpur Madrid Melbourne Mexico City Nairobi
New Delhi Shanghai Taipei Toronto

With offices in
Argentina Austria Brazil Chile Czech Republic France Greece
Guatemala Hungary Italy Japan Poland Portugal Singapore
South Korea Switzerland Thailand Turkey Ukraine Vietnam

Oxford is a registered tradé mark of Oxford University Press
in the UK and in certain other countries.

Published in India
by Oxford University Press, New Delhi

ISBN-13: 978-0-19-569305-8
ISBN-10: 0-19-569305-1

Typeset in Minion 10.5/12.5
by Eleven Arts, Keshav Puram, Delhi 110 035
Printed in Ram Printograph, Delhi 110 051
Published by Oxford University Press
YMCA Library Building, Jai Singh Road, New Delhi 110 001

for Eleanor Zelliot

Sketch by S.Y. Waghmare

CONTENTS

ILLUSTRATIONS

PREFACE

We are proud and happy to present this first of two volumes in honour of Eleanor Zelliot. We two editors are among the many contributors to these volumes whose lives and careers she has profoundly affected. As Manu Bhagavan's undergraduate professor at Carleton College, Zelliot opened up for him the world of committed, analytical historical inquiry, and after he graduated from college she continued to discuss his work with him and to follow his career actively. Anne Feldhaus was not Zelliot's student, but met her as a graduate student in India. Generous as always, Zelliot introduced Feldhaus to numerous friends and colleagues, both in India and in the United States. Most importantly, Zelliot took the young Feldhaus and her work seriously. Not only did Zelliot recommend her for numerous research fellowships, teaching positions, and posts on professional organizations, she also read the manuscript of Feldhaus's first major postdissertation project and made her own written contribution to it ('The World of Gundam Raul', in *The Deeds of God in Ṛddhipur*, translated by Anne Feldhaus. New York: Oxford University Press, 1984).

The two of us are not alone in our debt to Eleanor Zelliot. We are joined in gratitude by the many contributors to this volume and its companion (*Claiming Power from Below: Dalits and the Subaltern Question in India*. New Delhi: Oxford University Press, 2008), and also by many other students, protégés, and colleagues of Professor Zelliot who were eager to felicitate her but whose scholarly work does not fit the themes of the two volumes. To quote one of them, Irina Glushkova of the Institute of Orientology, Moscow:

Though not sharing Bai's [Zelliot's] focused attention to Dalits, I believe that the nature of that attention is far beyond the professional frames, that giving a hand whenever possible is another way of involvement, that going deep into Ambedkar movement studies, contributing to Cokha Mela's legacy, and writing an introduction to Vasant Moon's *Growing Up Untouchable in India: A Dalit Autobiography* was a historian's as well as a humanist's commitment. There are grades of 'oppression' which are sometimes recognized by scholarly analysis, and sometimes by a shrill pain in one's own heart, and Bai is an expert in both. 'Oh well, don't despair, Eleanor' is a lovely melody I have learned from her email letters—the implicit teaching and encouragement she addresses to herself has had a profound impact on each of us. Bai, you are a great optimist, moreover, you are a trained optimist, with energy and vigour both imagined and unimagined, constructed and intrinsic, and invariably brought into life and put to creation....

I remember once asking Anne Feldhaus, 'What will happen to us when we are older?' The answer was, 'Don't worry, we'll be like Eleanor.' Will we manage?

Irina Glushkova's words come from a message that she sent to be presented to Zelliot with the very first draft of these two volumes. In October 2004 we presented our first draft to Professor Zelliot at a surprise party held in conjunction with the annual Conference on South Asia at the University of Wisconsin, Madison. The book has gone through many changes and much editing since then. We are grateful to our editors at Oxford University Press for their interest in the work, and most especially to the contributors, who have been extremely cooperative and patient.

The optimism that Irina Glushkova points to in her message is the key theme of this volume. We have chosen as our title 'Speaking Truth to Power' because we believe it captures not only a basic theme of this volume but also a powerful thread of Eleanor Zelliot's life and work.

INTRODUCTION

Manu Bhagavan and Anne Feldhaus

The release in 1982 of the first volume of the *Subaltern Studies* series is regarded as a watershed in scholarly inquiry of the South Asian past and present. Ranajit Guha, in the preface to this volume, stated that the

> word 'subaltern' in the title stands for the meaning as given in the *Concise Oxford Dictionary*, that is, 'of inferior rank'. It will be used ... as a name for the general attribute of subordination in South Asian society whether this is expressed in terms of class, caste, age, gender, and office or in any other way.... There will be much ... which should relate to the history, politics, economics and sociology of subalternity as well as to the attitudes, ideologies and belief systems—in short, the culture informing that condition (Guha 1994: vii).

Subaltern Studies followed on the heels of the 1978 release of Edward Said's masterpiece, *Orientalism*, a work that linked knowledge, and its construction and dissemination, to power and exploitation, and the two methodological schools laced together over the following years to dramatically influence the way in which the study of South Asia is itself approached (Said 1994a). In 1994, Said released *Representations of the Intellectual*, in which he argued that the intellectual's true role was to 'speak truth to power', that is, to speak out against injustice and to stand morally with, and advocate for, the world's dispossessed and marginalized (Said 1994b). All of this work represented, innovative approaches in the academy and, at the same time, a harsh indictment of the academic establishment itself, for its role in maintaining and creating hierarchies of power.

Unquestionably the subaltern and Saidian methods came as shocks to the system, there were, as Ranajit Guha acknowledges in his preface, others who had been 'equally unhappy about the distortions and imbalances generated by ... [the elitist] trend in academic work on South Asian questions (1994: viii).' Indeed, since the early 1960s, one of the pioneers of modern scholarship on South Asia had been doggedly working on bringing the condition of oppressed people in South Asia to the attention of elites in the region and the world. Eleanor Zelliot studied subalterns long before it was fashionable to do so. While the 'Untouchable' or Dalit ('the oppressed', literally, 'broken to pieces') movement in India has been the principal focus of her attention, she also foresaw Guha's insight that culture informs the condition of subalternity. Her research attempts to understand as much of the caste condition as possible, and encompasses diverse topics such as mystical devotionalism (bhakti), the practice of religion (particularly Buddhism) and its political implications, the goals of political leaders and movements (especially B.R. Ambedkar and the movements he started or inspired), and the power of poetry and literature simultaneously to resist and to rejoice.

The essays in this volume and in its companion, *Claiming Power from Below: Dalits and the Subaltern Question in India*, are a tribute to the life and work of Eleanor Zelliot. Not only did Zelliot break new empirical ground, she also laid the foundation for methodological breakthroughs that occurred nearly two decades after she began her work. Importantly, Zelliot has avoided the pitfall for which Said scathingly rebuked the institutional academy. In some measure as a result of her Quaker background, Zelliot has single-mindedly 'spoken truth to power'[1] through her work. That is, rather than seeking merely to study passively and objectively the 'others' who have been the focus of her work, Zelliot has sought to involve herself in their plight, their lives, their misery, and their hope, and she has used her position and her writing to advocate their cause. Yet Zelliot has also made considerable efforts to 'let the subaltern speak' for themselves. In this, she preemptively hewed to Gayatri Spivak's later words of warning for subaltern studies, that such a postcolonial scholarly project might, in recovering subaltern subjects, re-commit acts of violence against 'them', by eliding differences, speaking for the subalterns, and locating such a voice within a hegemonic, western discourse.[2] Zelliot has chosen to work in both English and Marathi; she has collected and edited various 'subaltern' narratives in both languages, allowing her subjects to tell their own stories from their own perspective.[3] Elsewhere she has added her own judicious and careful reading and analysis, making every effort to write or speak as often as possible within fora accessible to, or administered by, Dalits specifically and South Asians more generally. As the Association for Asian Studies noted in its citation naming her the recipient of the 1999 Award for Distinguished Service to Asian Studies, Eleanor Zelliot '"changed the paradigm" in the study of South Asia'.

All of the contributors to our two volumes have been touched by Eleanor Zelliot in some way. For all of them she has been a teacher, a mentor, a generous colleague, and/or someone whose scholarly writings have influenced their work. The pieces presented over the course of our two books have been brought together in each of the areas in which Zelliot has made major contributions, so that they build on and move forward from her Earlier work. We have roughly arranged the chapters of the two volumes around the themes that Zelliot herself used in presenting her own work *From Untouchable to Dalit* (Zelliot 2001a), a collection of the most significant essays from the first three decades of her scholarly career.[4] The overall layout of the two volumes, thus, reflects the arc and coherence Zelliot herself saw as binding her publications together. *Claiming Power from Below* will explore, from a variety of angles, issues related to Dalit politics and literature. The present volume focuses on the large question of religion—in all its forms, encompassing beliefs, ethics, ritual, and artistic expression—and its role in the construction and deconstruction of caste and power in India.

In an important essay on the relevance of the bhakti movement's impact on social change in the modern world (Zelliot 2001b), Zelliot examined Chokhamela, a thirteenth- and fourteenth-century Mahar[5] saint from western India, and Eknath, a sixteenth-century Brahman saint from the same region. Chokhamela criticized the treatment of 'Untouchables', but he did not attempt to delegitimize the structure of caste as a whole. He sought to humanize Mahar suffering and to show how God's grace could be delivered to and through all manner of people, regardless of the position in which they found themselves born.

Eknath, similarly, made efforts to break down caste barriers, both in his life and through his writing, especially his *baruds*, or drama poems; he also cited Chokhamela frequently and liberally.

Both these became important figures in social reform and social justice movements of the twentieth century, though differently by clearly differentiated camps. Chokhamela was heralded by 'Untouchables'[6] in the early twentieth century, while Eknath was the preferred hero of elite, intellectual agents of social change. Devotionalism therefore served as an avenue in which change could be imagined and lived. But the lives and deeds of Chokhamela and Eknath served respectively as inspiration to very different wings of society, illustrating both the possibilities and the limitations of modern anti-caste movements: the desire for solidarity across caste lines, and the inherent problem of such unity, given the disjuncture produced by the lived reality of caste hierarchy.

Several chapters in our volume build off Zelliot's examination of bhakti to investigate ways in which devotionalism, popular narratives, and ritual can either inform socio-religious movements of liberation or act to consolidate unjust structures of power and inequality. Gail Omvedt leads off by exploring more fully the role of the early seventeenth-century 'bhakti radical' Tukaram and his role in the Varkari movement, which had been established earlier by the fourteenth-century saint Namdev. She locates her analysis in contemporary historiographical and human rights debates, arguing both that Tukaram and other bhakti radicals were crucial agents of reform and revolution and that the act of understanding this is critical to current efforts to bring about social change. Christian Novetzke picks up one strand of this thread, to focus on ways in which the saint Namdev has been remembered and reconstructed. Namdev has been compared to the western philosopher Desiderius Erasmus, a practice Novetzke illustrates here, in the process reclaiming an indigenous humanism, a significant theme in modern Indian nationalism.

Janet Davis deals with a different form of 'devotion', devotion to the lives and welfare of animals. She focuses on the relationship between American animal welfare activists and India in the late nineteenth and early twentieth centuries. Resonating with issues raised by Novetzke, Davis argues that these activists, influenced by Hindu and Jain attitudes, sought to build a 'radical humanism', one that saw in kindness to animals the foundation for a larger world vision free of racism and empire. At the same time, American animal-rights activists provided a way of 'policing the working poor' in India and the United States. In India they also played into and perpetuated a Brahmanical understanding of Hinduism, while simultaneously accepting and advocating the colonialist 'white man's burden'.

Ann Gold, Jeffrey Brackett, and Michael Youngblood turn our attention from devotional literature to folk culture, and to some other religious contexts in which hierarchy is expressed, reinforced, or opposed. Gold's contribution relays to us a sampling of narratives of oppression and resistance found in the village context. Illustrating how various narrative genres advance different social agendas, Gold not only relates stories whose theme is the moral superiority (and ultimate triumph) of Dalits, she also reminds us that not all low-caste narratives seek to circumvent power and injustice. Indeed, some continue to use chauvinistic stereotypes to mock and diminish other groups. Brackett examines an important case of the dynamics by which a rural 'folk' (that is, low-caste) god becomes urbanized and Brahmanized. Brackett shows how the monkey-god Hanumān (Mārutī) has moved from local, rural origins to become one of the most popular deities in the subcontinent. He has even become a patron divinity of Hindu nationalists, who link him with another seventeenth-century saint, the Brahman Samartha Ramdas Swami, and the Maratha king Shivaji. Youngblood explores how the 'demon king' Bali, important throughout the subcontinent but particularly in Maharashtra, is invoked differently in urban and rural settings and by members of different castes. Youngblood shows how Bali serves as a means through which economic, social, and cultural hierarchies are 'debated, challenged, or asserted'.

The contributions by Donna Wulff, Gail Minault, and Paula Richman refer to another kind of power construction: the hierarchy of gender. This is another theme that Zelliot has addressed extensively in her writings, and one that is significant for understanding her own life and academic career. In addition to a thorough and insightful bibliographical essay on English scholarship about women in Maharashtra (Zelliot 1998), Zelliot has written on the lives of medieval women bhakti saints (for example, Zelliot 2000b and 2000c), on Ambedkar's work for women's empowerment (Zelliot 2003), on the leadership roles of women in Buddhism to which he led his people in converting (Zelliot 1992 and 2000a), and on women's contributions to Dalit literature (Zelliot 1996a and 1996b). In her work on these topics, Zelliot is interested, to be sure, in injustices done to women, especially Dalit women, and the sufferings they have undergone, but her focus is more often on the personal and political actions that women have taken on their own behalf, and most especially on their creativity in expressing their experiences and aspirations in literary form.

The chapters by Wulff, Minault, and Richman examine aspects of gender hierarchy in three different religious traditions (Hindu, Muslim, and Catholic Christian) and three different regions (Bengal, urban north India, and Tamil Nadu), all in modern times. Wulff considers the case of twentieth-century women singers of West Bengali *padavali kirtan*, a type of Hindu devotional performance. Focusing on two particular women, Wulff argues that the opportunities afforded by the kirtan were constrained by existing patriarchy, and that they created a dynamic tension between domination and freedom for the performers. Minault's chapter deals with the lives of Muslim women living in purdah in the late nineteenth century. Because these women were not allowed to learn to write, we do not have direct records of their own thoughts about their lives. Reading 'between the lines' of male Muslim reformers' writings about such women, Minault is able to show that they had a language and a ritual life of their own, ways of managing interactions within their courtyard and outside it as well, and, above all, a sense of their secluded world of purdah as the central, primary world in which the things that were important took place. Finally, Richman presents a study of Bama, a south Indian Tamil Dalit writer from a village where most of the Dalits converted to Catholicism in the early twentieth century. Richman discusses significant episodes from Bama's autobiography and from a collection of Bama's stories about Dalit women. Richman organizes her discussion around three themes drawn from Zelliot's work on Dalit lives and culture: transformation, narratives, and rhetoric.

All of these chapters point to the larger role of religion in both structuring and disassembling modes of discrimination. The effort to understand such processes consumed much of Eleanor Zelliot's early work. In her broadest examination of the 'religion question', Zelliot sought to understand how practice and faith were used to legitimize various attempts at redress in the Mahar movement (Zelliot 2001d). This set the stage for several other pieces that focused more specifically on Buddhism. Buddhism is the tradition to which the great twentieth-century Dalit champion B.R. Ambedkar led his followers in an attempt to escape the burden of the caste system and the unwillingness of the Indian government to mandate reform of this system through the power of law. Much of the impact of the conversion was psychological, though this does not at all mean that it was pointless. In a careful but brief piece (Zelliot 2001c), Zelliot showed how all classes of converted Buddhists found relief in their act of conversion, from uneducated (but celebrated) singers and folk artists, to professors of Marathi language; from the Communist wing of the Dalit Panthers, the social arm of the Dalit movement, to the Ambedkar faction of the same group. Still, this relief, while providing 'a fresh sense of identity and a newly acquired confidence' (*The Times of India*, cited in Zelliot 2001c: 219), did not extend to the material poverty inflicted upon the Dalit community as a whole. Zelliot thus warns that the

rationale for conversion was psychological, but it is clear that this is not enough. Economic improvement for the masses, freedom from village harassment and urban prejudice, room at the top for the ambitious and the able—all this must come through some other path (Zelliot 2001c: 220).

Keeping this limitation in mind, Zelliot fleshed out various aspects of contemporary Buddhist practice, to further highlight the way in which Dalits live Buddhism, in the process reinscribing older 'traditions' and incorporating a host of new practices. For instance, *viharas*, the residences of Buddhist monks, have been reconfigured as meeting places to serve the social and political needs of the masses of Buddhist lay people. Of the four major 'holidays' observed by contemporary Buddhists, only one is 'traditional', the Buddha's birthday. The others commemorate the Dalit mass conversion to Buddhism in 1956 and the birth and death anniversaries of Ambedkar. Indeed, even the Buddha's birthday observance is linked with the modern Dalit movement, since its celebration was initiated by Ambedkar himself in 1950. Zelliot's work, thus, has been instrumental in highlighting the ways in which religion generally, and Buddhism specifically, has been claimed, modified, and practiced by the marginalized in order to carve for themselves spaces of dignity and solidarity.

Guy Welbon, Laura Jenkins, Gary Tartakov, and Gopal Guru offer essays in this spirit. Welbon takes us to the beginnings of the Buddhist tradition to examine Buddhism's early relationships with the low-caste and despised. Re-reading some early Pali texts, he discusses the representation of the barber Upali, 'the first great master of the discipline', and briefly contrasts this hero with another barber, Subhadda, seen as villainous for having rejoiced at the Buddha's death. Jenkins writes about more modern Buddhists. Focusing specifically on the Dalit conversion led by B.R. Ambedkar, Jenkins listens to the voices of some of the converts who followed him into Buddhism. She is thus able to flesh out in greater detail what Zelliot termed the 'psychological' impact of the conversion.

Tartakov picks up this point, and moves us to an investigation of the ways in which Ambedkar's followers reinterpreted older Buddhist symbols and concepts and blended them with newer tropes and iconography to create innovative ways of expressing their identity. In addition to revisiting some of Zelliot's work on viharas, Tartakov also examines a wide range of Dalit Buddhist artistic expression, to argue that such aesthetics are radical forms of social change, indeed revolutionary in the truest sense. One aspect of Tartakov's chapter centres on statues of Ambedkar that have sprung up in public places all over Maharashtra and beyond. Gopal Guru's essay refers to these statues as well as to other portrayals and idealizations of Ambedkar among Dalits today to discuss the ways in which 'Babasaheb' Ambedkar has himself become an object of belief. Guru delineates and criticizes popular Dalit imagery of Ambedkar as a superhuman, as a saviour, and as a model modernist, while commenting on how class can affect the constructions and reading of such a 'champion'.

We close this volume with Syed Akbar Hyder's presentation of examples of the devotional performance genre called *qawwali*. This poetry from the Sufi, mystical devotional tradition returns us to the point at which we began this book: Zelliot's trust in bhakti—mystical devotionalism—to open up new avenues for communication, justice, and equality. Through the poems, Hyder illustrates how literature and alternative religious discourse often combine to provide a framework that can be more accommodating of difference and less rigidly hierarchical than that produced by more formal, orthodox religious authority.

NOTES

1. 'Speak truth to power' holds a prominent place in Quaker history, and is often associated with a meeting between George Fox and Oliver Cromwell in 1653.

2. Spivak 1988. See also a cogent synopsis at: *http://postcolonialweb.org/poldiscourse/spivak/spivak2.html*, accessed on 27 April 2007.
3. See the bibliography of Eleanor Zelliot's works at the end of this volume.
4. While *From Untouchable to Dalit* serves as the source for many of Zelliot's works referred to in this Introduction, in order to provide a sense of the chronology of her scholarship we also include in the bibliography the year each essay mentioned was originally published.
5. Mahars are an 'Untouchable' caste.
6. This was the term used in English common parlance at the time. From this point forward we will simply use the term 'Dalit' to refer to oppressed castes at any point in South Asian history, in measure to deny the validity of the idea of untouchability. However, as untouchable-ness as a concept and a term marked a particular formation of tyranny, we shall use it as appropriate when quoting from a caste-ist, discriminatory view.

REFERENCES

Bhagavan, Manu and Anne Feldhaus. 2008. *Claiming Power from Below: Dalits and the Subaltern Question in India*. New Delhi: Oxford University Press.
Guha, Ranajit (ed.). 1994 [1982]. *Subaltern Studies I*. New Delhi: Oxford University Press.
Said, Edward. 1994a [1978]. *Orientalism*. New York: Vintage Books.
_____. 1994b. *Representations of the Intellectual: The Reith Lectures*. New York: Pantheon Books.
Spivak, Gayatri Chakravorty. 1988. 'Can the Subaltern Speak?'. In Cary Nelson and Lawrence Grossberg (eds). *Marxism and the Interpretation of Culture*. Urbana: University of Illinois Press, pp. 271–313.
Zelliot, Eleanor. 1992. 'Buddhist Women of the Contemporary Maharashtrian Conversion Movement'. In José Cabezón (ed.). *Buddhism, Sexuality and Gender*. Albany: State University of New York Press, pp. 91–107.
_____. 1996a. 'The Poetry of Dalit Women'. In Saral K. Chatterji and Hunter P. Mabry (eds). *Culture, Religion and Society: Essays in Honour of Richard W. Taylor*. Delhi: Indian Society for Promoting Christian Knowledge, pp. 227–38.
_____. 1996b. 'Stri Dalit Sahitya: The New Voice of Women Poets'. In Anne Feldhaus (ed.). *Images of Women in Maharashtrian Literature and Religion*. Albany: State University of New York Press, pp. 65–93.
_____. 1998. 'A Bibliographic Essay on Women in Maharashtra'. In Feldhaus (ed.). *Images of Women in Maharashtrian Society*, pp. 256–71.
_____. 2000a. 'Religious Leadership among Maharashtrian Buddhist Women'. In Ellison Banks Findly (ed.). *Women's Buddhism: Buddhism's Women*. Sumerville, MA: Wisdom Publications, pp. 259–74.
_____. 2000b. 'The Untouchable Women Saint-poets of Maharashtra'. In

Mariola Offredi (ed.). *The Banyan Tree: Essays on Early Literature in New Indo-Aryan Languages.* New Delhi: Manohar, pp. 273–82.

_____. 2000c. 'Women Saints in Medieval Maharashtra'. In Mandakranta Bose (ed.). *Faces of the Feminine in Ancient, Medieval, and Modern India.* New York: Oxford University Press, pp. 192–200.

_____. 2001a [1972]. *From Untouchable to Dalit.* New Delhi: Manohar.

_____. 2001b [1980]. 'Chokhamela and Eknath: Two Bhakti Modes of Legitimacy for Modern Change'. In Zelliot. *From Untouchable to Dalit,* pp. 3–32.

_____. 2001c [1977]. 'The Psychological Dimension of the Buddhist Conversion'. In Zelliot. *From Untouchable to Dalit,* pp. 218–21.

_____. 2001d [1978]. 'Religion and Legitimization in the Mahar Movement'. In Zelliot. *From Untouchable to Dalit,* pp. 197–215.

_____. 2003. 'Dr Ambedkar and the Empowerment of Women'. In Anupama Rao (ed.). *Gender and Caste.* New Delhi: Kali for Women, pp. 204–17.

1

THE BHAKTI RADICALS AND UNTOUCHABILITY

Gail Omvedt
Translations from Marathi
by Gail Omvedt and Bharat Patankar

TUKA AND THE VARKARIS

The Varkari movement centred on the god Vithoba, located at Pandharpur on the banks of a tributary of the Krishna River in southern Maharashtra, a god with Kannada 'hero-deity' origins, identified with Vishnu/Krishna in the Brahmanic tradition. The story is that the God (Krishna/Vishnu) came from Dwarka to the semi-mythical original devotee, Pundalik; Pundalik however was so engrossed in service to his parents that he told the God to wait, throwing a brick for him to stand on. The brick has been ever since a unique symbol of Vitthala or Vithoba (an important historical survey is given in Zelliot 1990).

The Varkari movement began with the *shimpi* (tailor) Sant Nama (Namdev) in the fourteenth century (Novetzke 2002). In spite of some impressive scholarship, we still do not have the full history of the movement. Although various groups and villages apparently maintained sites within Pandharpur, described as *phad*s in one of Tuka's *abhang*s (song-poems) (#190), the *palkhi*s (processions) we know of today, which organize the pilgrimage centred around particular sants identified with different castes, really only began during the colonial period. As Engblom has pointed out, the first major palkhi was that of Dnyaneshwar (the Brahman outcast Sant, also fourteenth century), organized by a Brahman 'nobleman from Satara district' at the very end of the eighteenth century; the same man also established the first official *dindis* or bhajan-singing groups and set the order of the songs. This obviously was a further form of social control of how the sants' teachings were to be understood. Engblom also emphasized that the Varkari tradition, centring around the pilgrimage, exists even today quite separately from the ritual life of the temple itself, which is highly Brahmanized (Introduction to Mokashi 1990: 8–11, 18–19).

Another sign of Brahmanization is similar to that stressed in Parita Mukta's study of Mirabai (1997): the existing most popular cassettes and CDs by and large use a style of singing that is classical or semi-classical, which must be far from the rhythmic, popular forms used by the sants themselves. The greatest sants must have been powerful, rhythmic singers, capable of awakening and inspiring listeners who were not aristocrats lounging on cots or pillows but women and men farmers and labourers tired from long days of toil; their songs must have been very different from the 'raga' forms we hear in cassettes and CDs today.

The fact that in spite of egalitarian traditions, the palkhis are now identifiable with particular sants and joined primarily by people of the *jati* (caste) of that sant, is one of the signs of the continued hold of jati in the society. The predominance of the Dnyaneshwar palkhi indicates clear Brahmanization. Nevertheless, the annual pilgrimage to Pandharpur still draws hundreds of thousands of people and represents a vibrant tradition of equality and openness towards Muslims even in the face of Hindutva efforts (Youngblood 2003).

METHODOLOGY

There are crucial methodological issues in analysing any of the bhakti sants. This is a general problem of Indian social history, that of sources. This lies in the fact that almost all of its documentation—and thus interpretation—was in the hands of upper castes. In the 'early-modern' period, in spite of a symbiosis among Sufis and radical bhakti sants, Brahmanic dominance and caste hierarchy remained consolidated in much of India. Muslim rule, it was true, opened up some space for dissidence, but Brahmans dominated also within the administrations of the Mughals and other Muslim rulers, and these administrations thus were as ready as Hindu overlords to enforce *varnashrama dharma*.

In contrast to Buddhism and Jainism, and later Sikhism, which succeeded in establishing an independent political structure, the whole process of interpretation and maintenance of records of the bhakti movement has been in the hands of Brahman men. Where the movements were centred around a particular temple or place of pilgrimage, the priests have been Brahmans. The biographies of the sants were written by Brahmans. In the case of the north Indian sants, an early account was by Nabhadas around 1600, with the most influential commentary that of Priyadas in 1712. As for the Varkaris, the most influential account was written by Mahipati in the eighteenth century, though the first biography of Tuka was written by his grandson. As More (1996: 86–90) describes the history of the family, it is clear that they compromised with Brahmanic powers within that generation.[1] The problem of a 'critical edition', of identifying which of even existing song-poems of the sants are authentic, is immense, even where, as in the case of Tuka, who himself kept notebooks, there are clear examples of interpolations.

This upper-caste control has had several important consequences. First, it meant a downplaying of the conflict with traditional authorities. The Marathi Varkari tradition, for example, has been argued to be one of *mahasamanvay*, a 'great harmonious conjunction' or 'coming together' by Dhere (1984) and, even more, G.P. Deshpande (2002). It would be accurate to say that the Varkaris brought together a mahasamanvay that included Muslims and sants from other regions of India, but that this meant a fight with Brahmanism.[2] But the usual interpretation of the mahasamanvay makes it a 'Maharashtrian' tradition (ignoring the links with a broader northern and western Indian radical bhakti trend) that involves a compromise with Brahmanism.

Second, upper-caste control meant a tendency to overemphasize the role of upper-caste sants (for instance, making Dnyaneshwar the founder of the Varkari movement). It is striking that the abhang most quoted here—'Dnyandev laid the foundations.... Tuka became the pinnacle', though attributed to Tuka's woman disciple Bahenabai, cannot be found in any of her collected verses (see More 1996: 28, Bahenabai 1979).

Third, the process of linking the movement to more orthodox Brahmanic traditions is done partly by giving the sants Brahman gurus. Thus Kabir and Ravidas were both said to be followers of the south

Indian Brahman Ramanand, while, on the basis of what is likely an interpolated abhang, Tuka is said to have had one Babuji as his own guru, linking him to Chaitanya. The well-known poet and translator Dilip Chitre (1990, 1991) is among those who accept abhangs like this one without any discussion of the problems of interpolation. All this attribution of Brahman gurus goes on in spite of the fact that there is little evidence within the poems of the sants themselves. Ravidas, for instance, himself never mentions Ramanand, who seems to have lived a full century before him. In the case of Kabir, there is little indication in his existing song-poems that he knew Ramanand, let alone as a guru. The 'Ram' in his poems is abstract, simply a name for the divine, and he roundly attacks the whole theory of avatars, including the hero of the Mahabharata (Hawley and Juergensmeyer, 1988: 35–49; Hess 1983: 3–6). The claim that Babuji was Tuka's guru goes against other claims for 'gurus' and is vigorously contested by one of his important recent interpreters, A.H. Salunkhe, who goes into the issue at length (Salunkhe 1997: 137–69). Most importantly, Salunkhe points out that the whole tone of Tuka's thinking was—like the early Buddhists', in fact—to emphasize one's own experience and thus reject the very notion of a guru. The abhang that says this, in other words, can hardly be taken as valid without further justification.

Fourth, we can see the attempt to 'uplift' the Dalit sants in *varna* terms; for instance, Ravidas is said to have been a Brahman in his previous life, but because he offered Ramanand some food that had been given by a merchant who had dealings with Chamars, he was reborn as a Chamar. This itself indicates the degree of purity-pollution behaviour observed even by Brahman ascetics; but worse if anything is the story that as a baby Ravidas would not accept the milk of his Chamar mother, but only that of a Brahman woman (Hawley and Juergensmeyer 1988: 15–16)!

Finally, there has been a clear reluctance to admit Muslim influences on the bhakti movement—a major problem for scholars today. Many of the famous sants of north India (Kabir and Dadu, for instance) came from Muslim backgrounds. In Maharashtra, the guru of Eknath, one of the most important of the Maharashtrian Varkaris, was Janardana, himself a disciple of Sufi Canda Bodhale (van Skyhawk 1992: 67). This link with Islam, however, has been systematically downplayed from both sides of the current Hindu-Muslim divide;[3] as Ikram points out,

The metamorphosis which the life story and teachings of Kabir and Dadu have undergone ... is symptomatic of the general movement of separation that became common in both Islam and Hinduism in later centuries. As the Muslims grew more orthodox, they turned away from men such as Kabir and Dadu, while the Hindus accepted them as saints but forgot their Islamic origin (Ikram 1964: 128).

Whereas it is said that Hindus and Muslims fought over Kabir's ashes, within a century or so the Muslims were ignoring it and Brahmanic Hindus claimed this and other movements, but distorted them in the process. Thus orthodox Muslims and *dvija* (twice-born) Hindus, both of whom Kabir had solidly attacked, each responded in their own way to his challenge to their religiosity. Today, the surviving institutions of almost all the sant-traditions are dominated by Brahmanism and are heavily Sanskritized, from the Kabir Panth to the 'official' Varkari organization in Maharashtra, which is controlled by the Vishva Hindu Parishad (VHP) (Youngblood 2003).

If we look at the history of the Varkari movement, Dnyaneshwar is normally considered its founder. In the popular tradition today, his name is coupled with Tuka's—'Gyanba-Tuka'. Dnyaneshwar wrote abhangs, but his most influential writing was what is called the *Dnyaneshwari*, a Marathi philosophical commentary on the Bhagavad Gita. Dnyaneshwari *parayan*s (readings) are a normal practice in Maharashtrian villages today, sponsored usually by the village elites, while the more genuinely popular abhangs of Tuka and others are rarely heard. Yet most scholars today believe that it was Nama (Namdev), the fourteenth-century shimpi sant, who really made Vitthala of Pandharpur the centre of the movement, wandering all over India and writing poems in various languages/dialects now comprised under Hindi, as well as having his poems in the Adi Granth of the Sikhs. It is Nama also who is projected by Tuka himself as the real founder in another abhang on the 'game' theme (#190). Here Nama is mentioned first, 'He made Vitthal the leader, ho!' and then come 'Dnyandev, Muktabai, Sopan, Changa Vateshwar', who 'made the cowherd Kanho [Krishna] the leader in their game'.[4] This appears to be historically and sociologically accurate—Namdev focusing on Vithoba, and Dnyaneshwar and others identifying the god (originally a Kannada 'hero-devata') with Krishna.

Thus there is a problem of recovering the 'authentic' song-poems (bhajans, abhangs, *dohas*, *shabda*, etc.) of all of the sants. In the case of Kabir, Ravidas, Cokhamela, and Mirabai, none were written down until long after their deaths. Tuka was able to write in spite of the tradition against it, and at great cost kept his own notebooks. But while over 4700 songs exist in the current official government collection (Tukaram 1973), there has never been even an attempt to do a critical edition. Some are clearly not his (that is, they are 'signed' by his brother, 'Tukyabandhu', or disciple, 'Tukyasevak'); some are clearly interpolations, for example, an abhang to Shivaji (#1886) which describes the king as *chhatrapati* (which would have been impossible considering that Tuka met Shivaji at the very beginning of his career!).

I have, in my own selections from Tuka here, used fairly simple criteria to look for the authentic abhangs: first, it is likely that the most anti-caste, anti-Brahmanic ones were genuine—since this went against the interests of the record keepers. There are some abhangs whose metaphors obviously contradict his otherwise strong views on issues of caste equality, and these I exclude on grounds of simple rationality. Second, there is a more amorphous question of feel and style—Tuka's language was sharp, his metaphors strong and compelling; abhangs with vague, abstract, metaphysical imagery simply do not ring true. Third, I exclude abhangs in which he describes himself in very deprecatory terms—all his work indicates that he did not have a low self-image; when he described his caste status as low he was simply critiquing the social view of him.[5]

Finally, I am simply bracketing most of his references to the Vedas and Puranas. Tuka very often takes the position of not critiquing the Vedas as such (in contrast to Kabir, who very sarcastically and frequently does so). Rather, he claims that he knows what the Vedas really say and that he is expounding them. This is itself a radical claim for someone who could not by tradition even read the Vedas—and it has satisfied most scholars, with More (1996: 182) claiming that Tuka is therefore *vedapramanya* (accepting the primacy of the Vedas) and Salunkhe (1997: 57–60) also arguing that it shows his greatness. It seems to me that Tuka would have had to be very naïve to believe that he really knew what the Vedas said. There are thus several possibilities. First, it is possible that he changed his views with time—starting out with the faith, inherited from many earlier Varkaris, that the Brahmanic scriptures were after all on his side, but then changing it as he gained experience and self-confidence. Second, referring to the Vedas as justification could have been a conscious political strategy. It should be noted that Tuka's position here differed from that of Kabir, who lived under long-established Muslim rule; while the Bijapur kingdom in the South was indeed Muslim at the top, its entire administration was filled with Brahmans, and the political regime was thus extremely dangerous for Tuka. Trying to 'moderate' his open radicalism with some bow to tradition was a means of simple survival—and one that, in the end, did not work. And lastly, one might argue that some of the Vedic-Puranic references are later interpolations.

With this as a background, let us look at some characteristics of caste and untouchability in the song-poems of the bhakti radical sants, and especially Tuka.

TERMINOLOGY: THE IDENTIFICATION OF JATIS AND THE REALITY OF THE CASTE SYSTEM

God ignores our hierarchies
showing loyalty only to devotion.
He eats the food of the slave's son Vidur,
gives protection to Prahlad in the demon's house.
He helps Rohidas in dy[e]ing leather,
and Kabir in weaving on the loom.
He helps Sajanak to sell his meat,
and weeds the field with Savata,
helps goldsmith Narhari to heat the metal,
with Cokhamela hauls dead cattle.
With Nama's Jani he gathers dung,
and waters the tree in the house of Dharma.
He feels no difficulty in dining with Nama,
and pulls Dnyana's wall on his body,
He holds the reins of Arjun's horse,
and eats the loving breakfast of Sudam.
He tends the cow in the house of the Gawlis,
became a guard at Bali's door.
Rishikeshi pays the debt of Yankoba,
suffers the pregnancy of Aamarishi.
He drinks the poison meant for Mirabai

and becomes the Mahar messenger for Damaji,
carries the clay for Gora on the wheel
and fills the bill of exchange of the Mahanta.
For Pundalik he is standing still in wait—
says Tuka, his accomplishments are great. (#2820)

Blessed the lineage, holy the land,
Where the servants of Hari are born ....
Karmadharma's become Narayan,
it's he who has purified the worlds. [refrain]
Who is purified by pride
of varna, tell me if you know!
Untouchables are saved by hymns to Hari,
legendary stories become their bards.
Tuladhar Vaishya, the potmaker Gora,
the leatherworker Rohidas,
The momin Kabir, Latif the Muslim,
the barber Sena are Vishnudas.
Kanhopatra, Khodu, cotton-carder Dadu,
sing hymns to Hari without discord.
Banka, Chokhamela, by caste Mahar,
have united with the Lord.
What is the worth of Nama's Jani,
when Pandhari's lord eats in her company?
Can you tell the lineage of Mairala?
What greatness did he have, do tell!
Vishnu's servants have no caste,
the Veda's science so decrees.
Tuka says, which of your books
have saved the fallen—I know of none. (#4299)

These two abhangs show a notable feature of Tuka's (and much
other Varkari) poetry, that is, a very specific use of jati names along with
the general varna terminology. Thus, in the above abhangs we have
not only the theme of a wide identification of the Varkari movement—
so that not only the known Maharashtrians, but also Puranic figures
and Kabir, Rohidas, and Mirabai become part of the movement—but
there is also specific jati identification. Savata is a Mali, Narhari a Sonar,
Gora a Kumbhar, Ravidas a Chambhar, Kabir a Momin, Sena a Nhavi,

Dadu a Pinjari (a Muslim 'cotton carder'), and Cokhamela a Mahar. The terminology is Maharashtrian, as can be seen in the case of Kabir (who would be a 'Julaha' in north Indian terms) and Ravidas (who would be 'Chamar'). It seems here that we are not simply talking about occupation, but about jati itself. Similarly, just as Eknath has a whole series of voices of village characters (Zelliot 1987), so did Tuka, with varying dialects and varying names (see Tukaram 1973 #127–9, 429–77. Many of these are translated in Fraser and Marathe 2000).

In many other places the varna terms are used, sometimes with five categories: 'Brahman, Kshatriya, Vaishya, Shudra, and Chandala' (#1142)—that is, the four varnas with Untouchables as a separate category. 'Chandala' is the normal abstract term for Untouchables, but in at least one place *shvapac* is used (#1471). Thus there are two types of categories—the varna ones, which are abstract and ideological, and the 'empirical' jati categories, which refer to actual caste-communities. Tuka himself clearly differentiates these, speaking of 'varna' and *'yaati'* (a variant form of 'jati') at many points.

It is fashionable to argue today that caste is constructed (in a process of discourse, like all social phenomena). It is even more fashionable to say that it was constructed during the colonial period by British processes of enumeration, classification, and other administrative practices. Dirks (2001) is the most recent exponent of this point of view, and Champalakshmi (2002) sees him as saying that

Caste endures and is so significant today because it has been the precipitate of a powerful history, in which colonial role (and rule) has been very significant. Caste...became a core feature of colonial power/knowledge.

A sociological methodology can easily refute this position. All social phenomena are constructed not by one set of actors only, but by all the members of society. And they are constructed within a context with an outcome that is not determined by the intentions of any individual or set of individuals. Weber called this the 'unanticipated consequence' of social action; Adam Smith spoke of an 'invisible hand'; and, as Marx put it, 'Men make history but they make it under conditions not of their choosing'. This means that in social analysis it is not enough to take into account the meaning of the action to the actor; the 'material' social structure must be analysed.

As for the unique role attributed to the colonial period, processes initiated then certainly affected the structure and practices of the caste system, but the hegemonic actors in the process were the Indian elite as much as the British.[6] And the system itself existed long prior to the colonial period, however loose and flexible it may have been. Just as 'race' in the United States is a social reality, a socially constructed category with real consequences, one with amorphous and shifting identifications, so is caste in India. The boundaries of any jati may be amorphous; people may be able to move between jatis by 'passing' in various forms. But the system remains, and it is a system that exploits and humiliates those considered low.[7] The very antagonism with which the radical bhaktas condemned jati and varna, and often the Vedas and panditry behind them (and even in the case of Tuka, advaita itself), indicates the exploitativeness of the system.

'MY CASTE IS LOW'

Time and again Tuka declares the 'low' characteristics of his own caste: 'Born of shudra lineage and so, free from hypocrisy.... I have no right to read and write. In all ways poor [din]—Tuka says, my caste is low [hin]' (#2766). Strikingly, he was considered 'low' even though he was a Kunbi, of a *mahajan* or moneylending and landowning family which was well-to-do to begin with, though they lost wealth during the famine. His family remained poor as a result of Tuka's refusal to be a moneylender and his notorious tendency—criticized by his wife in many well-known abhangs—to give away whatever food came his way. As a Shudra, whether well off or poor, he was not supposed to be literate. So serious was the 'crime' of writing that it was one of the accusations against him when he was brought before the village council and his notebooks were thrown into the river Indrayani, a famous, much-debated incident recorded in abhangs and legends.[8] Nevertheless, he has an advantage over earlier sants in having acquired, somehow, writing skills and the ability to keep his own notebooks. He was in a better position with regard to social status than the Dalit sants, such as Chokhamela and Ravidas. In the case of all of these, I would argue that the sants recognized their social stigmatization, but did not internalize it. The pain of caste humiliation lies in the fact that stigma is normally internalized, and those who escape this have to do so through sometimes prolonged psychological struggle. There are many songs showing Tuka's opposition to untouchability and caste:

He's not a Brahman who abhors
the touch of a Mahar.
What retribution will suffice?
except to sacrifice his life! [refrain]
He won't touch a Chandal,
it's his heart that's defiled.
Tuka says, his caste's defined
by what fills his mind. (#55)

Short and simple, this is perhaps Tuka's most famous abhang on untouchability, referring to both the symbolic (Chandala) and the actual jati (Mahar). An even more famous abhang, sung by Lata Mangeshkar and reproduced on many cassettes and CDs, expresses the theme of forgetting varna and caste, and emphasizes that the Vaishnavas triumph because they fall at each other's feet, humbling themselves before each other—rather than the 'low' humbling themselves before the 'great':

They've organized a game on the river sands.
The Vaishnavas are dancing, ho!
Pride and wrath they trample underneath their feet,
at one another's feet they're falling, ho!
They dance in thunderous joyousness,
singing holy songs and names, ho!
To the dark ages challenging,
one is stronger than the other, ho! [refrain]
Sandal paste on foreheads, rosaries and garlands,
they parade themselves with pride, ho!
Cymbals and tabors, a showering of flowers,
an unparalleled festival of joy, ho!
Engrossed in music and entranced
are my simple sisters and brothers, ho!
Pandits, meditators, yogis, Mahanubhavas,
all have won unequalled powers, ho!

Forgotten is the pride of varna and of caste,
each humbling himself before the next, ho!
Minds have become as pure as melted butter,
The stones themselves will melt at last, ho!
Cries of victory reach up to the sky.
The Vaishnava heroes feel their power, ho!
Tuka says, you've made an easy road,
To cross the oceans of our life, ho! (#189)

Tuka's egalitarianism, however, just as often expresses itself in bitter, oppositional terms. In an abhang that refers to Ravidas, Tuka says:

He's a devotionless Brahman, let his face burn.
From what concubine was he born?
Blessed is the mother of the Vaishnava Chambhar;
his lineage and his caste is pure. [refrain]
It is not simply what I say—this is the decision given anciently.
Tuka says, let this greatness burn up in fire,
I don't want to even see these evil men. (#1319)

In other words, egalitarianism and the achievement of self-respect for Untouchables and Shudras required a rejection of caste and Brahmanism itself.

The cunning grab for coins and sell
their daughters as concubines.
Such is the dharma of our time,
the good is slave, the evil strong. [refrain]
Leaving righteousness,
Brahmans have become vile thieves.
They hide the tilak on their face,
and dress in Muslim clothes.
They sit on thrones oppressing
to keep the people starving.
They manage public kitchens,
living on oil and butter.
They're servants of the base;
get beatings for mistakes.

The king exploits the people,
holy places nourish evil.
The Vaishyas, Shudras, and all
are naturally so low.
These are all the outer colours,
the green inside is masked by sham.
Tuka says, O God,
don't sleep, but run to help! (#267)

This roundly attacks both kings and Brahmans, as well as almost all powerholders (a whole series of abhangs is also scathingly critical of the *shakta* cults). It could, of course, be read as arguing that the king should be (and thus could be) just, that Brahmans should be (and could be) meritorious, challenging the degradation of an ideal, not the ideal itself, and thus accepting the role of the Brahman and the king. Sometimes in fact an 'ideal Brahman' is described. However, actual Brahmans and kings as depicted throughout the song-poems are so consistently bad that this seems a problematic interpretation. If we compare this way of handling the *kaliyuga* theme with an obvious interpolation that I call 'The Brahman's Lament' (#3035), we can see that Tuka interprets degradation not just as falling into evil ways, but in terms of exploitation as such.

Call him pandit, he's in bliss,
yet everywhere he looks an ass.
What will you do by muttering
the Vedas, wasted sputtering. [refrain]
He does not do what the Vedas say,
Brahma's equality is kept away.
Tuka sees the good in life,
This is his experience. (#1622)

It is also important that while the typical hardline Brahmanical tendency downgrades the Varkari movement by stressing the softness and non-violence of the sants in contrast to the hard-core militant orthodoxy of Ramdas (see the discussion in More 1996: 657–64), Tuka's song-poems, as well as his life, indicate not simple non-violence but a militant opposition to injustice:

We servants of Vishnu are softer than wax,
but hard enough to shatter diamonds.
Dead but alive, awake while asleep,
whatever is asked of us we go on giving. [refrain]
We give away the clothes off our bodies,
but we'll give a blow to the knaves.
We are more loving than mother or father
but ruthlessly destroy our enemies.
Amrut has no sweetness compared to us,
and poison has no bitterness.
Tuka says, we are sweet all through,
we give what everyone has longed for. (#987)

As Zelliot has noted, 'With this poem we cannot but help entertain ideas about bhakti in the modern world—the bhakti poets as moralists, as crusaders against casteism and evil, as agents of change' (Zelliot 1987: 45). Far from the 'non-violence' of the Varkaris making them helpless, as orthodox Brahmanic propaganda has it, it is clear that they were militant fighters of their time.

THE FOUNDATION OF 'HUMAN RIGHTS' IN INDIA: AGAINST CASTE AND UNTOUCHABILITY

The debate today about the foundations of modernism, secularism, and human rights is particularly intense. Many Indian intellectuals still argue that the major dilemma of India today is that these are somehow 'western'; having been brought from the west during the colonial period, they can find little real acceptability. These intellectuals pose a supposedly collective tradition (which does not separate Brahmanic and inegalitarian from non-Brahman/egalitarian aspects) against western 'individualism'.[9] This has been a fashionable 'post-modern, post-colonialist' approach, and today it finds most of its sincere proponents standing horrified at the power of the Hindutvavadis, who condemn the proponents of equality as westernized Indians and 'pseudo-secularists'. The response to this from most Indian left-progressives has simply been to reassert Nehruvian or Gandhian secularism. While sincere Nehru-Gandhian secularism may be the best hope in current conditions at the political level, in the long term and at the theoretical level it is not enough. For the Hindutvavadis are right in saying that there is no real difference between 'Hindutva' and 'Hinduism'; the 'Ram Rajya' of Gandhi has led easily to the 'Ram Rajya' of Hindutva in Gandhi's home of Gujarat. In fact, 'secular' human rights and equality requires a moral basis that is best found in tradition.

What the 'secularists' of today fail to see is that this tradition did not begin only in the colonial period, and it is not to be identified with an amorphous Hinduism that allows Vedic sanctity, Brahmanical authority, and varna hierarchy to sneak in by the back door. Rather, the tradition of equality and rights had a foundation in India in Buddhism (and other shramanic traditions) in the ancient period—and in the 'early modern' period, the bhakti sants began to give it a new direction by linking it to hopes that the world could be transformed. In other words, they fought the political priesthood with demands for a new world, to be realized not in the next life through *karma* or in escape from *samsara* to union with the absolute, but in the empirical world, here and now—if only in the future.

Thus, Tuka in the early seventeenth century—the same period when Galileo was confronting the Inquisition and Grotius was giving the initial formulation of the moral basis of modernity at the socio-political level—sang this:

Hear, O people, the mark of your welfare!
Keep the lord of Pandhari in mind.
Then how can we be bound
when we speak and sing Narayan?
who understands the world
will reach this side. [refrain]
Time will submit to slavery,
Illusion's bonds will broken be;
Everyone will be
powerful and prosperous.
Brahman, Kshatriya, Vaishya, Shudra,
and Chandalas also have rights [*adhikar*],
women, children, male and female,
and even prostitutes.
Says Tuka, through experience

we have torn down every fence.
Many are the divine joys
taken by the devotees. (#1142)

Some might argue that Tuka was seeing slavery in spiritual terms, that 'breaking illusion's bonds' refers to the illusoriness of the existing world standing between the soul and the Absolute. This interpretation goes against all the core features of Tuka's writing. His bhakti—and the bhakti of other radicals such as Ravidas, Cokhamela, Kabir, Eka, Nama— is similar to the great emotional and theological contributions to the tradition of freedom made by African Americans under slavery. Today their 'Negro spirituals' (now clearly emerging as 'Freedom Songs') are recognized as among the greatest songs of the American musical tradition. Such songs—those who heard by some chance BBC's full coverage of Jimmy Carter's acceptance of the Nobel Peace Prize would have heard a beautiful rendering of one of the most popular of these— had both a spiritual and a very concrete, empirical meaning. The same is true of Tuka's abhangs. Even more noteworthy, the claim to rights— the word used is adhikar, the very term used today in *manavadhikar* (human rights)—is very specific. It claims rights not only in varna terms, but specifically includes the untouchable, and stands at the height of equality of the twentieth century in claiming rights for children and women and for the section of women seen as most degraded.

Thus the foundation of human rights in India can be found with the linkage of equality—specifically directed against the caste system and untouchability—to an urge to transform the world. The process of realizing this hope requires, in part, a recovery of the radical tradition of India, taking it back from its appropriation by Sanskritic-Brahmanic forces.

NOTES

1. Sadanand More, one of the main Marathi interpreters of Tuka and a defender of the 'orthodox' mahasamanvay approach, is a descendent of this family; for his dispute with Salunkhe, see More (1996) and Salunkhe (1997). Chitre, the major writer on Tuka today in both English and Marathi, has sided with More in this debate. Which newspapers these various views have appeared in is also significant. In today's India, interpretation of the Varkari movement, indeed of any sant tradition, is inevitably political.

2. The mahasamanvay is usually interpreted—for instance, in the writings of More, Chitre and above all Deshpande—to argue that while 'Brahmans' were often opposed, the sants, including Tuka, did not oppose advaita or the basic social framework of varnashrama dharma. It also involves seeing the Varkaris and the orthodox sect of Ramadas as part of one great all-encompassing Marathi tradition—an interpretation begun by no less than M.G. Ranade.

3. For a description of the Muslim contribution in regard to the Varkaris, see Dhere (1967). This however is a little-known book in comparison to his others and one with an obscure publisher.

4. This is a pure Pali form of the name of Krishna.

5. For instance, in the famous 'Good you made me a Kunbi, otherwise I'd have died of hypocrisy' (#520), the Marathi *bar kunbi kela* suggests irony, not that he really liked being considered low.

6. As critics of this now fashionable 'post-modernist post-colonialism' have pointed out, attributing so much influence to colonial rule and a Western-imposed framework deprives colonized/dominated people of any significant agency (see Sarkar 1997 and Nanda 2002).

7. This process of humiliation was discussed by Dalits and others for perhaps the first time in a seminar on Caste and Mental Health, Pune, 14–15 December 2002.

8. The story is that he threw them in himself and then waited thirteen days praying until Vithoba restored them, with fervent poems of humility and forgiveness afterwards (see Tukaram 1973, #2222–45). Salunkhe's interpretation (1997: 193–230) is that they were simply thrown in by the powerful judges, with the resulting loss of many valuable works.

9. In fact such generalizations miss the way in which Western individualism was 'collective' (see Taylor 2002, on the individual and society in 'modern social imagery') and, conversely, Indian tradition—both Buddhist and Brahmanical—was individualistic.

REFERENCES

Bahenabai. 1979. *Sant Bahenabainca Gatha va Samiksha*. Shalini Anant Javadekar (ed.). Pune: Dharmik va Sanskritic Prakashan Mandal (Marathi).

Callewaert, Winand M. and Peter G. Friedlander. 2001. *The Life and Works of Raidas*. New Delhi: Manohar.

Champalakshmi, R. 2002. 'Cultural Technology of Colonial Rule'. *The Hindu*. 3 November.

Chitre, Dilip (ed.). 1990, *Punha Tukaram*. Mumbai: Popular Prakashan.

———. 1991. *Says Tuka: Selected Poetry of Tukaram* (Translated from Marathi and with an Introduction). New Delhi: Penguin Books.

Cokhamela. 1987. *Sant Cokhamela Abhangvani*. M.S. Kanade and Bhalchandra Khandekar (eds). Pune: Snehavardhan Publishing House.

Deshpande, G.P. 2002. 'Philosophical Discourse in Modern Marathi'. *Economic and Political Weekly*. vol. 37, no. 21, pp. 1987–91.

Dhere, R.C. 1967. *Musalman Marathi Santkari*. Pune: Jnanaraj Prakashan.

_____. 1984. *Shri Vitthal: Ek Mahasmanvay*. Pune: Shri Vidya Prakashan.

Dirks, Nicholas. 2001. *Castes of Mind: Colonialism and the Making of Modern India*. Delhi: Permanent Black.

Fraser, J. Nelson and K.B. Marathe. 2000 [1909]. *The Poems of Tukarama, Translated and Rearranged with Notes and Introduction*. Delhi: Motilal Banarsidass.

Hawley, John Stratton and Mark Juergensmeyer. 1988. *Songs of the Saints of India*. New York: Oxford University Press.

Hess, Linda. 1983, *The Bijak of Kabir*. Translated by Linda Hess and Shukdev Singh. San Francisco: North Point Press.

Ikram, S.M. 1964. *Muslim Civilization in India*. New York: Columbia University Press.

Javale, B.G. 1999. *Pandharica Pandurang Bodhisatva Hota*. Bid: Dolas Prakashan.

Mokashi, D.B. 1990. *Palkhi: An Indian Pilgrimage*. Translated by Philip C. Engblom. Albany: State University of New York Press.

More, Sadanand. 1996. *Tukaram Darshan*. Pune: Gaj Prakashan.

Mukta, Parita. 1997. *Upholding the Common Life: The Community of Mirabai*. New Delhi: Oxford University Press.

Nanda, Meera. 2002. *Breaking the Spell of Dharma and Other Essays*. New Delhi: Three Essays Press.

Novetzke, Christian Lee. 2002. 'One Nation Under Nama: A Cosmopolitan Marathi in the National Imagination'. Paper presented at Ninth International Conference on Maharashtra, Minneapolis, Minnesota, USA, June.

Salunkhe, A.H. 1997. *Vidrohi Tukaram*. Pune: Gopal Mokashi.

Sarkar, Sumit. 1997. *Writing Social History*. New Delhi: Oxford University Press.

Taylor, Charles. 2002. 'Modern Social Imaginaries'. *Public Culture*. vol. 14, no. 1, pp. 19–24.

Tukaram. 1973. *Shri Tukarambavancya Abhangaci Gatha*. Mumbai: Shaskiya Madhyavati Mudranalay.

van Skyhawk, H. 1992. 'Sufi Influence in the Ekanatha-bhagavat: Some Observations on the Text and Historical Context'. In R.S. McGregor (ed.). *Devotional Literature in South Asia: Current Research, 1985–88*. Cambridge: Cambridge University Press, pp. 67–79.

Youngblood, Michael. 2003. 'The Varkaris: Following the March of Tradition, Dissent and Identity in Maharashtra'. *Critical Asian Studies.* vol. 35, pp. 287–300.

Zelliot, Eleanor. 1987. 'Eknath's Bharuds: The Sant as a Link Between Cultures'. In Karine Schomer and W.H. McLeod (eds). *The Sants,* Delhi: Motilal Banarsidass, pp. 91–109.

_____. 1990. 'A Historic Introduction to the Varkari Movement'. In *Mokashi, Palkhi,* pp. 31–53.

_____. 1995. 'Chokhamela: Piety and Protest'. In David Lorenzen (ed.). *Bhakti Religion in North India.* Albany: SUNY Press, pp. 212–20.

2

HUMANISM, RELIGION, AND THE NATION
Sant Namdev as a *Mānavatāvādin*

Christian Lee Novetzke

Postcolonial scholarship has powerfully critiqued the modern discourse of nationalism and its forms of democratic humanism as they were perverted in the colonial context, often refigured by colonialist thinkers to justify colonialism's rapaciousness. Given the deep investment with the idea of the nation among scholars of postcolonialism, we find the notion of humanism sometimes drawn up and quartered. On the one hand, humanism in this context has been subjected to the critiques of postmodernity (most explicitly attributed to Foucault 1966), which has so deeply influenced postcolonial scholarship from Said (1978) on down. In this context, what is often described as postmodernity's 'anti-humanism' attacks the idea of the human good residing at the heart of western moral philosophy and statecraft. On the other hand, postcolonial scholars have linked their criticism of western humanism to the way the postcolonial nation has been 'imagined' (see Anderson 1983) or 'derived' (see Chatterjee 1986, 1993) vis-à-vis western hegemonic modernity and political philosophy. The inadequacies of the western nation-form in these contexts are matched to a suspicion of western humanism. In both the political genealogy of the nation-state in Europe and the scholarly genealogy that surrounds the nation as a key term, the idea of humanism, and in particular, secular humanism, arises as inherently linked to the ethic of the democratic nation and thus is subjected to the same criticisms.[1] Yet sustained engagements with humanism in the context of modern Indian public culture are rare. This essay is a brief dip into this relatively still water.

Many key European and early American political philosophers of the nation, such as Johann Gottlieb Fichte (1762–1814), Johann Gottfried von Herder (1744–1803), Jean-Jacques Rousseau (1712–78), David Hume (1711–66), Thomas Paine (1737–1809), Ernest Renan (1823–92), and John Stuart Mill (1806–73), were also humanists. Likewise, many of the significant figures of Indian nationalism were associated with humanism by declaration or proclivity: Rammohan Roy (1772–1803), who founded the Brahmo Samaj; Vivekananda (1863–1902), founder of the Ramakrishna Mission and the Vedanta Society; Syed Ahmed Khan (1817–98), founder of the Muhammedan Anglo-Oriental College; Annie Besant (1847–1933); Debendranath (1817–1905) and Rabindranath Tagore (1861–1941); Muhammad Iqbal (1877–1938); Mohandas K. Gandhi (1869–1948); Jawaharlal Nehru (1889–1964); and Mohammed Ali Jinnah (1876–1948), to name only a few. The language of the nation was shared by elites, whether in Europe, India, or America, and this was also often the language of humanism.

Although the idea of humanism has received little attention from postcolonial scholars of South Asia, there are a few important exceptions, such as Ranajit Guha and Gayatri Spivak. Both authors explore humanism in the context of colonialism as one of the defining ideas of western modernity and historiography. Spivak finds in humanism a self-serving explanation for the creation of colonial markets and the spread of imperial 'democracy' in the colonial period as she deconstructs many of the primary statements of western humanism from the late eighteenth to the twentieth century.[2] Guha (1993) turns to a familiar source in India, one of the final articulations of Bankimchandra Chattopadhyay, the *Dharmatattva*, published in 1888, and finds in it a 'challenge to the universal pretensions of Western humanism' and hence to universal history; Guha thus presents Chattopadhyay's collection of essays as a brief example of the 'prose of counterinsurgency' enunciated by a figure positioned as 'subaltern' in the context of colonial hegemony, but of a class and social position in India that allowed him the power to 'speak', an impossibility for the quotidian subaltern, as Spivak's famous essay asserts (in Nelson and Grossberg 1988). What Guha chooses not to emphasize in his treatment of *Dharmatattva* is

Chattopadhyay's resonant use of bhakti or devotionalism in his formulation of a uniquely Hindu and Indian humanism. Indeed, one could read *Dharmatattva* as more explicitly about a recovery of the term 'bhakti' in a new global context than a challenge to western ideas of 'humanism'.[3] Despite these strong denunciations of western humanism by two key figures of the postcolonial study of South Asia, Indian nationalists, literary critics, and others in the Indian public sphere generally have used the term in a more nuanced way.

A brief treatment of one example of the meeting of western humanism with 'Hindu' devotionalism, bounded not by colonialism but rather by a postcolonial context, is the aim of this essay in honour of Eleanor Zelliot. In order to focus the essay, I will engage with two subjects well-observed by Zelliot. The first is the legacy of the Marathi Vārkarī tradition, a subject Zelliot has studied in detail. In particular, I will look at the remembrance of one key figure, Namdev, who is attributed to the fourteenth century and is said to have been both a friend to, and the key hagiographer of Cokhamela, the first 'Untouchable' or Mahār sant-poet in Marathi, about whom Eleanor Zelliot has eloquently written.[4] Namdev is remembered as having been born a tailor or Śimpī, and hence as being a 'Śūdra' according to the Brahmanical varṇa echelon. In Indian public memory, he is portrayed as having travelled all over India, composing in Punjabi, Hindi, and other languages as well as in Marathi, and thus he is vital not just to Maharashtrian religious life, but also to Dādū Panthīs, Kabīr Panthīs, Sikhs, and others in northern India. The second subject, then, will be the subaltern or Dalit (a term Zelliot would prefer) perspective that is recovered from this historical voice, and how this voice is articulated in the language of humanism in English and its equivalent in Marathi, *mānavatāvāda*. We will see how, both by critics and in Marathi public culture, Namdev's humanism has been imagined to be part of the proto-history of the Indian nation and part of the long history of expressing Dalit concerns in Marathi cultural contexts.

In the later years of the independence movement and in the postcolonial period in India, particularly from the middle of the 1960s onwards, Namdev increasingly entered the Indian public sphere (in English, Hindi, and Marathi) as a national 'integrator', or a 'saint of the nation' (*rāṣṭrīya sant*). This was due to biographical and ethical features of his remembrance, especially his legendary travels throughout India in the fourteenth century and the social egalitarianism of his community of fellows, which is remembered to have consisted of Brahmans, Śūdras, and Untouchables, men and women, Marathi-speakers and others. His position within a larger pantheon of proto-nationalist heroes was framed by the ideals of Gandhian pluralism, Nehruvian social democracy, and a kind of Hindu secularism or Hindu modernity, of which Gandhi is also emblematic. In contrast to this politically centrist lineage of secular and religious humanism, Namdev has not maintained much social capital in the world of majoritarian Hindu politics espoused by the Hindu Right under the rubric of Hindutva. This is important because Namdev's position within one articulation of the Indian nation is 'humanistic', not religiously chauvinistic, and this contrast highlights the way humanism in the Indian public sphere can map onto one popular representation of modern Hinduism worldwide, that of a 'tolerant' and accommodating religion. Discussions of religion, politics, and nationalism in India, as well as elsewhere in the world, are often dominated by a discourse of extremism, fundamentalism, and the forces of the radical Right within the political spectrum. But religion also has a strong effect on the politics and nationalist imagination of more centrist political actors, an interaction regularly overlooked by scholars and critics of contemporary politics in India. Instead, when one sees 'religion' and 'nation' or 'politics' together, one often assumes a Rightist ideology, but the discourse on humanism contradicts this assumption. The fields of religion and nation conjoined come to characterize Namdev's legacy in the public sphere of central, western, and northern India from the twentieth century to the present, and this characterization is championed by the same social and political forces that espouse secularism, humanism, and democratic socialism.

One can see this invocation of the religious genealogy of the Indian nation in a 'Hindu secularist' mode in multiple ways. For example, in 1964 the Government of India commissioned a series of lectures on issues of national cultural cohesion, which were later aired on All India Radio and published by the Ministry of Information and Broadcasting. These lectures commemorated the legacy of Sardar Vallabhbhai Patel (1875–1950), a freedom fighter, nationalist leader, and chief architect of India's post-independence integration of princely states into the new state-union of India. One of the lectures, delivered by V. Raghavan, a Professor of Sanskrit at the University of Madras, concerned a pan-Indian hagiography that reflected the activities of 'great integrators' among the 'saint-singers of India' (1966: 15). Namdev appears in

Raghavan's roster of integrators (1966: 123–8), which includes Tukaram (seventeenth century), Ramdas (seventeenth century), and Jnandev (thirteenth century) from Maharashtra, with the other sants and holy figures drawn from all regions of the modern nation. Namdev here is positioned as a cosmopolitan, polyglot Maharashtrian in the national imagination of India, and his presence in national public memory is due to several facets of his legacy, the core of which must consist of the legend of the sant's travels. This is the root of his position as an 'integrator' of literary devotionalism in central, western, and northern India over the past seven centuries, of the so-called 'bhakti movement', and by extension, of India as a Hindu secularist nation.

The public memory of Namdev's travels is found more as the 'background' story to the wide circulation of his songs and biography in central, western, and northern India, and less in any specific text that recounts this voyage. Indeed, the most common source for Namdev's travels, the *Tīrthāvaḷī*, can be found in almost all editions of Namdev's verses in Marathi, yet the story itself only hints at travel outside the immediate area of Pandharpur. Whatever travel is narrated in this version finds its completion within the first third of the story, and takes the protagonists (Namdev and Jnandev) no further than Dwarka before they return to Pandharpur. This most common version of the *Tīrthāvaḷī* is a cautionary tale *against* pilgrimage to any place other than Pandharpur, and is difficult to read as a story that presents a 'united' India.

A second, little-studied version of the *Tīrthāvaḷī*, which dates to 1581 CE and has almost never appeared in print,[5] seems to contain the only textual account of this remembered pan-Indian voyage. In the popular story of Namdev's journey, which is detailed in this version of the *Tīrthāvaḷī*, the sant does literally chart out the contours of what would become the modern Indian nation, going no further to the northwest than Rajasthan and no further east than Puri, thus avoiding what would become the postcolonial nations of Pakistan and Bangladesh while voyaging as far north as the Tibetan plateau, near Nepal, and to the southernmost town of Kanyakumari. Furthermore, Namdev's travels do enact a *pradakṣiṇā* of the 'heart' of India, which is to say he charts a clockwise course consistent with ritual practice at temples and other holy sites, and this pattern has been read by some scholars and popular writers as a prognostic benediction of the Indian nation— one encapsulated by a 'saint of the nation' and of 'national integration', not of Hindu chauvinism. Writing the preface for the Maharashtra-state-sponsored *Nāmdev Gāthā* in 1970, the Minister of Education M.D. Chaudhari asserted that Namdev had circumscribed the territory of 'the heart of India' (*āntara bhāratī*) through his travels.[6] One Marathi yogi and *kīrtankār*, K.G. Wankhade, even embarked on a journey to retrace Namdev's footsteps throughout India as a living symbol of Namdev's nationalist proclivities.

The 'truth' of this story in Indian public memory is not invested in any recorded version of the *Tīrthāvaḷī*. Instead, what gives credence to the idea of Namdev's ability to integrate the Indian nation is the distribution of his legend in hagiography and his songs in various regional literatures, and the physical presence of sites of remembrance, *lieux de mémoire* (Nora 1989), throughout India. The sites of memory that make up the historiographic cairns of Namdev's legacy also mark the domain of influence of the sant's 'humanism'.

Amid numerous celebrations and symposia held across India in 1970, a number of publications heralded Namdev's importance in the history of the nation, phrased in vaguely religious terms. The Maharashtra Information Center and the Government Central Press of Maharashtra produced a short essay in English on Namdev by the Marathi scholar M.A. Karandikar. The preface to the essay sums up the contents of its thirty pages:

National integration is the need of the hour and Saint Namdev by virtue of his crossing the linguistic and geographical barriers to enlighten the people in areas far away from Maharashtra can truly be called Apostle of National Integration (Karandikar 1970: i–ii).

Intertwined in this simple description is a unified idea of religion, secularism, and nationalism that came to characterize the post-Nehruvian period of Congress rule at the Centre and in many states. I would describe this idea as Hindu secularism. It is similar to the secularism of the United States, which remains deeply characterized by Christianity, heard in common mottos such as 'One Nation Under God' and 'In God We Trust', yet is ideally set at a safe distance from actual Christian practice, which would be characterized as 'the Religious Right' or Christian fundamentalism. Karandikar uses terms that reference Western Christianity, such as 'saint' and 'apostle', yet these religious appellations are applied to 'national integration' across boundaries of language and geography, the secular map of a nation. This statement was made almost two decades before the full rise of the Hindu Right in Indian national politics, when political discourse indulging in religious metaphors was replaced by the explicit public use of religion, and particularly chauvinistic Hinduism, in ways far removed from the impulse of 'national integration'.

Namdev's influence within the trajectory of the Indian nation certainly might appear to be a form of 'religious nationalism'. However, the kind of religious nationalism associated with Namdev is not that of the so-called Hindu Right. Instead, Namdev's legacy constitutes one of many 'secret histories', as Partha Chatterjee uses the term, of the Indian nation embedded in a field often identified by Western scholars and others as 'spiritual' or 'religious', but by reference to sentiment rather than doctrinal content. In this case, Namdev's religious contribution to the nation suggests one of the key features of Hindu secularism in general, a reference to the ethics of humanism, a notion that in Western history has its own long and complicated relationship to Christian thought.

Several key elements of Namdev's hagiography appear to have become seamlessly enmeshed in the eighteenth century and carried into the twentieth century. What is worthy of preservation from this earlier hagiographical tradition is the general character of Namdev as a figure who represents the downtrodden, helpless, landless, and powerless, and whose position is reinforced by caste and class—a position designated in contemporary scholarship as 'subaltern'. Yet this designation in the Marathi public sphere, when associated with bhakti figures, is also conditioned by a sense that humanism or mānavatāvāda is defined in relation to the subjectivity of the subaltern, not the elite; to be a humanist, in this sense, is to suffer the pains of human life without the mediation or comforts afforded by wealth and power. It is the humanism at the root of Nehruvian socialism or within Ambedkar's repeated efforts to legislate amelioration for Dalits under the rubric of 'Scheduled Castes and Tribes'. In both cases, Indian humanism visualizes a particular kind of ethical analeptic state that is influenced by a nation largely composed of those who have suffered the domination of colonialism, caste discrimination, or other kinds of oppression. The Indian nation-state, though imagined by its most elite members, projected a vision of itself as subaltern from its very inception in the early twentieth century and its actual political creation in 1947, thus wedding a particular kind of Indian humanism with the unique Indian state newly engendered.

Namdev's mānavatāvāda is expressed in two ways: through the ascription to him of opposition to caste, class, or gender discrimination; and through a motif, which I feel is in part borrowed from Kabir because of its relatively late appearance in Namdev's pan-Indian hagiography, that Namdev assuaged the rivalries of Hindus and Muslims. In a volume of Marathi essays published in 1970 by the Government of Maharashtra and intended as a companion to its edition of Namdev's songs, Dhananjay Keer writes of the 'Humanist Namdev' that his travels throughout India served to 'spread the light of wisdom'. This refers to an oft-quoted verse attributed to Namdev in which he proclaims, 'let's dance with passion in the kīrtan, and spread the light of wisdom in the world' (Kavitkar et al. 1970: 111). Keer cites Marathi and Hindi songs that reiterate Namdev's lowly status, his opposition to Brahmanical orthodoxy and orthopraxy, his rejection of caste and class, and his inclusive social politics. Keer quotes a Hindi song attributed to Namdev, 'My caste is low and debased, Lord of Pandhari. Why did you make Nama the Tailor this way?' (ibid.: 112). In a Marathi verse, contained in manuscripts from the eighteenth century, Keer quotes, 'These [Hindu] Gods, they are broken by the Turks, drowned in water [by Hindus], yet they never utter a single complaint.'[7] While this song, also present in the Marathi corpus, is clearly of the nirguṇī variety, it is often used to express Namdev's 'balanced' assessment of orthodox religious culture: he is neither dogmatically Hindu nor sympathetic to dogmatic Islam.[8] Similarly, Ashok Kamat and R.C. Dhere quote a Hindi song attributed to Namdev, 'Hindus worship in the temple and Muslims in the mosque. Namdev happily serves the lord, neither in the temple nor in the mosque,' (Kamat and Dhere 1970: 105) a couplet that one would not be surprised to find within Kabir's corpus of songs.[9] The demonstration of Namdev's 'non-denominational' position, entwined with the biographical persona of Kabir, is implied in another quotation: 'Hindus are blind and Turks can't see straight. A smart man is better than both' (ibid.). Namdev here is carefully construed as someone who worships humanity itself.

In a copious collection of essays entitled Śrī Nāmdev Darśan, D.K. Sant wrote an essay on 'Namdev's Humanism' (Relekar et al. 1970: 712–26). Sant attributes to Namdev a sentiment of temporality or worldliness (aihikatā) that helped develop a sense of the historical (*aitihāsik*) in India. The author insists that Namdev assisted Maharashtra in becoming part of the nation of India by balancing cosmopolitanism and regionalism in his own biography and corpus of verses, a balance made with the help of a historical impulse. Sant also draws a striking analogy, asserting that Namdev was the Erasmus of Maharashtra, thus making the connection with humanism unmistakable (ibid.: 715–16). Desiderius Erasmus Roterodamus (1466–1536) was a Dutch philosopher whom many consider to have been the founding voice of modern humanistic thought. The comparison between him and Namdev is made on the basis of several perceived similarities. Both figures were considered devout in their faiths, but were also reformers; both travelled widely—Erasmus lived in the areas of the modern-day nations of the Netherlands, Italy, Germany, Switzerland, and England; both composed in several languages.

Yet what was particular about the *mānavatāvāda* Namdev espoused? It sometimes rejected orthodox Islamic and Hindu practice, perhaps, but was surely invested with Hindu religious language and actions. What kind of nation is imagined through the eyes of Namdev's humanism? In order to answer these questions, I would like to turn to two films about Namdev produced within the context of his invocation as a representative of humanism and nationalism, that is, within the latter half of the twentieth century. Rather than using songs attributed to him or biographies of him written before the twentieth century, I refer to film in order to maintain a historically consistent context and to comment on the way Namdev's legacy is invoked in public memory. The 'modern' portrayal of Namdev, in the modern medium of film, is one of the best ways to see the interaction of humanism and nationalism in the legacy of the sant.

Keshav Talpade made *Sant Namdev* in 1949, two years after Independence. *Sant Namdev* represented a departure for this Marathi director, who was more famous for his large-scale commercial Hindi film, the Fearless-Nadia hit *Tigress* (1948). Produced in a period of uncertainty about the shape of the future constitution of India and the division of its states, the film, though invoking a figure of the fourteenth century, appears to engage concerns of the twentieth century. By noticing these concerns, we can see how Namdev's humanism was imagined.

Talpade's film begins in an undisclosed narrative time in the context of a *kīrtan*; this immediately marks the moralizing ethos of the film.

In Marathi a kīrtan is a performance of song, dance, exposition, and music that focuses on the hermeneutics of a particular verse or moment from the life of a sant, presented to elucidate some moral position. Namdev is considered the first Marathi kīrtan performer, and this narrative entrée suggests a link to him as well as a link to the ethical injunctions the audience is about to receive. In other words, the film is contextualized by delivering Namdev's humanistic message itself.

Namdev is first portrayed as a child, various stories are recounted, and we meet the adult sant at the door of the Vitthal temple, where he and others are denied entry by a group of Brahmans who are counting bags of money. They lock the door to the temple to be sure the Śūdra stays out. Namdev stands forlornly at the door and sings to Vitthal a song about how the deity saves the fallen and most wretched of the world: 'Hearing the name of the One Who Saves the Fallen (patitapāvan), I have come to the door [of the temple]. But because He is not there I have turned back again' (NG: 659, song 1691, verse 1). Abandonment by one's deity is a perennial theme in bhakti throughout India, and Namdev voices this anxiety here. At the song's conclusion, the doors open, to the amazement of all, including the Brahman priests. This episode does not appear in Namdev's received biography. Instead it seems to invoke debates about temple entry for low-caste and Untouchable Hindus. In early 1950 the Indian Constitution was ratified, carrying with it in Article 25 the mandate to allow Hindus of all castes free access to temples. As we will see, this film reinvents many aspects of Namdev's remembrance in order to address issues that pertain to the film's present.

Intervening scenes depict Namdev's family life, made difficult by economic hardship, until the narrative introduces a key figure in Namdev's public memory, his orthodox Brahmanical interlocutor, Parisa Bhagavat. The two carry out a debate about caste difference. In this debate, well-documented in Namdev's literary corpus, Namdev betters the Brahman, who hurriedly leaves the scene humiliated. In Talpade's film, Parisa is not fully redeemed; he is merely humiliated into renouncing his casteism. In other words, the tide of public opinion, represented by the many observers of the debate (and, by extension, the viewers of the film), turns against the Brahman and his orthodox position. The encounters between Namdev and Parisa Bhagavat were important enough to the film's appeal that the producers used a still from one of these scenes for publicity purposes (Fig. 2.1).

Fig. 2.1 Encounter between Sant Namdev and Parisa Bhagavat. Still from Talpade, *Sant Namdev*, 1949. Courtesy: National Film Archives of India

This particular encounter solidifies the non-Brahman character of this film. Following the assassination of M.K. Gandhi on 30 January 1948 by a Maharashtrian Brahman, Nathuram Godse, India saw riots and violence directed at Brahmans, in rural areas as well as in cities like Bombay and Pune. Marathi anti-Brahman sentiment has a long history, including among such social luminaries as Jotirao Phule (1827–90) and B.R. Ambedkar (1891–1956), and draws much of its anger from resentment over the Brahman-dominated Peshwa rule of the Maratha Confederacy. The events of 1948 refocused attention on non-Brahman sentiment in Maharashtrian public culture. Made one year after Gandhi's assassination, Talpade's film was no doubt viewed in light of these events and of aggressive anti-Brahmanism in the Marathi-speaking regions of India. Yet the film does not depict violence, and Parisa is not ostracized, but merely coerced into recognizing his own folly. Anti-caste humanism makes a space for redemption within the narrative of the film, and thus also within the ethics of Namdev's character. Thus, the film presents Namdev's humanism with regard to caste from both a subaltern position and an elite one, concerned with maintaining civil society.

While these concerns are not necessarily those of the nation, but rather of Maharashtrian public culture in the late 1940s, both the energy of newly-won independence and Namdev's own cosmopolitan legacy required the film to address in some way Namdev's peregrinations over the length of India, the key narrative at the heart of his position as a 'national integrator'. This is done only briefly, with a montage depicting Namdev walking along a road in an undefined terrain, followed quickly by an image of Namdev, singing and walking, superimposed over a clay replica of the new political area of post-independence India. Interestingly, Namdev's image is also divided into five identical images, and their translucency allows us to see India through Namdev's multiple forms. The song he sings invokes unity and oneness (Fig. 2.2). The hint of the impulse toward 'national integration' is thus present but muted, subjugated to the more pressing local concerns of Bombay State (later to be divided into Maharashtra and Gujarat) rather than to the needs of the 'nation', itself still in the process of becoming 'imagined'. It is not until the 1990s that a film is made on Namdev with an explicit nationalist agenda.

Fig. 2.2 Multiple images of Sant Namdev superimposed on a map of India. Still from Talpade, *Sant Namdev*, 1949. Courtesy: National Film Archives of India

This film, also called *Sant Namdev*, was made by Yashwant Pethkar in 1991. Pethkar's career began in 1947 with Hindi films of a non-religious nature. In 1951, he made his first Marathi film, *Vitthal Rakhumai*, about the deities of Pandharpur. His most well-received film was *Keechaka Vadha* (1959), 'The Slaying of Keechaka', a retelling of a popular vignette from the Mahabharata. Pethkar continued to make Marathi and Hindi films, both widely commercial and devotional, until the middle of the 1970s. *Sant Namdev* was his first film in almost two decades. It was shot half in Marathi and half in Hindi, half in Maharashtra and half in northern India. The multiple locations of the film, as well as its bilingualism, immediately signal its nationalist proclivities.[10] Pethkar's narrative, like Talpade's, follows in the main the standard recollection of Namdev's life. Here too we have the famous encounter between Namdev and Parisa, but the resolution reveals a slight shift in the 'non-Brahman' ethos so readily apparent in Talpade's film—and, indeed, in the corpus of songs and stories about or attributed to Namdev in the pre-modern period. Here Parisa and Namdev debate, but the compulsion for Parisa's ultimate metanoia is not public humiliation but personal transformation. In this case, Parisa is moved both by Namdev's words and by those of the famous Untouchable Sant Cokhamela. The humanistic impulse against caste-ism is represented here as shared by Namdev and his companions and is undertaken in public discourse, but it relies not on civil society but on personal conviction, on human ethics, the human individual choosing the ethically righteous.

While the first half of the film largely establishes Namdev's ethics and narrates the denouement between Parisa and Namdev, the second half shows Namdev travelling and living in northern India. The locale of the Punjab is made explicit, and the characters, including Namdev, speak Hindi, though Namdev's Hindi remains stilted and odd, emphasizing that it is a second language to him. Yet his status as a stranger in the Punjab also lends him an outsider's point of view—a device found often in Tamil films that comment on issues in northern India.[11] In one scene, Namdev intervenes on behalf of a poor, starving man who stole an ear of corn to feed his family. Namdev produces a bag of grain to pay for the one ear of corn, and it is left ambiguous whether the grain has been produced as a 'miracle' or Namdev has purchased it—after all, it is only one bag of grain he offers, not an endless stream.

This story, like several in Talpade's film, is invented entirely for this scene, and its novelty comments on the director's intent to establish Namdev's humanism in somewhat realistic rather than magical or mythical terms. Though poor himself, Namdev helps the poor, and the means of that help is modest, yet somehow divinely invested.

In the final scenes of the film, Namdev has reached an advanced age. He tells his now-copious crew of followers that they should no longer serve him but rather 'serve the poor, humble, and suffering', Namdev's humanistic imperative. One follower delivers a short speech:

Since [your] coming to Ghuman [in Punjab], there has been no violence between Hindus and Muslims. Brahmans, Kshatriyas, and Jats—they all eat together. All the Muslims worship Ram and all the Hindus perform Muslim prayers. Because of your kīrtans, everyone has forgotten their caste and has become one community (jāti).

This is a key summation of the film, enunciated by a devotee of Namdev's, a former criminal whom Namdev brought back to lawfulness. We hear of bhakti, but not of a particular deity or even practice. Instead, we hear of social cohesion, of peace among castes and religions. These final iterations of Namdev's humanism wed a secular Hindu nation to the ethics of anti-caste-ism, and convey the thesis of this film's morality tale.[12] The film's clear social message seems aimed at the concerns of 1991, both caste and religious, though here the latter seem paramount. The state of Indian communal politics was highly volatile at the time when the film was made, given that the general elections of late November 1989 had been followed by some of the worst communal violence in northern India since the Partition or the Emergency. Since 1986 the Vishva Hindu Parishad and the Bharatiya Janata Party had been calling increasingly vociferously for the Babri Masjid to be razed; 1990 saw the self-immolation of Hindu Right protestors over the Babri Masjid, and L.K. Advani's first *ratha yātra* ('chariot pilgrimage') was carried out in September of that year. In 1991 Rajiv Gandhi was assassinated by a Hindu woman who opposed Gandhi's withdrawal of support for Hindu Tamil separatists in Sri Lanka. Between 1989 and 1991 India had four prime ministers, with two governments that each lasted less than a year. Pethkar seems to have been deeply influenced by this social and political turmoil, and Namdev's humanism, as depicted in the film, may have been an artist's response to the darkness of the times.

Pethkar's film was first screened not in India but in Israel, in 1995, at the behest of a Marathi-speaking Bene Israeli (Jewish) organization. Thus the first audience for the film was neither in India nor predominantly Hindu. In this context, perhaps, a reminder of the sovereign nation, as defined by the peregrinations of a historical figure, was deemed important, both to Indians in India and to those abroad. Pethkar, who embraced the idea that Namdev's travels unified India, made his film at a time when not only was there turmoil in India, but India was moving toward neo-liberal reforms and embracing the transnational economies of 'globalization', opening its markets and, as a result, its public culture to the influences of the global cultural economy. It is only in this context, one that circumscribes the Indian nation as an entity amid many global competitors, that Namdev's perceived humanism so explicitly invokes the Indian nation. Yet it retains all those hallmarks of Namdev's ethics that have compelled Marathi and English commentators to refer to him as an Indian humanist—his position against caste, class, and gender injustice. The two films, by Talpade and Pethkar, can be viewed as two perspectives on the single subject of the nation and humanism, constructed in historical contexts that required shifts within, but not radical departures from, the quotidian representation of Namdev's social ethos. The legacy of Namdev's representation as a humanist is deeply intertwined with the imagination of a Hindu secular nation. But it is the ethics of this humanism, not the demands of the nation, that have remained the enduring interpretive lens through which contemporary artists and cultural critics in India have sought to refine Namdev's public memory.

NOTES

For assistance or encouragement in one way or another, I would like to thank Anne Feldhaus, Manu Bhagavan, Gayatri Chatterjee, Shobha and Sharad Kale, Rivka Israel, K. Shashidharan and the wonderful staff of the National Film Archives of India, Suvir Kaul and the participants of the India Cinema Conference at the University of Pennsylvania in the Spring of 2006, Rana Dasgupta, Ashok Kamat, and Sunila S. Kale.

1. See, for example, Hobsbawm 1996: 22, 234, and 243.

2. See Spivak 1999 and Spivak and Guha 1988: 3–32.

3. This mapping of humanism onto bhakti is not uncommon. In the 25

August 1997 edition of *Outlook*, a popular Indian magazine, Ravinder Kumar, then-director of the Teen Murti Nehru Memorial Library and Archive in Delhi, India, commented that 'In our society, humanism is shaped by bhakti and devotional theism.'

4. See Zelliot in Lorenzen (ed.) 1995 and Lele (ed.) 1981.
5. I know of only two times this text has been printed: in Babar 1970 (*NG*) and in Nikte 2000. The version reproduced in both anthologies is dated to 1581 CE.
6. *NG*: '*nivedan* [preface'], 1.
7. Ibid. See also *NG*: 640, song 1630, verse 2.
8. See Nemade in Lele (ed.) 1981.
9. I could not find this song attributed to Namdev or Kabir, but Gorakhnath's *sakhi* literature does include an almost identical song (Callewaert and Op de Beeck 1991: 491, song 58).
10. At one point, Namdev even briefly speaks Gujarati with a dacoit who hails from the Gujarati-speaking region. This may refer to the popular story that Namdev met, and influenced, Narsi Mehta, a famous sant-poet of Gujarat from the fifteenth century.
11. For example, Mani Ratnam's films *Roja* (1992) and *Bombay* (1995).
12. It is important to note that though Namdev is a *bhagat* within the Sikh tradition, and this particular film was financed by both Sikh and Maharashtrian devotees of Namdev, the film is careful not to imply a nascent Sikh community, and thus Hinduism is clearly the mode of religious expression even as Namdev is in Ghuman, in Punjab, the central location of his public memory in Sikhism.

REFERENCES

Anderson, B. 1983. *Imagined Communities*. London: Verso.

Babar, S., *et al.* 1970. *Śrī Nāmdev Gāthā*. Bombay: Maharashtra State Government Printing Press (*NG*).

Callewaert, W. and B. Op de Beeck. 1991. *Devotional Hindi Literature*. vol. I. New Delhi: Manohar.

Chatterjee, P. 1986. *Nationalist Thought and the Colonial World: A Derivative Discourse?* London: Zed Books for the United Nations University.

_____. 1993. *The Nation and its Fragments*. New Delhi: Oxford University Press.

Foucault, M. 1971 [1966]. *The Order of Things*. New York: Pantheon Books.

Guha, R. 1993. *A Construction of Humanism in Colonial India*. Amsterdam: Centre for Asian Studies Amsterdam.

Hobsbawm, E.J. 1996 [1962]. *The Age of Revolution*. New York: First Vintage Books.

Kamat, A. and R.C. Dhere. 1970. *Eka Vijay Yātrā*. Pune: Varda Books.

Karandikar, M. 1970. *Namdev*. New Delhi: Maharashtra Information Centre.

Kavitkar, G.V., D. Keer, H. Inamdar, N. Relekar, and N. Mirajkar. 1970. *Śrī Nāmdev: Caritra, Kāvya āṇi Kārya*. Bombay: Government of Maharashtra Press.

Lele, J. 1981. *Tradition and Modernity in Bhakti Movements*. Leiden: Brill.

Lorenzen, D. (ed.). 1995. *Bhakti Religion in North India: Community, Identity and Political Action*. Albany: State University of New York Press.

Nelson, C. and L. Grossberg (eds). 1988. *Marxism and the Interpretation of Culture*. Urbana and Chicago: University of Illinois Press.

Nikte, P. (ed.). 2000. *Śrī Nāmdev Gāthā*. Pandharpur: Sant Namdev Seva Mandal.

Nora, P. 1989. 'Between Memory and History: Les Lieux de Mémoire'. *Representations*. vol. 26 (Spring), pp. 7–24.

Raghavan, V. 1966. *The Great Integrators: The Saint-Singers of India*. Delhi: Government of India, Ministry of Information and Broadcasting.

Relekar, N.N., H. Inamdar, and N. Mirajkar (eds). 1970. *Śrī Nāmdev Darśan*. Kolhapur: Namdev Samajonnati Parishad.

Said, Edward. 1978. *Orientalism*. New York: Pantheon Books.

Spivak, Gayatri. 1999. *Critique of Postcolonial Reason*. Cambridge: Harvard University Press.

———— and R. Guha (ed.). 1988. *Selected Subaltern Studies*. Oxford: Oxford University Press.

Zelliot, Eleanor. 1981. 'Chokhamela and Eknath: Two Bhakti Modes of Legitimacy for Modern Change'. In Jayant Lele (ed.). *Tradition and Modernity in Bhakti Movements*. Leiden: E.J. Brill, pp. 136–56.

————. 1995. 'Cokhamela: Piety and Protest'. In David Lorenzen (ed.). *Bhakti Religion in North India: Community, Identity and Political Action*. Albany: State University of New York Press, pp. 212–20.

3

PROPAGATING THE GOSPEL OF ANIMAL KINDNESS
Sacred Cows, Christians, and American Animal
Welfare Activism with Reference to India at
the Turn of the Twentieth Century

Janet M. Davis

On 23 April 1866, a New York shipping heir named Henry Bergh
charged through the crowded streets of New York City in hot
pursuit. Wearing a badge and a dark blue cape, the towering, spindly
Bergh chased down an immigrant German butcher who was driving a
cart loaded with calves 'piled up like wood ... and one of them so disposed
of as to bring his eye in contact with a sharp stick, thereby destroying
his sight....'[1] Acting in his official capacity as officer and president of
the newly incorporated American Society for the Prevention of Cruelty
to Animals (the nation's first organized animal welfare group), Bergh
arrested the butcher, thus marking the first of thousands of confrontations
and arrests over the next several decades in New York City and beyond.
By 1874, virtually every medium-sized and large city north of the
Mason-Dixon Line had an animal welfare society. Variously, these
organizations (also known as humane societies) sought to regulate
and 'civilize' the urban animal economy by creating decent conditions
for labouring horses, oxen, and cart dogs; abolishing cock fighting,
dog fighting, and pigeon shoots; banning vivisection; prohibiting the
sale of unadulterated milk; lobbying in state legislatures for the humane
railroad transport of animals bound for the stockyards; and enforcing
'noiseless' and painless methods of euthanasia for unwanted strays.

In its earliest years, the American animal welfare movement was largely a local affair, situated squarely within specific urban environments: the street, stockyard, dairy, laboratory, and fighting pit. Detractors charged that Societies for the Prevention of Cruelty to Animals (SPCAs) were simply a collection of nervous, native-born power brokers, hell-bent upon controlling working-class immigrants whose livelihoods were dependent upon animals. One letter writer to the *New York Times* sharply criticized Henry Bergh: 'Mr Bergh had a laboring man sent to the Penitentiary for three months for killing a cat although the man, who had no counsel, urged that he had a wife and three children dependent upon his daily work for support. On which side is the cruelty in this case?'[2] Yet, by the turn of the twentieth century, several SPCAs used animal kindness as the foundation for an expansive radical humanism that denounced child labour, racial violence, and rising American militarism overseas. George Angell, the deeply religious president of perhaps the most activist SPCA in the nation, the Massachusetts SPCA (MSPCA), vigorously condemned European imperialism, and attacked US policymakers for their forays into empire-building during the Spanish-American War (1898), the war with the Philippines (1898–1903), and the formal annexation of Hawaii, Puerto Rico, Guam, and the Philippines.

Although the United States had no formal colonial relationship with India, the subcontinent figured regularly in the MSPCA's activist agenda—as an exemplary site of animal kindness among 'proper' Hindus and Jains. Moreover, India constituted an important part of the organization's radical humanist vision. In keeping with the MSPCA's larger attack on imperialism, Angell bitterly criticized the British Raj and sought alliances with Indian nationalists to promote his educational organization, the American Humane Education Society (1889), which sought to combat poverty, inequality, and violence through moral persuasion to achieve its larger goal of empowering the dispossessed. At the same time, however, MSPCA representations of India succinctly articulated broader American ideologies of empire that envisioned the United States playing a dominant role in global affairs as a moral rather than military power. Furthermore, they tacitly supported colonial notions of the 'white man's burden' by reifying existing power structures. Infused with evangelical fervour, MSPCA activists worked hand-in-hand with missionaries in South Asia to propagate the twin gospels of animal kindness and Christianity. Yet paradoxically, American animal activists also idealized Brahmanical Hinduism—particularly cow worship and vegetarianism—thus participating in the discursive formation of an increasingly homogenized, modern Hindu subject.

The MSPCA magazine, *Our Dumb Animals*, contained frequent coverage of South Asian religious life, animals, and society. Founded upon the premise that 'we speak for those that cannot speak for themselves', *Our Dumb Animals* began publication in 1868, shortly after the MSPCA was incorporated by the state legislature. With a splashy initial print run of 200,000 copies (considerably fewer thereafter), the MSPCA used much of its budget to circulate free copies of this magazine among a local and international network of law enforcement, politicians, and missionaries. In addition to its treatment of India, the magazine discussed international politics, expressed support for the anti-lynching movement, reported on local SPCA responses to cases of animal cruelty nationwide, and chronicled the legislative status of state and local animal welfare bills worldwide.

Much of the India reportage focused on Hinduism, positing in orientalist terms that Indian civilization was 'ancient', 'immutable', and understandable through a study of caste, vegetarianism, and cow worship. *Our Dumb Animals* reverentially described India as 'A Country Rich in Cattle':

It is in India that we learn really the dependence of man upon cattle .... The sacred bulls still wander unharmed, the oxen are the wealth of the people, and the milch kine their dearest possession. Here, in the West, where every large house is a gaping mouth into which dead cattle are shoveled by the ton, and where the cow, which has mothered our children, is fatted up and sent to the butcher so soon as her milk supply ceases to bring in its full pennyworth of profit, it would need a slaughter of the Innocents, indeed, to bring home to us the vast debt of gratitude we also owe to the 'Red skinn'd kine in the red tipped clover.'[3]

Vegetarianism had not yet become a barometer of one's commitment to the animal welfare cause in the United States (as it has become at the turn of the twenty-first century in organizations like PETA and the Animal Liberation Front). Still vegetarianism was an important part of various secular dietary movements from the antebellum era onward (Green 1986: 48, 135). Some vegetarian organizations did express their explicit concern for healthy diet and kindness to animals. For example, John W. Scott, the president of the New York Vegetarian Society, denounced SPCA euthanasia policies, particularly the ways in which activists 'went around catching cats and putting them to death'.[4]

South Asian and American vegetarian religious movements often spoke directly to animal welfare issues. After Swami Vivekananda spoke in 1893 at the World Columbian Exposition's Parliament of Religions in Chicago as part of a national speaking tour, the vegetarian Vedanta Society flourished in the United States. While lecturing at the V Club in New York City, Vivekananda trumpeted Indian vegetarianism and animal kindness as evidence of India's spiritual 'superiority' over the 'decadent' United States:

Nearly three-quarters of the people of India are vegetarians. They are so because they are too kind to kill animals for food. In this country, when animals are injured, it is the custom to kill them. In India, it is the rule to send them to a hospital. In approaching Bombay, the first thing the traveler comes across is a very large hospital for animals. This has been the practice for 4,000 years.[5]

The Theosophists also brought Hindu-based prohibitions against meat-eating to an American audience. Created in New York City in May 1878 by a Russian, Madame Blavatsky, and an American Civil War colonel, Henry Steel Olcott, Theosophy was a syncretism of American spirit rapping, Hinduism, and Blavatsky's vivid visions of 'Himalayan Masters' who guided the universe. Collectively, the Theosophists argued that the East (specifically India) represented the basis for all spiritual thought. Consequently, in February 1879, Olcott and Blavatsky sold everything they owned to move permanently to India. Although many Indians—particularly members of Dayananda Sarasvati's Arya Samaj— soon denounced the Theosophists as charlatan mystics, this organization gained a wide following in India, Sri Lanka, and Britain (van der Veer 2001: 55–7). Theosophist Anna Kingsford asserted in 1884 that meat-eating promoted alcoholism, polygamy, and crime, while vegetarianism made people more civilized (Kingsford 1884: 5, 11, 16–17). Theosophists also protested the medical establishment's practice of vivisection— that is, performing experimental surgery on conscious animals without any form of sedation. In March 1904, for example, Theosophists called upon fellow followers around the world to participate in a day of global prayer against vivisection.[6]

At the turn of the twentieth century, images of 'peaceful' Indian vegetarians and antivivisectionists on the pages of *Our Dumb Animals* represented a stark contrast to the United States' expanding overseas empire. After President McKinley blamed Spain for the accidental explosion of the US battleship *Maine* off the coast of Havana in the Spring of 1898, the US Congress promptly declared war; in four short months, the US dismantled the remains of the Spanish empire, and subsequently took formal possession of Guam, Puerto Rico, and the Philippines, while maintaining virtual sovereignty over Cuba and other Caribbean countries. Although US officials argued that the war with Spain was an anti-colonial struggle intended to promote self-determination among former Spanish colonies, the American military was soon embroiled in a guerilla war against Filipino nationalists fighting for their independence. Articles such as 'The Present War Craze', 'The Philippines are Expensive', and 'Shooting Boys in the Philippines' articulated the MSPCA's anti-imperialist sentiments.[7]

Our Dumb Animals argued that American military appropriations, instead, should be used to help starving people in India:

If we could have had our way, every dollar our government has been spending in the Philippines, and every dollar the British government has been spending in South Africa, should have gone to the starving in India. From our moderate means we have thought it our duty to make several contributions.[8]

Indeed, India had been triply hit by hard times at the turn of the century: a fall in world silver prices had severely devalued the Indian rupee in the 1890s; a series of monsoon failures had plunged the Deccan into famine, and a plague epidemic had further decimated the population. From 1895 to 1905, India's total population declined for the first and only time since census figures had been taken (Wolpert 1989: 267–8). These catastrophes made British ceremonial celebrations of empire all the more repugnant. When, for example, King Edward VII was crowned the Emperor of India at the Durbar of Delhi in 1903, Angell roundly condemned the lavish affair in *Our Dumb Animals*:

[A]nd then the royal message of Edward speaking of '*his empire*' and '*his subjects*' as an American would speak of his personal property .... Then our thoughts go back to the calls made on us ... to send money to the starving millions of India, and then we take up dispatch from London this January 10th telling that all this folly has cost nearly *five millions of dollars*, while '*the majority of the people of India are continually on the threshold of starvation*'....[9]

Although vehemently opposed to military expansion, American humane activists believed fervently in US economic expansion as a vehicle for global peace and prosperity. And, while guided by philanthropic concerns, famine aid also dovetailed nicely with broader calls for economic development and the cultivation of world markets, all of which would ideally serve as an antidote to unemployment, starvation, and endemic class warfare. Echoing industrialists such as Andrew Carnegie and John D. Rockefeller, *Our Dumb Animals* argued that new markets must be found for American goods in order to combat the dangers of overproduction and resulting unemployment.[10]

Such sentiments also complemented American animal welfare activity in India. American SPCA activists arrived in India with an organization created by the MSPCA in 1882 called the 'Band of Mercy'. Based upon organizational antecedents created by the Royal SPCA in England, George Angell and an English minister named Thomas Timmins of Portsmouth, England, inaugurated this broadly defined humanitarian organization comprised of local bands around the world which worked primarily with children. All who joined were required to abide by the following pledge: 'I will try to be kind to all harmless living creatures, and try to protect them from cruel usage.'[11] Issues of *Our Dumb Animals* triumphantly declared that this 'army' was several hundred thousand strong within a few years of its creation.

The spread of this enormous 'army' abroad—particularly in India— was made possible by the close relationship between American animal welfare activists and missionaries, a logical nexus given the humane movement's deep roots in evangelical Christianity. George Angell was the son of a Baptist minister father and a mother who spent two hours alone each day in silent prayer (Angell 1883: 2). Francis Willard, the president of the Woman's Christian Temperance Union, praised the SPCA movement: 'I look upon your mission as a sacred one, not second to any that are founded in the name of Christ.'[12] India was a popular location for American Protestant missionaries ever since 1813, when the British government's Charter Act lifted a ban on missionaries in its Indian provinces. Thereafter, American Baptist, Presbyterian, Methodist, and Methodist Episcopal missionary reports contained a plethora of sensational, exoticized representations of Indian religious icons and practices: the tongue-lolling Goddess Kali wearing a garland of skulls and dancing on Shiva's corpse, hook-swinging devotees, roving bands of murderous thugis, and more. As greater numbers of American women attained a college degree in the 1870s, more American women arrived in India as single missionaries (M.C. Singh 2000: 5). Although a few high-caste Hindus like the Bengali writer Michael Madhusudan Datta converted to Christianity, the majority of Hindu converts were lower-caste (Spear 1978: 163–4). And Hindus and Muslims as a whole were generally unreceptive to proselytizing. Missionaries found better reception among India's peripatetic hill tribal communities, particularly in the isolated northeastern regions of current-day Assam, Nagaland, Manipur, and Mizoram—places where there was no centralized state or religious apparatus in place. Missionary efforts there were so successful that Nagaland, for example, has a Christian majority today.[13]

Missionaries often worked hand-in-hand with anthropologists and Crown administrators in producing colonial knowledge about the peoples of India and corresponding systems of colonial control. The historian Nicholas Dirks has demonstrated that such representations collectively emphasized the 'corrupt' and 'idolatrous' nature of Hinduism, and the 'barbarism' of hill tribal groups (Dirks 2001: 173–7). Both missionary and official representations repeatedly generated lurid images of animal sacrifice and cannibalism. Lockwood Kipling described ritual Hindu animal sacrifices in orgiastic terms:

When we talk of sacrifice we think of the grave and decent solemnities described in the Bible or in Homer. Such ideas are rudely dispelled by the reality in India. The goat and buffalo sacrifices to Kali at Kali ghat in the highly civilised metropolis of Bengal are not to be mentioned in connection with any slaughtering we know of, for there may be seen thousands of people gloating in delirious excitement over rivers of blood (Kipling 1891: 8).

Band of Mercy likewise produced discursive images of 'savagery' in support of their mandates to 'civilize' and Christianize the Indian masses. N. Agnes Robb, an American missionary in Sura, Assam, who was the leader of her local Band of Mercy, proudly reported her success to *Our Dumb Animals*:

Not much more than half a century ago these people were wild savages and cruel head-hunters, though they were not cannibals so far as we know. Now there are many schools and more than 5,000 Christians. There are forty-one members, big and little, in the Band, and would be more if I could give more time to it. Some of the big boys and girls who joined have graduated from our school here this year and gone home to their villages. Some of them, I feel sure, are interested enough to teach along humane lines if they do not really organize Bands. The seed has been sown and I pray the good work may spread.[14]

Another Band of Mercy in Ferozepore, Punjab, was created in 1911 and became the Animals' Friend Society by 1914. In addition to its animal protection activities (with a special emphasis on bird conservation), this Band of Mercy worked through what Booker T. Washington referred to at the Tuskeegee Institute as the 'gospel of the toothbrush', by promoting 'natural and humane diet' and good hygiene.[15]

Despite their growing ubiquity in the late nineteenth century, missionaries had occupied an ambivalent place in the early British Raj. In the late eighteenth and early nineteenth centuries, British officials banned missionary activity wholesale because they were worried that Christian zealots would incite indigenous hostility, thus thwarting the political peace and Company profit potential. British Orientalists like Sir William Jones, an East India Company judge in Calcutta, a comparative philologist, and the founder of the Asiatic Society in 1786, believed strongly in noninterference with indigenous religions. Yet Company opinion began to change as evangelicals gained greater political authority in England, and British missionaries made successful forays into nearby Danish Serampore, where evangelicals translated and taught the Bible in several Indian languages; seeing that such linguistic ventures could be invaluable in training Company servants, the British Parliament passed the Charter Act of 1813, which opened India to 'licensed' missionaries and private traders. In the words of the historian Stanley Wolpert, 'The spirit of Adam Smith's laissez-faire thus marched hand-in-hand with the gospel of evangelicalism through the narrow portals of company privilege ...' (Wolpert 1989: 207–8). Despite this change in official policy, evangelicals and Orientalist Company officials still clashed on numerous occasions. From 1817–63, Orientalists held sway in Madras, where British East India Company officials took over the administration and maintenance of Hindu temples; this move enraged evangelicals, who saw this form of governance as tacit support for Hindu 'idolatry'. Missionary anti-idolatry activists protested long and hard, culminating in 1863 with legislation that moved temple management into the hands of Hindu elites. As the historian Peter van der Veer notes, evangelicals like Zachary Macauley worked hand-in-hand with utilitarians such as his son Thomas Babington Macauley to create—in the words of the *Minute on Indian Education* (1835)—'a class of persons, Indian in blood and colour, but English in taste, in opinion, in morals, and in intellect.' According to van der Veer, 'Indians did not conceive the colonial state as neutral and secular but rather as fundamentally Christian' (van der Veer 2001: 23).

Similarly, animal welfare activism—despite its promise of serving as a radical humanist critique of empire—could serve as an agent of imperial policing. The Legislative Council of India, under the authority of Sir Andrew Scoble, passed Act XI of 1890 on 21 March, for the prevention of cruelty to animals. Lockwood Kipling devoted much of his treatise *Beast and Man in India* (1891) to showing that such legislation was urgently necessary in India:

The Hindu worships the cow, and as a rule, is reluctant to take the life of any animal except in sacrifice. But that does not preserve the ox, the horse, and the ass from being unmercifully beaten, over-driven, over-laden, under-fed, and worked with sores under their harness; nor does it save them from abandonment to starvation when unfit for work, and to a lingering death which is made a long torture by birds of prey, whose beaks, powerless to kill outright, inflict undeserved torment (Kipling 1891: 1–4).

In 1887, the *Annual Report of the Calcutta SPCA* noted that Calcutta had the highest number of arrests for animal cruelty in the world, leading to 7,126 prosecutions and an extraordinarily high 7,042 convictions in 1886.[16] (By contrast, in New York City in 1885, the ASPCA investigated 2,846 cases of suspected animal cruelty, out of which 722 were prosecuted in the courts.)[17] Although *Our Dumb Animals* treated the Calcutta SPCA statistic as further proof of India's vigilant animal kindness, one could read such reportage in a different way: as a sign that animal welfare activism in India—as in the United States—could serve as a means of policing the working poor. SPCA prosecution efforts in the subcontinent targeted lower-caste Hindus and labouring Muslims whose livelihood was dependent on animals.

Ultimately, American animal advocacy with respect to India was a paradoxical phenomenon. As a progressive platform, *Our Dumb Animals* consistently denounced formal empire in India and attempted to build relationships with Indian nationalists. In particular, George Angell established solid ties with the Maharashtrian Christian educator, scholar, nationalist, and child-widow-protection advocate Pandita Ramabai Sarasvati, who lectured in the United States from March 1886 to November 1888. Midway through Ramabai's US tour, in December 1887, progressive American reformers founded the American Ramabai Association in Angell's hometown of Boston in order to fund Ramabai's Indian educational initiatives. In *The Peoples of the United States* (1889), Ramabai chronicled in Marathi her views of American society, culture, democratic politics, the status of women, race relations, and American attitudes toward animals. Ramabai wrote a letter to Angell denouncing the feather trade and fashionable bird hats; her letter became the basis for an MSPCA pamphlet that the organization used to raise funds around Boston: 'As I travel around this country I see thousands of young ladies and old women, as well as little children, wearing whole and half bodies of birds on their bonnets. It shocks and grieves me.'[18]

Our Dumb Animals happily noted that Pandita Ramabai's support for animal welfare had boosted the magazine's circulation rates in the subcontinent.[19] Moreover, she infused the curriculum at the Sharada Sadan (her boarding school for widowed girls and women in Kedgaon, Maharashtra) with Angell's tenets of humane education as 'a monument to our dear friend Mr Angell, God bless him! Through him I learned what a good influence this has over children. In India, though people worship animals, they are not humane; and they treat animals most cruelly' (Kosambi 2003: 250, n. 48).

Yet such progressive forays on behalf of animal welfare also contained reactionary strands. The MSPCA's contradictory fusion of support for vegetarianism, sacred cows, anti-colonialism, and Christian missionary work resonated with the formation of a proto-Hindutva nationalism in the late nineteenth century that was predicated upon a politics of exclusion. American missionaries in India naturally supported the evangelical dimensions of Britain's colonial project—which in turn helped spawn an explosive, reactionary new identity politics among many Hindus who felt that their religious identity was under siege. And animals played a central role in defining and sustaining this new nationalism. After the British North-West Provincial High Court declared in 1888 that cows were not sacred and consequently could not be covered by Section 295 of the Indian Penal Code, a volatile Hindu cow-protection movement took shape, first in the Punjab and then across Uttar Pradesh, designed to 'save' the lives of cattle slated for religious sacrifice, and in some cases, ordinary butchering. Cow protection societies targeted Muslims who sacrificed cattle as part of Baqar Id (in ceremonial observance of the near sacrifice of Ishmael by Ibrahim), and low-caste Hindus who sold cattle to Muslims for sacrificial purposes, slaughtered cows themselves, or worked with leather. The historian Sandria Freitag observes that this movement helped consolidate the formation of a wider Hindu public and supported broader nationalist organizations such as the Indian National Congress. Moreover, cow protection was spearheaded by Hindu elites, took shape in urban environments, and spread into rural areas via printed materials and itinerant orators like wandering holy men. At one large meeting in Azamgarh district, an influential zamindar (landholder) and priest passed around a picture of a cow standing next to a menacing sword-bearing Muslim (Freitag 1989: 150–3). In some instances, cow activists were mostly peaceful—simply purchasing cattle destined for slaughter and placing them in well-funded cow sanctuaries. At other times, this activism turned violent. Hindu leatherworkers, in addition to those engaged in the cow trade with Muslims, were harassed, beaten, and legally bullied in the courts. And in 1893, approximately a dozen Muslims practicing their right to sacrifice in eastern Uttar Pradesh, along with Muslim bystanders, were killed by Hindu mobs (Freitag 1989: 169–70).

Many colonial officials declared that the cow riots were simply another form of anticolonial agitation. According to one administrator, Oday Pertap Singh, 'A taste for harassing the Government is springing up in the country, and the cow agitation has more as its motive than appears on its surface. The time is not far distant when there will be Nihilists here in India as well as in countries farther west' (O.P. Singh 1894: 667). *The New York Times* reported that the cow riots evoked memories of the Indian Rebellion of 1857, and called for heightened British force in India through liberal use of 'the stick'.[20] Certainly nationalism played an enormous role in shaping the cow-protection movement; yet this particular strand was also animated by marginalizing and demonizing a Muslim and low-caste Hindu 'Other', foreshadowing the rise of violent Hindutva groups like the Rashtriya Svayamsevak Sangh (RSS) in 1925 and beyond (Freitag 1989: 171).

In contemporary India, animal welfare issues are still often integrally tied to a politics of exclusion, much as they were a hundred years ago. As the Quit India movement accelerated during the 1920s and 1930s,

American animal activists applauded Mahatma Gandhi's brand of vegetarian nationalism and nonviolence. Founded in the United States in 1980, the animal rights organization People for the Ethical Treatment of Animals (PETA)—like its antecedents a hundred years ago—has strong ties to India. PETA's South Asian counterpart, PETA India, has a website sprinkled profusely with ahimsa epigraphs from Gandhi in addition to updates on its many campaigns (for example, against KFC).[21] Yet this organization, similar to its predecessors, marginalizes dispossessed people even as it simultaneously attempts to promote a progressive agenda. In 2001, PETA India launched a huge campaign against the Indian leather industry, claiming that Indian cows were abysmally treated. As a result, American retailers like Gap and L.L. Bean have decided to abandon their trade with Indian leather exporters. PETA India spokeswoman Porva Joshipura noted that this boycott had cost Indian producers around $20 million in 2001. Yet the boycott has had a devastating human cost among the 2.5 million impoverished Chamar leatherworkers whose ability to make a living is dependent upon a healthy leather trade.[22]

Conservative Hindus have resorted to legal harassment to protect animals as part of defending a 'purer' form of Brahmanical Hinduism. Although a law banning animal sacrifice had been on the books in the state of Tamil Nadu since 1950 (the Animal and Bird Sacrifices Prohibition Act), it was not enforced until August 2003, when—out of ostensible concerns for animals—state Chief Minister Jayalalitha Jayaram ordered district-level officials to enforce the ban rigorously after police stood by doing nothing as 500 buffaloes were sacrificed at a Hindu temple in the district of Tiruchirapalli.[23] Animal rights activists like former Union Environment Minister Maneka Gandhi applauded both this move and Jayalalitha's order two days earlier to give temple elephants a mandatory one-month rest every year. Other advocates supported the ban in Whiggish, neo-liberal terms: that animal sacrifice was a vestige of the past, akin to other now-unacceptable social practices like sati and untouchability (Viswanathan 2003). But the state's Dalit constituents regarded the ban as yet another example of caste oppression because animal sacrifice was integral to Dalit folk-deity temple worship. Dalits defied the ban by continuing their practice of animal sacrifice (even though many were arrested as a result) and by challenging the ban in the courts on grounds of unconstitutionality. The religious scholar A. Sivasubramaniam observed that the ban was clearly a bow to Brahmanical Hindutva forces who had long wanted '... to homogenize the temples of folk deities[, which] would only lead to the end of the plurality of Hindu society,' and place village temples under Brahmanical control, thereby standardizing religious practices, removing village deities, and replacing them with images of mainstream gods like Shiva (Viswanathan 2003). Dalits, however, protested most effectively with their feet. After Jayalalitha's All India Anna Dravida Munnetra Kazhagam (AIADMK) Party was trounced in the Lok Sabha polls, AIADMK leaders lifted the 2003 enforcement order in February 2004, and introduced a bill in July 2004 to repeal the 1950 Act altogether as a way to woo disaffected voters back into the party fold.[24]

The Bharatiya Janata Party (BJP) made vegetarianism and cow worship a central part of its Hindu nationalist agenda. During his tenure as prime minister, Atal Bihari Vajpayee stated on numerous occasions, 'I prefer to die rather than eat beef,' while fellow party members and allied conservative political groups such as the Vishva Hindu Parishad lobbied to pass a national bill prohibiting cow slaughter.[25] Although the Congress Party (now again the ruling party after Vajpayee's BJP was defeated in national elections in 2004) was founded upon Jawaharlal Nehru's commitment to secular freedom, Congress Party officials have also participated in the communalist Hindutva movement. Even before the BJP introduced the bill for a nationwide ban on cow slaughter in August 2003, the Congress Party chief minister in the state of Madhya Pradesh jumped into the fray in January 2003, calling for a nationwide ban. The journalist Jyotsna Singh observes, 'The debate has taken a remarkable turn as the country's two main political parties have begun battling over which one is the more "Hindu"' (J. Singh 2003). In this battle for Hindu authenticity, gruesome assaults on low-caste leather-workers and meat-eating Muslims have made headlines in recent years (see, for example, Sullivan 2003: A33). Given the shadow of historical precedent, it remains to be seen if animal protection can ever be separated from the exclusionary Hindu nationalist objectives that have long nurtured and sustained this movement.

NOTES

1. 'Cruelty to Animals: First Case of Punishment under the New Law'. *New York Times* (hereafter, *NYT*). 25 April 1866: 8.
2. 'A Strange Affair'. *NYT*. 6 February 1875: 4.
3. 'A Country Rich in Cattle'. *Our Dumb Animals* (hereafter, *ODA*). vol. 47, no. 4 (September 1914): 50.

4. 'View of a Vegetarian'. *NYT*. 15 September 1895: 9.
5. 'Had No Meat at the Dinner'. *NYT*. 2 May 1894: 5.
6. 'Theosophists Pray Against Vivisection'. *ODA*. vol. 36, no. 11 (April 1904): 140.
7. 'Shooting Boys in the Philippines'. *ODA*. vol. 35, no. 1 (June 1902): 2; 'The Present War Craze'. *ODA*. vol. 30, no. 11 (April 1898): 134; 'The Philippines are Expensive'. *ODA*. vol. 33, no. 4 (September 1900): 38.
8. 'For the Starving in India'. *ODA*. vol. 33, no. 2 (July 1900): 15.
9. 'Delhi, India'. *ODA*. vol. 35, no. 9 (February 1903): 106 (emphasis in original).
10. 'A Great Danger'. *ODA*. vol. 38, no. 7 (December 1905): 94.
11. 'Two Kinds of Armies'. *ODA*. vol. 21, no. 4 (September 1888): 49.
12. 'Francis E. Willard'. *ODA*. vol. 30, no. 11 (April 1898): 145.
13. *www.mapsofindia.com/stateprofiles/nagaland/*accessed from the World Wide Web on 18 November 2007.
14. 'Band of Mercy in India'. *ODA*. vol. 46, no. 11 (April 1914): 170.
15. 'For Kindness in India'. *ODA*. vol. 47, no. 3 (August 1914): 45.
16. 'Annual Report of the Calcutta SPCA'. *ODA*. vol. 20, no. 5 (October 1887): 52.
17. Published reports did not list the numbers actually convicted. 'Henry Bergh's Society'. *NYT*. 7 January 1886: 8.
18. 'Pundita Ramabai Humane Pamphlet'. Quoted from Kosambi 2003: 26.
19. 'India: Pundita Ramabai Request for Subscriptions to Our Dumb Animals'. *ODA*. vol. 20, no. 6 (November 1887): 65.
20. 'When Mussulman and Hindu Fight'. *NYT*. 17 September 1893: 19; 'England, India, and the Stick'. *NYT*. 1 October 1893: 22.
21. 'Amitabh Bachchan and Yana Gupta Voted Hottest Vegetarians Alive'. *www.PetaIndia.org* accessed from the World Wide Web on 21 October 2003.
22. Sanjeev Srivastava, 'PETA Skins India's Leather Workers'. *BBC News*, 23 August 2001 (*http://news.bbc.co.uk/2/hi/business/1506426.stm* accessed from the World Wide Web on 31 August 2004); 'Animal Rights Group Targets Indian Leather'. *BBC News*. 12 August 2002 (*http://news.bbc.co.uk/2/hi/business/2188876.stm*, accessed from the World Wide Web on 31 August 2004).
23. 'South Indian State Cracks Down on Sacrifice after 500 Buffalo Slaughtered'. Agence France Presse, 28 August 2003 (*http://lexis-nexus.com*, accessed from the World Wide Web on 31 August 2004).
24. 'Bill to Lift Ban on Animal Sacrifice in Temples Introduced'. *Worldwide Religious News*, 30 July 2004 (*http://www.wwrn.org*, accessed from the World Wide Web on 19 September 2004).
25. 'Maneka Gandhi Calls for a "Cow Protection Act"'. Hindustantimes.com.

10 October 2003 (*http://www.hindustantimes.com/online*); 'VHP Says it will Back Congress if it Pilots Cow Bill'. Hindustantimes.com. 10 October 2003 (*http://www.hindustantimes.com/online*, accessed from the World Wide Web on 31 August 2004).

REFERENCES

Angell, George T. 1883. *Autobiographical Sketches and Personal Recollections*. Boston: American Humane Education Society.

Dirks, Nicholas B. 2001. *Castes of Mind: Colonialism and the Making of Modern India*. Princeton: Princeton University Press.

Freitag, Sandria B. 1989. *Collective Action and Community: Public Arenas and the Emergence of Communalism in North India*. Berkeley: University of California Press.

Green, Harvey. 1986. *Fit for America: Health, Fitness, Sport and American Society*. Baltimore: Johns Hopkins University Press.

Kingsford, Anna. 1884. 'The Best Food for Man'. Bombay: International Book House Limited.

Kipling, J. Lockwood. 1891. *Beast and Man in India: A Popular Sketch of Indian Animals in Their Relations with the People*. London: Macmillan and Co.

Kosambi, Meera (ed. and trans.). 2003. *Pandita Ramabai's American Encounter: The Peoples of the United States (1898)*. Bloomington: Indiana University Press.

Singh, Jyotsna. 2003. 'India Targets Cow Slaughter'. *BBC News*. 8 August 2003 (*http://news.bbc.co.uk/go/pr/fr/-/2/hi/south_asia/2945020.stm*, accessed from the World Wide Web on 31 August 2004).

Singh, Maina Chawla. 2000. *Gender, Religion, and 'Heathen Lands': American Missionary Women in South Asia (1860s–1940s)*. New York and London: Garland Publishing, Inc.

Singh, Oday Pertap. 1894. 'The Cow Agitation, or the Mutiny-Plasm in India'. *The Nineteenth Century*. vol. 35, no. 206 (April), p. 667.

Spear, Percival. 1978. *A History of India: From the Sixteenth Century to the Twentieth Century*. vol. II. London: Penguin Books.

Sullivan, Tim. 2003. 'In India, Eating Cow Can be One Giant Political Misstep'. *Austin American-Statesman*. 22 March, p. A33.

van der Veer, Peter. 2001. *Imperial Encounters: Religion and Modernity in India and Britain*. Princeton: Princeton University Press.

Viswanathan, S. 2003. 'A Decree on Animal Sacrifice'. *Frontline*. vol. 20, no. 20 (27 September–10 October) (*http://www.flonnet.com/fl2020/stories/20031010001205000.htm*, accessed from the World Wide Web on 31 August 2004).

Wolpert, Stanley. 1989. *A New History of India*. 3rd edn. New York: Oxford University Press.

4

BLINDNESS AND SIGHT
Moral Vision in Rajasthani Narratives

Ann Grodzins Gold

Every picture has its shadows
And it has some source of light
Blindness, blindness, and sight

—Joni Mitchell, 'Shadows and Light'

This essay contemplates aspects of moral vision in diverse genres of Rajasthani narrative. Through examining the ways in which few oral texts offer fragments of cultural critique, I aim to honour Eleanor Zelliot's contributions to our understandings of South Asian hierarchy from below. In her pioneering work on the 'folklore of pride' (1992 [1986]: 317–33), Zelliot shows how contemporary Dalits in Maharashtra actively seek to reclaim a cultural heritage of achievement and self-respect in traditional proverbs and tales. In rural Rajasthan, where disadvantaged communities are generally less mobilized than in Maharashtra, persons at the lower end of ritual and social hierarchies also tell stories that decry oppression and deny degradation based on birth-given status. Such narratives often make powerful claims for human equality in religious terms—a possibility Zelliot delineates in her earlier writings on untouchable bhakti poets (ibid: 3–32). I shall also consider stories that humorously mock particular groups for particular stereotyped foibles, finding these too not wholly without moral insight.

The tales I treat emerge in highly varied performance contexts but have in common a broad concern with social hierarchy, identity, and difference. The first narrative I examine lends itself to an interpretation that allows me to make it this essay's thematic parable. It is quite literally about blindness and sight. It also suggests that those who choose to sustain society's judgements of the low-born reveal an inner blindness based on unwarranted self-regard. Ironically, god's granting physical vision to impaired eyes does not clear the lenses of the soul.

Music from my student years occasionally echoes in my aging brain, and Joni Mitchell's post-1960s lyrics about shadows and light surfaced through associative impulses beyond any intellectual control, as I thought about the stories I wished to discuss here. My epigraph from a non-Indic cultural world poetically implies that darkness is not hopelessly impenetrable; something always glimmers. Equally, light is never all there is, or nothing would be visible. I recall repeatedly listening to the album containing this song during the years before my first fieldwork in India. Who knows what cognitive loops are at play. Perhaps all my interpretations of village morality are based partially on values embedded in counterculture poetics, my own formative milieu (and one that was of course influenced by South Asian philosophies).

I proceed to offer minimal introductory background followed by three brief examples of Rajasthani oral narratives: the 'twice-blind carpenter', a pilgrimage miracle account told by a Regar (leatherworker) man in 1980; two stories about stupid weavers (*balai*) told by a male herder (*gujar*) in 1993; and a story about Raidas, cobbler saint and devotee of the goddess of purity, told by a Regar woman in 1993. My conclusions are appropriately tentative.

BACKGROUND

During about a quarter-century of engagement with north Indian oral traditions, I have—no matter what my formal research topic—assiduously recorded any myths, legends, folktales or lively anecdotes that came my way. My publications, spanning approximately the same period, often feature those tales that brilliantly subvert caste and gender hierarchies. Thus I highlight tales pointing to a divine morality that denies and punishes devaluation of any disadvantaged human being. I stress that although I selected such examples to translate and highlight, I never sought them in research. Rather, they came to me with delightful spontaneity. Such stories use humour and irreverence, earthy language and an encompassing devotional cosmology to show how the human spirit, affirmed by multiform divinity, prevails over many kinds of domination. Thus, for example, women claim ritual authority and superior knowledge and virtue in a patriarchal religious world (Gold 2002; Raheja and Gold 1994: 149–81); sweepers claim that their community, stigmatized by its work of cleaning excrement, is in truth the source of all food on heaven and earth (Gold 1998); Regars tell that the river goddess Ganga summarily punishes those who seek cruelly to exploit the triple vulnerability of young, attractive leather worker women (Gold and Gujar 2002: 206–9). This last is a striking tale that bears repeating for this essay's purpose.

Over the years, I have also happened to record but failed to publish a handful of humorous short narratives, indigenously labelled 'entertainment' (*manoranjan*) which are told by members of one community to mock and deride another. These made me laugh but squirm. I felt I had to disapprove of them. Of course, in the United States and the world over, there exist vast stores of folklore around ethnic and racial traits. Even in our times of rigorous political correctness, some of these still arouse laughter and some scholars of such humour argue that this is not necessarily unhealthy for society. I shall therefore consider here, together with stories displaying resistance to hierarchy, two entertainments that seem to support it. In what I suppose to be their disconcerting shadows, these stories flicker with lights of irony and comedy. Tales that support equality, as well as those that jokingly appear to reinforce discrimination, may be sources of positioned social commentary.

This is a brief work of limited scope. I have selected my examples to present varied takes on inequality, but I encountered them in the course of research on other topics: pilgrimage, agriculture, environmental history. I made no systematic collection of stories about hierarchy, and cannot claim that these are representative. Whether they critique conventions of social difference from a disempowered position, or reinforce them from a slight advantage, these portrayals of human difference inevitably reflect the teller's situation and the performance context. The narrative genres I treat include performed reminiscences based on recent experience ('the twice-blind carpenter'), humorous vignettes told to pass the time ('the weavers and the black snake' and 'the weavers who danced like peacocks'), and a tale about the low-born saint Raidas, which might be classified within hagiography.[1] Some stories play gleefully upon the human comedy's surface but others demand of their audience deeper and more compassionate vision. For each story I sketch the context in which I recorded it. In all but the last case, I was accompanied and assisted by my long-term research collaborator and sometime co-author, Bhoju Ram Gujar. His voice, contributions, and interventions will be apparent.

My understanding of these stories is helped, and unified, not only by Zelliot's foundational work on the social implications of untouchable religious sensibilities and Dalit transformations of tradition, but by James Fernandez and Mary Taylor Huber's musings on irony. Every example I offer has its ironic twists, and displays, I believe, what Fernandez and Huber call 'true irony' in contrast to 'malicious irony'.[2] It is worth examining their formulation of this distinction in full, for it expresses just what is most valuable in the Rajasthani stories:

> Militant or malicious ironists use parody or satire of the other to express their self-confidence and mock the others' lack of knowledge, and/or values and accomplishments. These expressions pretend to possess a sense of how the world works and what the causes and solutions are, and they use the tools of discrepancy positively or negatively, benignly or maliciously, to favour that confident worldview. 'True irony' on the other hand may be said to dwell in uncertainty, with a kind of comic sense of the finitude and impermanence of all things human. While it shares the generic sense of the discrepant it sees no easy solutions or definitive causes of the kind that can confidently, even maliciously, energize ridicule and sarcasm (Fernandez and Huber 2001: 21–2).

True irony, then, is also a play of shadows and light.[3]

THE TWICE-BLIND CARPENTER: A PILGRIMAGE MIRACLE ACCOUNT

Bardu Regar of Ghatiyali village belonged to the formerly 'untouchable' community of leatherworkers.[4] Bardu narrated the story of the twice-blind carpenter to Bhoju Ram Gujar and me in 1980 when I was in the midst of my doctoral research on pilgrimage. Although Gujars and Regars have a history of mutual disregard, Bhoju and I had ventured into the leatherworker neighbourhood on learning that a group of pilgrims had recently returned from a journey to Ramdevra in western Rajasthan. Ramdevra is the main sacred site dedicated to one of Rajasthan's legendary hero-gods, Ramdevji. Ramdevji is especially connected with untouchable groups, although members of the higher castes often worship him—especially when seeking relief from affliction. Ramdevji himself was born into a Rajput or aristocratic, ruling lineage, but an untouchable friend/devotee plays an important role in his legend.[5]

Ramdevji's tale asserts in a number of ways that he is a cosmic personage who disapproves strongly of all attitudes and behaviours encapsulated in the single Hindi term *chhutachhut* used to encompass matters of discrimination between touchability and untouchability. This hero-god is known also to give immediate 'proof' (*parchya*) to devotees—either of favour or displeasure. In the context of Ramdevji's lore the term 'proof' is used synonymously with miracle (*chamatkar*).

Bhoju and I were discussing with Bardu his experiences on pilgrimage to Ramdevra, and the nature of devotion to Ramdevji in general. Bardu had been talking about the curative power of bathing at the tanks near Ramdevji's temple and other places in the sacred geography of the pilgrimage route. These waters belonging to the deity were particularly famed for giving eyesight to the blind. Bardu then moved without any prompting into a more elaborated and specific miracle narrative. I give this narrative in Bardu's words as he told it to us, and as we recorded, transcribed, and translated it many years ago:

Before, on a previous pilgrimage, there were ten or twenty farmers with us. [By farmers he means higher caste, non-untouchables.] Among them were Narayan Khati [Carpenter] and Bhura Khati [his wife]. Narayan Khati was blind. We sat him on a stone seat, put all our stuff with him, and went to look around—at the place of Mandor Bhairu.

When we came back, Narayan Khati said, 'Now I can see.'

People asked him, 'What things do you see?'

So he said, 'There are horses,' and he counted them. He said, 'Over here is the gate.'

So everyone thought, it is very good if a miracle happens to one of our villagers. Everyone will praise Ramdevji. So everyone called 'Victory!'

I told him he should touch the feet of all the company. But he didn't do it. Perhaps there was hypocrisy in his heart.

In this company were Regar, Chamar, Khati, Mali, all together. [Regar and Chamar are both leather working 'untouchable' groups; Khati or carpenters and Mali or gardeners are from the middle-ranking 'clean' birth groups.] When he saw all the peoples' things mixed together, including food, Narayan said to his wife Bhura, 'Hey why are all the things put together?'

At that very instant, he became blind again. [Bardu concludes]: On this road, the road to Ramdevji, Untouchability should not be and should not be spoken.

Towards the end of this interview, Bardu Regar brought out some of Ramdevji's *prasad* and gave it to us to eat. I thought nothing of it, as the sharing of prasad is a major meritorious act enjoined upon returned pilgrims. Bhoju also casually swallowed the prasad. Later Bhoju told me that for him to consume anything at all in a leatherworker's house was a major violation of his own caste's dharma, and that he never would have done it except for fear of Ramdevji's anger. Perhaps Bardu deliberately tested the effect of his story by offering Bhoju prasad.

Although this is a miracle account and not a folktale as such, it nonetheless offers a nice variation on a 'folklore of pride'—taken generically as a reclaiming of self-worth. In this instance narrative closure firmly discounts prejudice and shows that God punishes unfounded discrimination. In its movement toward this outcome, Bardu's account plays between two obvious levels of vision and blindness—of the eyes and of the heart. Ramdevji gave the carpenter a chance to see reality, but he failed the test. To touch the feet of leatherworkers was not within his capacity because he lacked moral vision even when he regained his eyesight. He might as well, therefore, be blind in both senses. There is true irony in the carpenter's fate. We are left to imagine how he must have cursed his own failure of nerve and comprehension. But in his profound disappointment he is not totally isolated, for all the pilgrim company would suffer disappointment at a rescinded miracle. Deities live on their reputations in very real ways.

Bhoju Ram's response to the narrative reveals a performative breakthrough: of miraculous lessons into ordinary social interactions, changing them in this case to extraordinary ones. Thus a moral is enacted.

STUPID WEAVERS IN HERDERS' ENTERTAINMENTS

A herder, Dayal Gujar, now deceased, told us two funny stories about weavers. Dayal Gujar was a memorably sweet, articulate, and thoughtful man, suffering from ill health when we interviewed him extensively in 1993. No longer able to do the work he loved, caring for animals, he did not mind our taping him for several hours during which we covered every topic under the sun. The weaver stories emerged as simple examples he gave us of how herders pass the time. We recorded similar tales from other, younger herders, but the two Dayal told us endured in my memory so that when I thought about folkloric commentary on social difference, they leaped to mind and were not difficult to unearth in electronic fieldnote files.

Rajasthanis consider such stories—devoid as they are of didactic or devotional purpose—to be mere entertainment (manoranjan). Apte's anthropological, cross-cultural study of humour delivers some common sense advice on this type of humour, affirming a relatively benign view of its nature. He writes:

people who propose many theories of ethnic humor often ignore the fact that humor in general serves the purpose of entertainment and pleasure. Enjoyment of any humor, including ethnic humor, does not necessarily make individuals aggressive or hostile. Rather, a make-believe framework or state of mind is developed temporarily for sheer pleasure and is discarded when engagement in humorous exchange is over (Apte 1985: 145).[6]

Dayal Gujar clearly enjoyed telling these stories. They might not have troubled me had not a child who belonged to the weaver community, and who was Dayal's neighbour, been sitting and listening. My transcription of the interview includes Bhoju calling the child's attention to his own weaver identity. The boy assented without any evident discomfort or shame, but I found this particular breakthrough from story to context to be disconcerting.

Both weaver stories contain some subtle commentaries on social and religious practices. The first has to do with reverence for ancestral spirits who take the form of snakes.

The Weavers and the Black Snake

In the village of Motipura on the banks of the Banas River in the house of a weaver a black snake appeared. The weaver wouldn't let anyone kill it, thinking, 'it is my honoured ancestral spirit, and it wants to drink milk.' So he gave it milk.

So the weaver had a son who was a servant in someone else's house.

And one day the son's wife was grinding flour and that snake wrapped itself around her leg, and she started shouting. People came running. Then the snake raised its hood over her. But she said, 'don't kill it, don't kill it, it is our god!'

The people all wanted to kill it; they said, 'throw it aside so we can kill it.'
Then her father-in law came and he became possessed and said, 'don't
kill it, it is our forefather.'
And then the snake bit her twice and she died.
Even today the son cannot find another wife and the two of them, father
and son, are rolling flat-bread by themselves.
Weavers are so stupid!

There is considerable lore in Ghatiyali and elsewhere in India
about snakes inhabited by the spirits of deceased relatives (Gold 1988:
235–9). While living in rural Rajasthan, I heard many fabulous stories
of snakes who were ancestors. In one of these, an old man in the thrall
of acute psychological illness dashed out of the house with suicidal
intentions. He hurled himself down a well in a field belonging to a
community different from his own. Lurking in that well was a huge
black snake. Not only did the snake not bite the temporarily deranged
old man, but his nephew was able to extract him from the well with
no harm from the snake to either one of them. I heard this story both
from the nephew and from members of the community to whom the
well belonged. All agreed that the snake was an ancestral spirit of the
well-owner, and that it did not bite the two men because of old bonds
of friendship between their family and the well-owners' family.

In spite of this snakes-as-ancestors lore, fear usually prevails over
reverence in the everyday treatment of snakes. In my experience, I
found that when people encountered snakes in their houses or courtyards
they were generally inclined to pound them to death, and only afterwards
to offer milk to their lingering spirits. The comic irony here is that the
weaver couple irrationally clings to the mystical interpretation rather
than act pragmatically. Events prove them foolish in this stubborn
attitude. The wife's folly is influenced by her husband, but other women
will not be so easily duped and thus the story's ending leaves the surviving
males of the household with no women to cook for them—a socially
devastating, pathetically comic situation in village thought. However,
it is possible to imagine an entirely different outcome where the
protected benevolent snake deity showers the weavers with boons while
their neighbours look on enviously.

A pervasive cultural context in which snakes are ambivalently
perceived as immediate threats but potential deities endows the stupid-
weavers story with the kind of ambiguity that characterizes true irony.

How do we know if a snake is an ancestor? The stupid weavers guess wrong, but so might anyone. The next weaver tale has still more complex factors at play, for it touches on gender and sexuality as well as bearing vivid religious imagery, although I had initially failed to realize this.

Around the time I conceived this paper, I happened to be flipping through an art book containing Krishna paintings from the pilgrimage centre of Nathdwara. I was searching for imagery relating to nature, and there was plenty of it. I was suddenly arrested by a colour reproduction from the early twentieth century, in the Rajasthani miniature mode, entitled 'Radha and Krishna as peacocks, dancing with peacocks'. The book's author writes of this painting:

During the Rasa Lila plays [plays that enact episodes from the childhood and youth of Krishna], actors dressed as Radha and Krishna perform a very interesting dance, *ghutano ka nach* ['knees' dance'] in which kneeling on the ground, they whirl around with great speed. Their raised kachhni [loincloth drawn up high] and rhythmic movements recalling a peacock's dance, have provided much inspiration to the artist (Ambalal 1987: 81).[7]

Thus the story of the 'weavers who danced like peacocks' acquires another interpretive layer. I had assumed their folly to arise from their own stupid fancies, when it seems they were modelling their behaviour on Radha and Krishna. The joke is not that it is silly for lovers to dance like peacocks in the rainy season but rather that it is silly for an ungainly human couple to imagine themselves graceful erotic partners like the divine couple. The absurdity is enhanced, as is the tale's polyvalency.

The Weavers Who Danced Like Peacocks

Once a weaver and his wife were both home. It was the month of Shravan [the romantic month of the rainy season], and peacocks and peahens all dance in the month of Shravan.

The weaver and his wife said to one another, 'why don't we dance like that?'

So Mr Weaver tied a wooden cot [a heavy and cumbersome object] to his backside [like a peacock's spread fan]. And Mrs Weaver tied a winnowing basket to her frontside, and going 'ko-ko-ko-ko-ko', they danced together.

One neighbour was watching them from his roof. He wanted to get them to go outside. So he set their roof on fire.

So they started to run outside and the woman ran outside going, 'ko-ko-ko-ko-ko', and the man started to run but the cot got stuck in the door and he burned to death and fell into the filthy drain.

And Mrs Weaver never came back; she went to another house and married someone else. The peahen ran away!

Mr Weaver had fallen into the drain!

Many years later Mrs Weaver was passing through her first husband's village, and she thought she would go and look at her first husband's house. So she saw his skeleton there. And she thought, 'let me greet my husband.'

So she tried to embrace her husband's skeleton, but as soon as she embraced him a scorpion bit her cheek.

Then she said, 'O my husband, you died but still you didn't forget your habit' [of biting her cheek; in regional folklore this is explicit erotic love play; see Raheja and Gold 1994: 39].

I enjoyed this story immensely, I have to admit, but I cringed when Bhoju Ram turned to the small weaver boy who happened to be sitting and listening and smilingly asked him, 'Are you a weaver?' 'Yes', the child replied, without hesitation.

According to Davies' study of ethnic humour round the world,

Such jokes should reveal the areas of moral ambiguity and ambivalence in the society where they are told and illuminate the relationship between the joke-tellers and the butts of their jokes (1990: 322).

Thus Davies points to the same open-ended aspect of ethnic humour that Fernandez does in his attempt to delineate 'true irony'. Rather than put people in boxes, it leaves openings and provokes reflection.[8] Although they first struck me as outrageously mean, on reflection I see that the funny stories herders tell about stupid weavers share these more benign qualities.

RAIDAS AND THE GODDESS GANGA[9]

Accompanied by Lila Devi, a woman of the *damami* or 'royal drummer' community, I had gone into the Regar neighbourhood in search of knowledge about the past. Lila was a performer by profession; her community, like the Regars, was regarded as untouchable, due to drums being made of leather. Lila and I had settled down to talk with a group of various ages, although we had come particularly to find an old woman named Gendi. We spoke for quite a while with Gendi's grandson's wife, Sundar, who was in her thirties. Sundar told us that she and her family belonged to the 'lineage of the devotee Raidas'. I asked her if that was why Regars called themselves 'Raidasi' and she and her relatives agreed, laughingly. I felt the laughter revealed their ironic awareness that few in the village ever used this polite designation for members of their community. I told them, in a foreigner's attempt at flattery, that the name of Raidas, and his compositions of devotional poetry, had 'arrived in America'.[10]

Lila was always ready with a tale. She told a story of Raidas as a baby, first refusing to suckle from his untouchable mother's breast, but doing so after the midwife chastizes him and instructs him, 'Drink mother's milk; wherever you were born you are born, so drink happily, your name will be worshipped, you will be famed, no matter in which community you were born.'

Lila followed this with another episode in which Raidas, now a grown man, is tanning hides when a group of pilgrims pass on pilgrimage to the river Ganges. Raidas pulls a bangle out of the dirty water in his tanning pit and sends it with them as an offering to Mother Ganges. The bad odour of the tanning pit is an ostensible reason for leatherworkers' untouchability.[11] Mother Ganges herself emerges from the river to accept Raidas's bangle. She simultaneously grants Raidas a vision (*darshan*) of her form, while he is sitting at home working. He is such a devotee that he has no need to go on pilgrimage to meet divinity, which is present in his 'polluted' home.

I asked the gathered Regars listening to Lila's stories of their saint if they had heard these before, and they were non-committal. Such stories are within a common tradition of low-caste devotion—in which a great but simple-hearted untouchable devotee is recognized by a deity as more truthful and sincere and pure of heart than any high-caste devotees who perform appropriate rituals. But Lila's stories also hint that even Raidas was not very happy to be born a Regar.[12]

Gendi, the old woman we had come to see, now spoke up and told me that she did know not only these tales, but many others as well. She proceeded to tell another story, also about the pure goddess Ganges treating her devotee Raidas with favour. But this has a different and far more defiant ring to it.

One time Raidas had a wedding [in his family, of his daughter], so he brought Ganges [the goddess] to the wedding as a guest. In that village was a landlord, and the landlord went riding on his horse to the Regar's house. He said [to Raidas], 'I want to marry this girl [Ganges'.]

The landlord was riding around on his horse, and came to the Regars, and said, 'I will marry this girl.'

[*Were it not that the 'girl' is a goddess, and the proposal 'marriage', the landlord's proposition reflects some prevalent negative stereotypes about rulers' bad behaviour in the past: the Rajput on his horse looks over the untouchable women and demands that the most attractive be delivered to him.*]

Raidas said, 'This is my guest! How can I marry her to you?' Then Raidas beseeched Mother Ganges, 'O Bhavani, this landlord is bothering me! He wants to marry you, so what should I do? I have brought you as a guest to the wedding, and he is acting this way.'

She said, 'It doesn't matter, if he wants to marry me, accept his wedding coconut; accept it as if you agree, and have me married in a very nice way.'

The goddess continued, 'When the landlord's wedding party comes, then you should fill the leather tanning tank—fill it with water and have them sit down near it. After that, I will take care of everything. That is all you have to do.'

[*Lila explained, in an aside, that he was to seat the Rajput and Regar groups separately.*]

Well, Mother Ganges said all that. Then the wedding parties came. So, he filled the tanning tank, and he married his daughter to the Regar on one side, and he seated the Rajputs on the other [*as if to marry Mother Ganges to the landlord; all Rajasthanis will picture the demure, veiled bride seated next to the groom*]. Then Mother Ganges jumped into the tanning tank and the water rose up and washed away the whole wedding party! They were flooded away! She swept them away!

[*She didn't want to kill the Regars, Lila interpolates.*] The whole Rajput marriage party just flowed away!

Gendi chortled audibly on the tape at the story's satisfying ending: merciless and thorough divine vengeance. The Rajput men did not just drown, they drowned in water from the leather-tanning tank: a fitting filthy end to match their filthy lust, an appropriate overwhelming of their imperious arrogance, evidence that the purity of Mother Ganges resides even in the evil-smelling, hide-tanning pit.

This story appears to take up the theme of divine favour to Regars from the mother of purity begun by Lila with her stories. However, Gendi's tale struck me as ringingly opposed to established social hierarchy in a different modality from the two Raidas tales Lila had offered. It was the difference between 'God loves me even though I'm polluted' and 'those who prey on our seemingly disempowered and helpless community will be righteously destroyed by divine anger!' Versions of both stories Lila told are part of leatherworker lore throughout north India, but I have been unable to find Gendi's story within any published accounts of devotional traditions. It offers an example of a folklore of unmitigated defiance, one that the Dalit activists described by Zelliot would be likely to approve.

SEEING THROUGH FOLLY

If anything unites these stories beyond their concern with social hierarchy it is their implicit or explicit critique or ridicule of human folly. But location of the folly shifts from case to case. In the miracle tale, folly is believing in the divisive constraints of social structure rather than the unifying reality of divine grace. In the weaver jokes the essence of folly is reversed: the weavers' mistake in both stories is to attempt to live their lives on the level of divine truth—where snakes are ancestors and humans may be gods—when this is so obviously dissonant with their mundane surroundings. In the story of Raidas and the goddess Ganga, stakes are higher and the clash more violent. An attractive and apparently vulnerable girl reveals herself to be a singular death-dealing power beyond reckoning; the folly of not recognizing this goes unforgiven. Here where the shadows of history are darker, light's remedies are more painful.

Stuart Blackburn has recently argued that for Tamil tales, 'their moral perspective is paramount' (2001: 274). I would add, at least for the narratives gathered here, that they possess not only moral vision but an ironic edge. They do not deliver morals but unfold moral imagination (Fernandez and Huber 2001). To experience measures of light and darkness, to perceive with measures of blindness and sight, remains the human condition. To claim otherwise can lead to the riskiest blindness of all—closed-minded complacency. Luckily folktales rarely perpetuate such complacency. Rather, oral narratives such as those presented here—whether inspiring laughter, anger, fear, or satisfaction—can serve to provoke a shift of viewpoints, a jog to consciousness, an altered understanding of self and other.

NOTES

1. A genre similar to 'lives of the saints' exists in north India as 'garland of devotees'.

2. According to a footnote to the passage from which I quote, Fernandez and Huber's understanding of 'true irony' bears a 'passing resemblance' to Kenneth Burke's 'classic irony'. See also Boon, who defines Burke's 'true irony' as 'humble irony that does not assume superiority to the enemy ... but rather suffers a fellow feeling' (2001: 125).

3. Rapport and Overing (2000) offer a useful summary of irony's components: 'Its definition may be said to include an ontological premise that human beings are never cognitively imprisoned by pre-ordained and pre-determining schemata of cultural classification and social structuration. They can everywhere appreciate the malleability and the mutability of social rules and realities, and the contingency and ambiguity of cultural truths.'

4. Regar is the neutral name for this group; *dherh* is insulting and Raidasi flattering.

5. For Ramdevji's legend and pilgrimage, see Binford 1976; Gold 1988: 148–9.

6. On pointed humour in India, see also Narayan, who says of urban riddle-jokes with contemporary political references, 'Clearly, these jokes are not just light and funny. They address conflicts and concerns experienced by particular social groups' (1993: 196), and Kolenda, who sees rural untouchables' humour expressing 'a train of defiance toward the official social structure and proper cultural values' (1990: 116).

7. Ambalal writes of these paintings, 'they are painted in bright primary colours and radiate joy. There are hardly any traces of their having indulged in intellectual exercises or involved craftsmanship. The main quality that shines through these paintings is devotion' (1987: 81–2).

8. See, however, Boskin, who declares, 'Because of its aggressive aspect, humour is one of the most effective weapons in the repertory of the human mind' (1987: 256).

9. This section reproduces material that appears in Gold and Gujar 2002: 206–9).

10. On Raidas see Callewaert and Friedlander 1992; Hawley and Juergensmeyer 1988: 9–32.

11. Today Ghatiyali Regars no longer perform those tasks that were traditionally degrading; the smelly practice of tanning hides has completely ceased.
12. Variants are found in Briggs' study of Chamars from the first half of the twentieth century (1920: 208–10). Callewaert and Friedlander also report a version of the Ganga offering story (1992: 28–9), although it does not refer specifically to the tanning pit.

REFERENCES

Ambalal, Amit. 1987. *Krishna as Shrinathji: Rajasthani Paintings from Nathdvara*. Ahmedabad: Mapin Publishing.

Apte, Mahadev L. 1985. *Humor and Laughter: An Anthropological Approach*. Ithaca: Cornell University Press.

Binford, Mira R. 1976. 'Mixing in the Colour of Ram of Ranuja'. In B.L. Smith (ed.). *Hinduism: New Essays in the History of Religions*. Leiden: E.J. Brill, pp. 120–42.

Blackburn, Stuart H. 2001. *Moral Fictions: Tamil Folktales in Oral Tradition*. Helsinki, Finland: Suomalainen Tiedeakatemia, pp. 120–42.

Boon, James. 2001. 'Kenneth Burke's "True irony": One Model for Ethnography, Still'. In James W. Fernandez and Mary Taylor Huber (eds). *Irony in Action: Anthropology, Practice, and the Moral Imagination*. Chicago: University of Chicago Press. pp. 118–32.

Boskin, Joseph. 1987. 'The Complicity of Humor: The Life and Death of Sambo'. In John Morreall (ed.). *The Philosophy of Laughter and Humor*. Albany: State University of New York Press, pp. 250–63.

Briggs, George W. 1920. *The Chamars*. London: Oxford University Press.

Callewaert, Winand and Peter G. Friedlander. 1992. *The Life and Works of Raidas*. New Delhi: Manohar.

Davies, Christie. 1990. *Ethnic Humor Around the World: A Comparative Analysis*. Bloomington: Indiana University Press.

Fernandez, James W. and Mary Taylor Huber. 2001. 'The Anthropology of Irony'. In James W. Fernandez and Mary Taylor Huber (eds). *Irony in Action*, pp. 1–37.

Gold, Ann Grodzins. 1988. *Fruitful Journeys: The Ways of Rajasthani Pilgrims*. Berkeley: University of California Press.

———. 1998. 'Grains of Truth: Shifting Hierarchies of Food and Grace in Three Rajasthani Tales'. *History of Religions*. vol. 38, no. 2, pp. 150–71.

———. 2002. 'Counterpoint Authority in Women's Ritual Expressions: A View from the Village'. In Laurie L. Patton (ed.). *Jewels of Authority: Women and Textual Tradition in Hindu India*. New York: Oxford University Press, pp. 177–201.

_____ and Bhoju Ram Gujar. 2002. *In the Time of Trees and Sorrows: Nature, Power, and Memory in Rajasthan.* Durham, North Carolina: Duke University Press.

Hawley, John S. and Mark Juergensmeyer. 1988. *Songs of the Saints of India.* New York: Oxford University Press.

Kolenda, Pauline. 1990. 'Untouchable Chuhras Through Their Humor: "Equalizing" Marital Kin Through Teasing, Pretence, and Farce'. In Owen M. Lynch (ed.). *Divine Passions,* Berkeley: University of California Press, pp. 116–56.

Mitchell, Joni. 1975. 'Shadows and Light'. *The Hissing Of Summer Lawns track 10.* New York: Elektra/Asylum.

Narayan, Kirin. 1993. 'Banana Republics and V.I. Degrees: Rethinking Indian Folklore in a Postcolonial World'. *Asian Folklore Studies.* vol. 52, pp. 177–204.

Raheja, Gloria G. and Ann Grodzins Gold. 1994. *Listen to the Heron's Words: Reimagining Gender and Kinship in North India.* Berkeley: University of California Press.

Rapport, Nigel and Joanna Overing. 2000. *Social and Cultural Anthropology: The Key Concepts.* London: Routledge.

Zelliot, Eleanor. 1992. *From Untouchable to Dalit: Essays on the Ambedkar Movement.* New Delhi: Manohar.

5

THE UPWARDLY MOBILE MONKEY-GOD[1]
Village and Urban Mārutīs in Maharashtra

Jeffrey M. Brackett

Hanuman is at any rate the most popular god in the whole countryside....
The real worship of the people is paid to the shrines of Hanuman and of the
village goddesses. The former abound and *there is a saying that there is no
village without a cock and a Hanuman temple.*[2]

In this brief essay, I address some issues connected with Hanumān-
Mārutī's movement from 'folk' (that is, 'low-caste') practice in
villages to his broad appeal within large cities. The distinctions between
urban and rural, like other categorizations, ought also to be viewed as
tendencies along a broad spectrum. Classification and categorization
of religion, religions, gods and goddesses—to name a few—runs the
risk of imposing Orientalist assumptions onto an imagined 'other'. In
opting to use, for example, the category 'folk' to describe Mārutī, I am
referring to *tendencies* that have variously been called 'popular', 'village',
'non-Brahman', 'non-Sanskritic', and so on. None of these labels is
unproblematic either. My aim is to highlight characteristics associated
with what might be called a 'pre-Rāmdāsicized Mārutī'. Hence, I will
use 'folk' more as a heuristic tool that describes family resemblances
or clusters of characteristics than as some reified 'thing' that would, in
fact, belie the very dynamism I am attempting to articulate. As I point
out in what follows, the 'folk' practices linked to Mārutī have not
disappeared; rather, they have been downplayed by the emphasis upon

Mārutī's connections to Samartha Rāmdās Swāmī. Mārutī, who may well have begun his 'upwardly mobile career' in the distant past as a folk deity in rural India, has long ago become insinuated into the fast-paced urban sprawl that is Pune, with its 'Rāmdāsicized' version of Mārutī.

Mārutī's appeal in Maharashtrian society cuts across boundaries of class, caste, sex, village, city, Brahman and non-Brahman, elite, educated, Sanskritic, popular, and folk. Nevertheless, in most of my conversations regarding Mārutī's regional importance Maharashtrians tended to present a fairly generic list of his characteristics: first, he has a temple in every Maharashtrian village; second, he is strong and courageous. While these first two themes appear in other parts of India, three region-specific themes directly contribute to Mārutī's perceived importance in Maharashtra: First, Samartha Rāmdās Swāmī, a seventeenth-century Maharashtrian Brahman sant, was an incarnation of Mārutī. Second, Rāmdās established the famous Akrā Mārutī, eleven Mārutī temples that are said to be important pilgrimage destinations. Third, Rāmdās was Chhatrapati Śivājī's guru; together these two heroes overcame the so-called tyrannical rule of the Muslims and restored Maharashtra Dharma, their vision of the proper social, political, and religious norms for the Marathi-speaking region.

These three themes appear rather late in the development of Mārutī traditions, as Rāmdās is a seventeenth century figure. Yet today Rāmdās' associations with Mārutī devotion often overshadow other important facts, namely, Mārutī traditions in village life that pre-date his 'Rāmdāsicization'. Moreover, some perceptions of Rāmdās's prominent position vis-à-vis Mārutī may, at times, present a selective reading of history that views the past through the lens of contemporary events. Rāmdās surely provides a regional stamp to Mārutī traditions, but there are also a number of other factors contributing to this god's significance in the region, factors that are most prominent at highly localized levels (that is, the village or neighbourhood). At this local level one finds the importance of Mārutī in everyday, practical Hinduism. That is, at the local level, Rāmdās may or may not be the primary reason a person chooses to worship Mārutī.

When one looks more, closely at the local level, a Mārutī more clearly connected with folk-god characteristics emerges. This folk-god is also very popular in cities, particularly as a god of extreme power, whose power is easily accessible. In addition, Mārutī has a special appeal for Brahmans, a group that on the whole might not clearly be associated with folk practices. The shift in the history or 'career' of Mārutī from possible roots in folk religion to his present position as an enormously popular god among all classes of Maharashtrians is not entirely clear.[3] Nevertheless, Rāmdās is apparently the figure most responsible for the process of 'upgrading' or 'classicizing' Mārutī traditions from an earlier 'folk' god into a largely Brahmanized deity. Whether Mārutī traditions themselves represent a pre-Hanumān or pre-Rāmāyaṇa cultus that itself becomes co-mingled with that Sanskritic set of myths is also unclear, but surely possible. Either way, the theme of power is common to most, if not all, Mārutī traditions.

There are certain characteristic ways in which Maharashtrians speak of Mārutī; power, broadly conceived, is most prominent. This power fits well with conceptualizations of Maharashtrian deities, one of which Maxine Bernsten (1988) describes as harsh and powerful (kaḍak). Kaḍak gods, such as Bhavānī Mātā and Khaṇḍobā, differ from milder (saumya: 'benign or gentle') gods like Rām and Viṭhobā. Bernsten notes that, although every devasthān ('place of god') functions as a centre of power, kaḍak gods control such shrines in a 'particularly alive and active' manner:

Such devasthāns are known as being kaḍak, or jāgrit (wakeful), or jājvalya (efficacious, powerful). The god of such a place has under his control, or perhaps himself constitutes, the forces of order and chaos that control human life. If he is the kuladaivat—the family deity—his worshippers look to him to ensure the well-being of the family, to provide sufficient food along with freedom from sickness and accident. The kuladaivat, generally though not always a kaḍak god, has in his hands not only the family's well-being but its very continuity (Bernsten 1988: 18).

Devotees particularly seek assistance from kaḍak gods during moments of crisis. Berntsen gives examples of childless women and persons suffering from illness. Ritual purity and ritual obligations, not ethical behaviour, are critically important when approaching a kaḍak god (ibid.: 19–20).

The concepts of kaḍak and saumya both apply to Mārutī. For example, people turn to him in moments of crisis, make vows (navas) to him, and perform various rituals in the hope of having a vow fulfilled, thereby placing Mārutī in the kaḍak category. However, Mārutī also fits the saumya category of deities: despite his monkey-form, he is not particularly fierce, at least not in relation to humans or devotees. His connection with Rām, a mild-mannered saumya god, further connects him with the non-kaḍak category. A person enlists Mārutī's help in repelling evil but does not fear Mārutī himself, even though Mārutī's *pratāp* form, with hand raised ready to strike a foe, is less than inviting. Mārutī is a powerful, fear-inspiring god, but it is the enemy—not his devotee—who must beware of Mārutī's raw power.

These popular notions of Hanumān's raw power differ substantially from his portrayal as Rām's humble servant in Vālmīki's Rāmāyaṇa or in devotional hymns, such as the ones composed in Hindi by Tulsidas. Along these lines, Leonard T. Wolcott notes:

Following the interpretation of the *Rāmacaritamānasa* and its widely acknowledged authority in north Indian religious practice, it appears that Hanumān is a popular figure because of his place in the *Rāmāyaṇa*, and that his significance derives from the fact that he is a *bhakta* (a religious server) of Rāma. But these conclusions do not square with folk religion and stories, or with popular use of the epic poem (Wolcott 1978: 655).

In Maharashtra, the servile Hanumān of Vālmīki's Rāmāyaṇa bears little resemblance to the popular perceptions of Mārutī. Mārutī aligns more closely with folk-religious themes in Maharashtra than with the less accessible deities of the Sanskrit epics.

P.B. Mande (1995) illustrates numerous ways in which Mārutī's characterization is typical of folk religion in Maharashtra. Mande notes that the unifying principle of folk beliefs is a desire to gain control over supernatural powers, whether good or evil. The types of gods approached are believed to be 'alive' (*jāgṛt*), a term that also translates as 'powerful' and 'awake':

By examining the corpus of beliefs, customs and rituals prevalent in Maharashtra, one may arrive at a theoretical formulation that underlies all these rites: the struggles of human beings to make life comfortable by creating the direct accessibility of live (*jāgṛt*) deities (Mande 1995: 154).

In order to accomplish this goal, devotees engage in different rituals depending on the situation and the preferred outcome. Sometimes specific gods are connected with particular illnesses, especially in rural areas where people regularly choose non-medical means for curing disease by trying 'various means of ascertaining prophecies' (*śakun*) (ibid.: 149).[4] Other common rituals involve taking a vow (navas), uttering potent words or verses (*mantras*), 'tying sacred threads and amulets (*gaṇḍā-dorā*)' or the use of medicinal herbs (ibid.: 148–9). One makes a vow not only when seeking a cure from illness, but also in order to have one's desires fulfilled (ibid.).

A telling example of folk perceptions of Mārutī that stand in stark contrast to the celibate, saumya servant of Rāma is found in a collection of *ovīs* (poetic verses, usually composed in stanzas of two lines). These ovīs, sung by village women, describe Mārutī's marital and celibate status. P.N. Joshi describes a number of such ovīs. The aim of Joshi's article is to illustrate Hanumān's popularity among what he calls 'the common folk'. He begins by stating, 'fantastic or extraordinary deeds have a powerful impact on people's psyche' (1973: 44). Since Hanumān's life is filled with such miraculous deeds, Joshi argues, people are drawn to his stories. Joshi then supplies a list of the widely-known feats of Hanumān. The following examples from among the numerous Mārutī ovīs he has collected illustrate these points (ibid.: 45):

Oh, Veśībāī, your husband is across the border/
There's red light on his body and his name is Mārutī//

Another woman also speaks of Mārutī as the husband of the border (Veśī, Veśībāī) (ibid.):

Oh, Veśībāī, your husband is standing right on the boundary/
His body is smeared with *śendūr*; his name is Māravatī//[5]

She gives a slight variation on this verse in the following (ibid.):

Oh, Veśībāī, your beloved[6] is standing on the border/
He's smeared with *śendūr* and his name is Hanumant//

The next example mentions Mārutī's celibate status (ibid.):

They say Mārutī is *brahmacārī*/
And all women salute him//

Finally, one reads of how barren women approach Mārutī with the hope of bearing a child (ibid.: 44):

I too said a vow to the Mārutī outside the village/
What is that vow for? I wanted a child in my womb//

Thus, Mārutī as the ideal brahmacārī empowers men and women in very different ways (Alter 1992: 203, 212–13).

Foremost among Mārutī's associations with folk religious practice are rituals that connect him to Śani, a generally malevolent deity whom only Mārutī has the power to defeat. Through these associations with Śani, one also sees the important role that time plays in rituals to Mārutī. Astrological time is the single most important factor in determining when one ought to seek Mārutī's protection from Śani. Devotees approach Śani himself less out of respect than out of fear; by enlisting Mārutī's assistance, they can lessen or even remove the potential danger of Śani's curse. The trait of removing obstacles is one that is more frequently ascribed to the elephant-headed Gaṇeśa, who himself is one of the most popular Hindu gods in Maharashtra, but this trait applies equally to Mārutī with regard to Śani.

It is not always so simple to delineate rural and/or folk perceptions of Mārutī from those located in Sanskrit texts. As the eleventh avatār of Rudra-Śiva, for example, Mārutī is connected to both scriptural and folk traditions. The two streams flow together, and are therefore indistinguishable one from the other in contemporary practice. Günther D. Sontheimer draws upon his research on the folk god Khaṇḍobā, a local form of Rudra-Śiva, in order to show that one cannot make a clear distinction between folk and scriptural traditions.[7] He highlights folk elements present in, for example, Vedic texts that persist in conjunction with later scriptural developments. In the following passage Sontheimer lays out the substance of his argument:

What I want to say here is that scriptural or high religion and folk religion including tribal religion should be seen as complementary, an organic whole and not exclusive to each other; that monotheism and polytheism are not incompatible with each other and that folk religion should not be written off as magic and superstition and not considered to be true Hinduism. Unfortunately we view and study tribal, folk, and scriptural religions as

separate entities and Vedic literature and other scriptures are interpreted with
the help of all kinds of sometimes far-fetched theories (Sontheimer 1992: 204).

As is frequently the case, the so-called 'high' religious traditions
absorb the 'folk' elements, making connections between the two.
Sontheimer is suggesting that such a process does not eliminate the
folk practices. The scriptures that incorporate folk gods do not tell us
about the continued presence of folk practices. Moreover, those who
participate in folk religious traditions, which are clearly polytheistic
in outlook, also accept the 'high' traditions of texts that are monotheistic
or monistic.

    Elsewhere, Sontheimer provides the following distinction between
what he calls a 'folk god' and other types of Hindu deities (1987: 1):

By 'folk god' we mean a god who is directly accessible to his followers, exists
on earth 'here and now', and is not preponderantly located in a distant
Purāṇic heaven.

    Sontheimer notes the following general features of Khaṇḍobā,
some of which are similar to those of Mārutī (1992: 206–8): Khaṇḍobā
is associated with forests (vanam) and mountains; he is believed to
live in anthills; the god may have been feared as a demon in the ancient
past; he is known for his hunting skills; and he is connected with
robbers. Mārutī also is linked to the forest, as it is there that he resides in
the Rāmāyaṇa. It is possible, as well, that his 'origin' may be as a folk
god. At times, the alleged origins of a Mārutī temple involve myths of
a snake hole, which shares features common to the anthill motif—a
rupture between terrestrial and subterranean realms that has a
heightened degree of power—and is frequently believed to be inhabited
by particular supernatural forces, such as are characteristic of folk
deities. Here, for example, is a story about an anthill/snake hole from
Sāp ('snake'), a village in Satara District:

About 4 km from Rahimatpur, and 1¹/₂ km from Āpśiṅga is Sāp village. There
is a small Mārutī mandir here. The Mārutī mūrtī inside of it is about three-
quarters of a meter tall. The people from there believe it is a jāgṛt devasthān.
Earlier there was an anthill on the place of this mandir. A cowherd used to
graze cattle next to this anthill. One of those cows stopped giving milk. The

cowherd couldn't understand the reason for this. He suspected that someone was constantly milking and stealing [the milk], so he decided to watch over that cow. At the usual time, this cow used to stop at the anthill and let out a stream of milk, and the snake in the anthill used to imbibe the milk. After seeing this incident, the cowherd tried to kill the snake. But when he didn't succeed in that, the snake suddenly disappeared. That night the cowherd dreamed, 'Without killing the snake, construct a Hanumān mandir on the spot of that anthill.' Following this advice, the cowherd built a mandir and established a Mārutī, so this village became named Sāp ('snake'). That cowherd used to bathe this Mārutī with cow milk (Gadgil 1983: 23).

Sontheimer adds that even though people commonly speak of Rudra's fierce nature—that is, his destructive, malevolent tendencies, his lack of concern for social norms, his living and/or dancing in cremation grounds, and so on—even in the Vedas one reads of his benevolence toward devotees. In other words, while Rudra is feared for his destructive powers, including bringing terrible diseases and death, he also bestows blessings upon devotees and is known for his healing powers (Sontheimer 1992: 213). In fact, Sontheimer notes that Rudra 'is the physician amongst physicians. Khaṇḍobā must have been feared in the past, but he has great healing power' (ibid.: 214). Each place is set apart from the settled life of villages and cities, suggesting a connection between the god's character and his place of 'origin'.

These specific examples tie in with another of Sontheimer's helpful paradigms for the study of Hinduism generally and folk religion in particular. Rather than promoting a 'monolithic conceptualization' of Hinduism, he suggests in an important essay that there are 'components' that have always interacted and that continue today to interact with each other (Sontheimer 1989: 197). The components that he addresses are: (1) the work and teaching of the Brahmans; (2) asceticism and renunciation; (3) tribal religion; (4) folk religion; and (5) bhakti ('devotion'). He offers the following comment to define further the goal of his essay:

Indian religious phenomena may partake of all of these components, but the important point is *which component is emphasized* and *which may be just secondary, subordinated, peripheral, or amounting to lip service in a particular case or at a particular time*' (ibid.: 198. Emphasis his).

The fourth element, which lays out beliefs, practices, and terminology applied specifically in the Maharashtrian context, is of particular interest in our examination of Mārutī as a folk deity (ibid.: 204–6).[8] Although not all of the elements Sontheimer provides apply to Mārutī, most of them in fact do. For example, a folk god is 'alive' (jāgṛt); it 'responds to the offerings and wishes of his devotees' (*dev pāvto*. Ibid.: 205); such gods are therefore often the recipients of a vow (navas); the god has specific festivals or fairs (*jatrā*),[9] and the god is his 'own form' (*svarūpa*). This last term sets apart images (mūrtis) of these gods from images—even if of the same god—artisans create. In the case of a *śiv-liṅg* (the aniconic representation of Śiva), which Sontheimer uses for his example, the 'self-form' (svarūpa) images are ones that frequently 'appear' in nature and are recognizable to devotees for different reasons, the most obvious being the morphological resemblance to the śiv-liṅg. Related to this 'self-form' term is another one frequently heard in Maharashtra: 'self-existent' (*svayambhū*). The two terms are interchangeable, it seems, with only minor variations in the meaning. The definition of the latter term is also 'self-becoming', though the two seem to suggest the same underlying intent: to set apart these types of images from created ones. More important, perhaps, is the added connotation that these images are especially—or even more—powerful than the created images.

Taken together, Mārutī's folk traits, his insinuation within everyday life, and his easily accessible power may all have contributed to his shrines outnumbering those dedicated to Gaṇeśa in the city of Pune. G.S. Ghurye reports that in the year 1810 there were 89 Mārutī shrines in the vicinity of Pune, while there were only 60 to Gaṇeśa.[10] Ghurye adds, however, that Gaṇeśa is considered 'the god of Maharashtra' (Ghurye 1979: 47, referring to Ghurye 1962: 123, 125, 235). When Ghurye breaks down the number of images into ones that 'were temples proper', as opposed to images such as roadside shrines, the numbers tilt in favour of other gods (ibid.: 163, see also 1962: 123–4): 'The numerical distribution of these temples among the principal deities was: 18 Mahadeva or Siva, 11 Rama, 11 Ganapati, and only 8 Hanumanta.'

However, the difference in these numbers suggests further Mārutī's importance at a sub-regional—or even neighbourhood—level. Moreover, as Ghurye points out, in terms of percentage of 'properly housed' images, Mārutī still fares better than Viṭhobā, even though two of the greatest Vārkarī poet-saints—Jñāneśvar and Tukārām— lived just outside Pune. Even though the Vārkarī movement had been established as early as the late thirteenth century, Ghurye concludes that an important factor contributing to the fact that there were more Mārutīs than Viṭhobhās was the work of Rāmdās:

[t]here was the active propaganda carried out by Samartha Ramadasa in favour of the power-packed deity ready to combat any aggression and to help any devotee [that he] was not only dynamic but, being militant, naturally appealed to the people of Maharashtra who were simply tired of the Muslim tyranny, so keenly observed and so deeply felt by Ramadasa (Ghurye 1979: 163).

Ghurye provides a further reason in support of his argument, saying:

Further, Chhatrapati Shivaji reportedly used to put up an image of Hanuman-Maruti carrying a mace in hand as usual, at the gates of hill forts so averred Rigvedi in 1924 .... Naturally Hanuman-Maruti prestige was boosted. This concatenation of circumstances I think explains the differential distribution of temples and/or other objects of religious tendance [sic] among different deities, yielding to Hanuman-Maruti the high rank that he received (ibid.: 163–4).

Ghurye conducted another survey of temples in the Pune area between 1954 and 1957. Both Viṭhobā and Gaṇapati had received many new temples since the earlier numbers recorded in 1810: Viṭhobā now had 52 temples, while Gaṇapati had 26, a large increase from the earlier figure of eleven back in 1810. Ghurye attributes the latter's increase to the work of Bal Gangadhar Tilak, who instituted the public Gaṇeśa festival in 1893 (ibid.: 164).[11] Yet it was the number of Mārutī temples that showed the greatest increase during that period, climbing from 8 proper temples in 1810 to 92 during the more recent survey (ibid.). In order to show further evidence of the regional popularity of Mārutī, Ghurye did yet another survey during the same period of 112 villages surrounding Pune. He found 139 of the 767 shrines observed to be dedicated to Mārutī (ibid.: 165).[12] Further research regarding annual village festivals suggests, however, that Mārutī normally only has a single large festival, unlike Bhairobā, a popular village deity whose annual fairs far outnumber those of all other gods (ibid.).[13] Ghurye concludes, therefore, that, 'Maruti Hanuman proves himself to be a popular deity for *daily appeal*, while Bhairoba receives annual pacification' (ibid.: Italics mine).

CONCLUSION

Given the connections that Mārutī has to folk religious practices, it may seem odd that Rāmdās, the main regional sant who emphasizes Mārutī devotion, is a Brahman. Yet it is perhaps because Rāmdās remains so popular today—especially among Brahmans in Pune— that one finds such a large number of devotees of this otherwise folk deity. Rāmdās' emphasis upon Lord Rāma, a god who is both saumya and a warrior at the same time, underscores the links to the pan-Indian, Sanskrit Rāmāyaṇa. At the same time, Rāmdās' call for *baeḷopāsanā* ('strength training' or 'worship of strength') highlights the folk-god powers of Mārutī. There are other ways in which Rāmdās may be viewed as partially responsible for the upward mobility of Mārutī from a folk god to a deity with broader appeal, especially among Brahmans. For example, Rāmdās' *Bhīmarupī Stotra* illustrates the continued importance among Hindu rituals of the efficacy of sound. In this instance, chanting, reciting, or singing of these verses in highly Sanskritized Marathi may also accentuate the associations with orthodox rituals that would more frequently incorporate Sanskrit verses. In short, Rāmdās appears to serve as a representative figure in the fluid process of transforming Mārutī from a folk deity into a god with wider allure.

Much of that allure seems directly related to Mārutī as a god of power available to devotees across all social classes. His power is especially consistent with the fierce, kaḍak type of deity found in Maharashtra. Perhaps the geographical location of Maharashtra as a 'region in the middle' contributes to the blending of kaḍak and saumya traits one sees in Mārutī. On the one hand, he is an avatār of the more kaḍak god Rudra-Śiva, while also being the servant of the saumya Lord Rāma. This 'taming' of a kaḍak deity by association with Rāma would not be unheard of in the Marathi-speaking region, as it is most likely the case that Viṭhobā of Paṇḍharpūr, a form of Viṣṇu, was initially a Śaiva god who was transmuted into a Vaiṣṇava deity as the rise of

Vaiṣṇava bhakti spread throughout the area. Yet, if one posits a symbolic 'taming' of a previously kaḍak god in Mārutī, it is a process that does not eliminate or even suppress his associations with power. His fundamental characteristic remains that of a jāgṛt god. Since he is linked to Rāma, Mārutī is connected to the Rāmāyaṇa, which increases his appeal to Brahmans and other groups whose traditions place high value on Sanskrit texts. Therefore, Mārutī gains further legitimacy in the eyes of some people while at the same time retaining his folk-religion ties.

NOTES

1. The content of this essay is largely adapted from portions (Introduction and Chapter 1) of my dissertation ('Practically Hindu: Contemporary Conceptions of Hanumān-Mārutī in Maharashtra', University of Pittsburgh, 2004). Of course, I go into much greater detail in that work.
2. Ghurye 1979: 152 (italics his; quoting from the 1916 Bellary District Gazetteer).
3. It is not unusual in Maharashtra for a god's 'career' to shift radically, as Charlotte Vaudeville (1974) demonstrates regarding the Vaiṣṇava god Viṭhobā of Paṇḍharpūr, who seems earlier to have been a Śaiva deity. For a presentation from Kerala of how perceptions of gods shift at various points in history, see also Clothey 1982.
4. There is a roadside Mārutī temple in Pune called Śakunī Mārutī. Devotees approach this particular image for 'prophecies', to use Mande's term.
5. Most of the verses in this group of ovīs use the name Māravatī as a variant of Mārutī.
6. 'Beloved' also can be translated here as 'husband', but the emphasis is upon a husband whom a wife *really* loves.
7. Sontheimer 1992: 201–16. He mentions in this essay that Khaṇḍobā shares much in common with the gods 'Mallana in Andhra, and Mailar in Karnataka and also with Murukan especially as described in the Caṅkam literature' (206). Elsewhere, Sontheimer writes in more detail about these connections (Sontheimer 1997).
8. Sontheimer notes that these beliefs and practices are not limited to Maharashtra, and can be found 'in other regions and languages' (1989: 204).
9. Here, Sontheimer uses the term jatrā in reference to 'participation in the god's divine play, e.g., in his hunting excursion or his marriage. In the Khaṇḍobā cult, for examples [*sic*], where devotees act like horses and dogs of the god' (1989: 205). In addition to this meaning for the term, jatra is also the term used more generally to speak of village festivals and fairs.

10. Ghurye's figures differ only slightly from those provided by B.G. Gokhale (1988: 177) for the same period (namely, 86 for Hanumān and 56 for Gaṇeśa).

11. For more regarding Tilak's role in this regard, see Cashman 1970 and 1975 and Courtright 1985: 202–47 and 1988.

12. Ghurye mentions that the same survey found 175 goddess temples, a larger number than the 139 for Mārutī, but these were distributed among a variety of goddesses.

13. For these figures, Ghurye surveyed 105 villages. Of the 108 annual fairs, Bhairobā had 66 celebrations.

REFERENCES

Alter, Joseph S. 1992. *The Wrestler's Body: Identity and Ideology in North India.* Berkeley: University of California Press.

Bernsten, Maxine. 1988. 'One Face of God'. In Eleanor Zelliot and Maxine Bernsten (eds). *The Experience of Hinduism: Essays on Religion in Maharashtra.* Albany: State University of New York Press, pp. 17–25.

Cashman, Richard I. 1970. 'The Political Recruitment of God Ganapati'. *Indian Economic and Social History Review.* vol. 7, no. 3, pp. 347–73.

_____. 1975. *The Myth of the Lokamanya: Tilak and Mass Politics in Maharashtra.* Berkeley: University of California Press.

Clothey, Fred. 1982. 'Śāstā-Aiyaṉār-Aiyappaṉ: The God as Prism of Social History'. In Fred W. Clothey (ed.). *Images of Man: Religion and Historical Process in South Asia.* Madras: New Era Publications, pp. 35–71.

Courtright, Paul B. 1985. *Gaṇeśa: Lord of Obstacles, Lord of Beginnings.* New York: Oxford University Press.

_____. 1988. 'The Ganesh Festival in Maharashtra: Some Observations'. In Eleanor Zelliot and Maxine Bernsten (eds). *The Experience of Hinduism.* Albany: State University of New York Press, pp. 76–94.

Gadgil, Amarendra (ed.). 1983. *Śrīhanumānkoś, 'Appendix 1'.* Pune: Shriramakosh Mandal.

Ghurye, G.S. 1962. *Gods and Men.* Bombay: Popular Book Depot.

_____. 1979. *The Legacy of the Ramayana.* Bombay: Popular Prakashan.

Gokhale, B.G. 1988. *Poona in the Eighteenth Century: An Urban History.* New Delhi: Oxford University Press.

Joshi, P.N. 1973. 'Lokagītāt Bhakta Hanumān' ('Devotee Hanumān in Folksongs') *Prasād.* vol. 27, no. 1, pp. 44–8.

Mande, P.B. 1995. 'Folk Culture, Folk Religion and Oral Tradition in Maharashtrian Culture'. In Günther-Dietz Sontheimer (ed.). *Folk Culture, Folk Religion and Oral Traditions as a Component in Maharashtrian Culture.* New Delhi: Manohar, pp. 147–64.

Sontheimer, Günther-Dietz. 1987. 'Rudra and Khaṇḍobā: Continuity in Folk Religion'. In Milton Israel and N.K. Wagle (eds). *Religion and Society in Maharashtra*. Toronto: University of Toronto, Centre for South Asian Studies, pp. 1–31.

———. 1989. 'Hinduism: The Five Components and Their Interaction'. In Günther-Dietz Sontheimer and Hermann Kulke (eds). *Hinduism Reconsidered*. New Delhi: Manohar, pp. 197–212.

———. 1992. 'Scriptural Religion and Folk Religion in India: The Case of Rudra, Śiva and Khaṇḍobā'. In Sitakant Mahapatra (ed.). *The Realm of the Sacred: Verbal Symbolism and Ritual Structures*. New Delhi: Oxford University Press, pp. 201–16.

———. 1997. *King of Hunters, Warriors, and Shepherds: Essays on Khaṇḍobā*. Anne Feldhaus, Aditya Malik, and Heidrun Brückner (eds). New Delhi: Manohar.

Vaudeville, Charlotte. 1974. 'Paṇḍharpūr, The City of Saints'. In Harry M. Buck and Glenn E. Yocum (eds). *Structural Approaches to South Indian Studies*. Chambersburg: Wilson Books, pp. 137–61.

Wolcott, Leonard T. 1978. 'Hanumān: The Power-Dispensing Monkey in North Indian Folk Religion'. *Journal of Asian Studies*. vol. 38, no. 4, pp. 653–61.

6

NEGOTIATING HIERARCHY AND IDENTITY
Cultural Performances on the Meaning of the Demon King Bali in Rural Maharashtra

Michael Youngblood

S cholars often render oppositional ideas and behaviour of 'the folk' as resistance to the dominant (and dominating) social, cultural, and religious norms of social elites. While resistance is a useful rubric for understanding the significance of heterodox cultural phenomena, there are two important points that are frequently neglected. The first is that, even when subaltern cultural productions and social meanings do embody opposition to elite ideologies, they are not simply or wholly reactions to dominant culture. They may be reactive to some degree, but they also emerge out of complex histories, embody multiple layers of meaning, and are cultural expressions that—as much as 'classical' cultural expressions—may satisfy and enrich the lives of those who identify with them. The second point, correlative with the first, is that dominant culture and ideology also express a sort of resistance. Although backed by greater social power in their assertion of 'orthodox' values and identities, these dominant forms are also in many ways structured by the heterodox values and identities to which they are opposed.

In the following pages, I will make a case for a more dialogical perspective on both the 'dominant' and the 'resistant' categories of cultural productions and meanings. My example comes from mythology and folk practice in Maharashtra, a region of India to which Eleanor Zelliot first introduced me when I was a student of the Associated

Colleges of the Midwest's India Studies Program in 1986. Almost a decade later, while back in Maharashtra conducting fieldwork on a major agrarian movement called the Shetkari Sanghatana, I became intrigued by divergent classical and folk representations of a mythological king named Bali. Within the multi-class, multi-caste context of the Shetkari Sanghatana, the dialogical character of some of these opposed practices and meanings was extremely significant. In this context, Bali was one of several cultural complexes of meaning through which differently positioned participants in rural society engaged in an indirect conversation on the meaning of community, the relative valuation of varied social segments within the community, and each segment's economic, political, and social priorities for collective political action. These dialogues were also extant within rural Maharashtrian society in general, and had been an integral component of larger debates on social identity and hierarchy long before being officially politicized in the movement.

The demon king Bali is a familiar character in Hindu folklore throughout India. Reputed to be of Shudra, or low-caste, genealogy, he is well known from Puranic accounts of his frequent challenges to the authority of the gods, most particularly the myth of his ultimate defeat and banishment to the netherworld *patal*. Familiar throughout the country, Bali occupies a place of distinctive cultural importance in Maharashtra, where his reign and defeat are a recurring theme in village ritual and daily life. Unlike in Kerala, where Bali is at the centre of the grand Malayali Onam festival, in Maharashtra Bali lives a relatively quiet cultural existence. There are no major festivals dedicated specifically to his memory, and urban Maharashtrian Hindus, though generally familiar with his role in one or more myths, might only rarely, and at best obliquely, acknowledge him within ordinary social intercourse or in their annual ritual calendar.

In rural Maharashtra, however, Bali is recalled and invoked in numerous community and household rituals, as well as in the normal fabric of day-to-day experience. In rural folklore and daily discourse, he is a generous and virtuous king who presided over a golden age of Maharashtrian village life. Bali's overthrow, many feel, ushered in a period of rural decline and formalized the social inequality that continues to define village life today. A familiar Marathi proverb calling for the restoration of Bali's realm reflects this attitude: 'May all evil go away, and may the kingdom of Bali be restored.' The association between

Bali and agriculture is so strong that Maharashtrian farmers commonly express personal identification with him. Many regularly greet each other as 'Bali', and village folk songs use the name 'Bali' to refer to cultivators or toilers. Even the bullocks that work in the fields are referred to in Marathi as 'Bali's helper' (*balivard*) and 'Bali's vehicle' (*balivahan*).

On the surface, Bali is a figure that all rural Maharashtrians can easily identify with and revere. On closer examination, however, we see that the boundaries of Bali-identity are complex, contested, and contextually shiftable. While many agriculturalists proudly address each other as 'Bali', more elite members of rural communities often deploy the name 'Bali' as a subtle tool for exercising control over the weakest sections of the village. Trimbak Narayan Atre (1915), a colonial revenue officer who documented village social relations, describes how rural Brahmans, landlords, moneylenders, and merchants often addressed poor villagers and members of the hereditary service (*balute*) castes by the name 'Bali' as a form of strategic flattery intended to extract from them ever greater degrees of service and subservience.

Bali, then, carries an extremely wide range of meanings in rural Maharashtra. Some of them are proud and positive, others servile and derogatory.[1] Considering the wealth of common associations that tie Bali to the soil, virtue, and strength, it is not surprising that Bali has more than once been adopted as a key symbol in rural Maharashtrian social movements. Most often he has been used as a symbol of low-caste demands for social reform from below. The social reformer Jyotirao Phule, for example, promoted Bali as a central symbol in the rural Satyashodhak movement during the late nineteenth century. In the twentieth century, Bali has been invoked in a number of smaller Maharashtrian agrarian movements and political organizations targeted at rural labourers—including, for example, the movement called the Shetmazur Shetkari Sanghatana, confined mainly to four heavily irrigated sugar-producing districts of the Desh subregion of the state. Others, however—most notably the Shetkari Sanghatana, which has been active across the state since the early 1980s—have used Bali as a platform for the social and economic grievances of *all* rural inhabitants, regardless of class or caste. Thus, while Bali stands for the downtrodden in one sense or another, the specific boundaries of 'Bali identity' are not fixed. They are negotiable in the context of a mass social movement, as they are routinely negotiated in rural Maharashtrian life, through ongoing assertions and counter assertions of his meaning.

BALI'S REALM AND HIS FALL FROM RULE

The central mythic event for which Bali is best known is found in a Puranic story called the *trivikrama* (the 'three steps'). In classical Puranas, the myth proceeds as follows:[2]

After Bali defeated the gods and extended his reign across the land, he asked his grandfather, the great demon Prahlada, how to govern the realm. Prahlada replied: 'Only virtue will always win. Rule the kingdom without deviating from virtue.' Bali, a devotee of Lord Vishnu, ruled his kingdom according to this advice and became famous throughout the three worlds.

The demons and the other subjects of the realm were happy and comfortable under Bali's rule—all except the gods and the Brahmans, who felt they were denied the privileges they deserved. One by one, gods began to leave the realm. Finally, Lord Indra approached Lord Vishnu and represented their grievances. Vishnu told them, 'Bali is devoted to me. Nonetheless, I shall help you to put him in his place.'

One day, as Bali was performing sacrifices to Vishnu on the bank of the river Narmada, Vishnu himself approached him in the incarnation of a dwarf Brahman hermit (Vamana), seeking alms. Bali was pleased with Vamana, whom he did not recognize as Vishnu, and offered to give him riches. But the hermit rejected Bali's offers, humbly requesting instead only three steps of ground on which to meditate and offer sacrifices. Bali eagerly granted his wish, and Vamana proceeded to measure the ground with his steps. As he did so, he simultaneously began to expand to the stature of a giant. Fearful, Bali's subjects began to attack Vamana with anything they could lay their hands on, but still he continued to grow, becoming an immense being. With his first step, he measured the whole earth. With the second step, he took all of heaven. With nowhere remaining to take the third step, he asked Bali how he would keep his promise. Bali, recognizing that this was Vishnu himself, replied that he now had only his physical body to call his own, and that the god might step on that to complete the promise. Thus Vishnu placed his foot on Bali's head and pushed him down to Patal, making him an inhabitant of the netherworld.

Although every oral account of the trivikrama that I have heard includes most of the key elements of this version, each is also distinguished by its own digressions and subtleties that interdigitate the myth with the beholder's broader world of cultural understandings, lived experience, and terrains of identity. In other words, the experiences and meanings signified in calls for the restoration of Bali's realm are complex, and they are open to many additional degrees of interpretation. Upper-class and upper-caste villagers may view Bali as an adversary of the Brahmanic pantheon, but also as a rural hero, or as an icon of distinctive virtue. Rural Shudras and Dalits on the other hand—disproportionately landless workers, marginal landholders, or holders of the poorest quality fields—while regarding the trivikrama myth as a story of upper-caste authority and domination, may also understand Bali as a devotee of one of those Brahmanical gods (Vishnu) and as a patron of all villagers, regardless of caste.

In order to better appreciate the dialectic between these meanings, which are not mutually exclusive, it is important to contextualize the trivikrama myth within the broader history of Brahmanical Hinduism. Bali can be interpreted as signifying the many non-Brahmanical village deities that were no doubt important in the past, as they are today, and Puranic narrations of the trivikrama reveal not only the conquest of the demon Bali, but also of the expansion of the Brahman theocratic social order over the village social structures and antithetical world views with which it was in competition. Bali is thus a metaphor for a wide array of heterodox village ideas and practices. For listeners and tellers sensitive to this interpretation, each of the three steps in the myth can be read as completing such a conquest. After revealing that the Brahman mendicant is, in essence, Vishnu himself with authority over all that the Brahmanical pantheon is entitled to command, the god proceeds to delineate the terrains of that control. In the first step, he encompasses the physical world; in the second, the rest of the physical universe and the spiritual domain of 'heaven'. The third and final step signifies the defeat of all contenders—particularly the unincorporated folk deities and demons venerated by the non-Brahman populace—and the ousting of these to a netherworld far removed from the domain of either humans or gods.

Of course, this is a myth—and, as a myth, it should not be read too literally or conflated with an accurate representation of historic occurrence. At the same time, myths are not meaningless tales or dead stories. They are 'operative fictions' (O'Flaherty 1988: 25)—stories that cannot be told or heard without an inherent act of interpretation that roots them in the beholder's understanding and experience of the world. Moreover, myths not only *reflect* experience, they can also *structure* it. From an ethnographic perspective, far less important than the question of a myth's original truth is the understood and experienced truth of the listener or teller. In rural Maharashtra, myths of demon conquest are far from dead stories, and the Puranas are still the dominant lens through which Brahmanically-influenced society—particularly the urban establishment and the Sanskritized rural elite—perceives and evaluates popular Hinduisms (Fuller 1992). This is significant in rural Maharashtra today, where local deities—many of them specific to different caste groups, villages, or areas of the state—continue to be more important in the fabric of everyday life than Brahmanical Puranic deities (cf. Feldhaus 1995; Karve 1968).

THE LIVED CONTEXT OF PURANIC WORLD VIEW IN MAHARASHTRA TODAY

In Maharashtra today, as elsewhere in the subcontinent, world view and practice are characterized more by pluralism than by a strict social homogeny of rules and ideas. While there are certainly similarities of practice within the Hindu world, local Hinduisms, particularly as practiced by the least Sanskritized rural communities, differ substantially in their understandings of the supernatural world and in the names, forms, and characteristics that they assign to supernatural beings. This is why most modern scholars refer to Hinduism as an orthopraxy, rather than a singular orthodoxy. Maharashtra exemplifies this complexity.

In the face of such diversity, ideas and practices that have the capacity to reinforce any identity group's worldview and distinguish it from those of other groups are particularly noteworthy. Upper-caste commentaries on the religious practices of rural Shudra, Dalit, and Adivasi communities are a good example. As Fuller (1992: 27) states with regard to popular Hinduism throughout India:

the Brahminical standard of Sanskritic Hinduism is neither monolithic nor unchallenged by alternatives. Nonetheless, it represents the single most important evaluative norm within Hinduism. By reference to it, higher-status groups tend to regard their own beliefs and practices as superior to those presumed to belong to lower-status groups (Fuller 1992: 27).

The operative nature of this evaluative norm is readily discernible in Maharashtra. This is not to say that subaltern practices and beliefs are actively prohibited at the village level. In most routine village contexts, attitudes toward less Sanskritic folk meanings and practices are highly contextual. Members of upper castes may refer to these practices and beliefs as examples of the irrationality of the lower castes, and sometimes hold them up as evidence of lower-caste peoples' inability to hold positions of responsibility or to escape adverse financial circumstances. But elite villagers who find themselves in extraordinary circumstances requiring alternative ('dangerous' or 'impure') supernatural interventions may also participate in lower-caste practices. Thus, in some respects, members of the upper castes value such practices and beliefs as the special culture and knowledge of their village Others—with the implicit understanding that these Others should remain peripheral to the public social and cultural life of the village.

CONQUEST AND RETURN OF BALI IN CONTEMPORARY VILLAGE PRODUCTIONS

Routine commentaries on the otherness of village Others, however, are not always so subtle or defined by such permeable frontiers, and many of these commentaries are revealed in public interactions with myth. As elsewhere in India, religious culture in Maharashtra is rich with stories in which demons appear as marauding Godzilla-like characters that are ultimately vanquished by one or more heroic deities. These myths are not only well known; they are also deeply embedded in the life of village Maharashtra. Some are dramatically enacted in major Hindu festivals celebrated during the course of the calendar year— reasserting, each festival season, the primacy of the Brahmanically 'orthodox' pantheon and the subjugation of the village deities and demons that many members of the rural communities in other contexts revere. These festivals create occasions for dramatizations of not only conquest but also alterity. In Maharashtra, much of this is couched in the image of the demon Bali.

The prominent annual festival of Navaratri, for example, which is held in Maharashtrian villages (as elsewhere) during the first nine nights of the bright lunar fortnight of Ashvina (September–October), celebrates the defeat of the buffalo-demon Mahishasura by the goddess Durga. This period in the calendar also coincides with another major mythological event, Lord Rama's killing of the demon Ravana, described in the epic Ramayana.[3] As in many other parts of India, Maharashtrian village celebrations on the final, tenth day of Navaratri (known as Dasara) are increasingly characterized by the celebratory burning of

Ravana effigies, often accompanied by firecrackers and other festival fanfare. Most introductory texts on Hinduism, as well as many upper-caste villagers, describe Navaratri and Dasara as a celebration of the victory of 'good' over 'evil'. In actual village practice, however, this festival complex reveals many deeper, far more complicated dimensions, intertwined with local assertions and counter-assertions on the legitimacy of spiritual, political, and economic inequality.

One such practice, as conducted in the large village of 'Gordpani',[4] in Ahmadnagar district, is a symbolic disembowelment of Bali. The ritual is a microcosm of the more public celebrations of demon conquest, and vividly ties together the mythological world of demon-killing and the village world of socio-economic hierarchy. Practiced by the small community of Brahmans that have historically ruled the village, the ritual is conducted in Brahman homes on the demon-killing day of Dasara.

As performed by Deshastha Brahman informants 'Vijaya' and her husband, Ashok, during my fieldwork in 1998, the ritual began with the couple seated on the stone kitchen floor of their prominent two-storey, wood-and-brick house. Reaching into a large store of uncooked rice, Vijaya measured out two handfuls of the grain onto two different stainless steel plates, then carefully fashioned each into an image of Bali. At this point Ashok turned his head away from the plates and Vijaya hid a small piece of gold jewellery inside one of the rice figures. All the while, Ashok narrated to me his own interpretation of the significance: 'You see, the rice represents agriculture, and the gold is wealth. Bali represents not just agriculture, but also the agriculturalists and the wealth that they produce.' When she had hidden the piece of gold, Vijaya asked her husband to turn around and try to guess which of the two images contained the symbol of wealth. Taking a sharp kitchen knife, 'Ashok' probed into the belly of one of the images and extracted the jewellery.

On the same day when the Brahmans of Gordpani symbolically extract agricultural wealth from Bali and villagers and townspeople across the state burn effigies of a demon, ordinary agriculturalists throughout Maharashtra are engaged in the culmination of a ten-day ritual that markedly contrasts with these activities. This ritual, called *ghatasthapana*, begins on the first day of Navaratri and continues through to the final day, each step of the way asserting the economic and spiritual autonomy of individual cultivators. Like the Bali-stabbing ritual, ghatasthapana begins within the household, but it involves no mediation by Brahmans or any other authorities.

As I observed the practice of ghatasthapana in the small, Brahman-less village of 'Neemgaon', just a few miles from Gordpani, it proceeds as follows. On the first day of Navaratri, non-Brahman agriculturalists and other low-caste villagers make a dish-shaped bed of leaves. Upon this bed, they place some soil from their own land (or, if they have no cultivable land, soil from the immediate area surrounding their home), and they seed this soil with several different grains. Finally, a *ghat*—a small clay or steel vessel filled with water—is sunk into the centre of the soil, and the whole fixture is installed in the small household *devghar* ('god-house'), nestled among the numerous images of Puranic and local gods. All of this is usually done by an older woman of the household. Over the course of the nine days of Navaratri, the soil is watered as needed for the seeds to sprout. On the tenth day—the culminating day in the celebration of the 'victory of good over evil'— the ghat and the sprouted soil are tossed onto or buried in the family's field while participants utter the words 'May all evil go away, and may the kingdom of Bali be restored'.

There are a number of ways that we could interpret ghatasthapana. The soil and ghat, placed in the devghar, suggest a veneration of the practitioner's own land and access to water—or a request for the acquisition of these. The burial of the soil and ghat in the field suggest an immanent birth—perhaps the birth and return of Bali, rising up from his exile in Patal. Most importantly, however, in the context of the demon-killing festival, the call for Bali's return suggests deep differences on the social meaning of the demon himself and all that he signifies.[5]

The other major festival in the same season is Diwali. This festival follows almost immediately on the heels of Navaratri and extends the narrative of Rama's victory over the demon Ravana. Diwali (often described as 'the festival of lights') is nominally dedicated to the worship of the Puranic goddess Lakshmi, in her aspect as Wealth— but it is also a continuing celebration of the homeward march of the kshatriya god-man Rama with his virtuous wife Sita (whom he had just liberated from the clutches of Ravana), and his return from exile to his rightful throne as king. A popular aspect of the festival, as celebrated in north India and many Maharashtrian towns and cities, is the lighting of bright candles and electric lamps—a practice that is variously described as a welcome to Lakshmi, a symbolic lighting of the route home for Rama and Sita, or a celebration of one's financial success in the preceding year. In this popular form, it is a relatively new urban borrowing in most of rural Maharashtra. But Diwali, which lasts four to five days,[6] includes a day of special significance to Maharashtrian lower castes: *balipratipada*, the day commemorating Bali's defeat, celebrated on the final day of the festival. According to older informants, this day has been significant in rural Maharashtra for much longer than the lighting of lamps, the public worship of wealth, and the other gala displays.

Balipratipada is commemorative in a number of different ways, each embodying different meanings for those who engage in the commemoration. In a number of villages, for example, informants have told me that on balipratipada Brahman or elite Maratha-caste men perform a brief ritual of crushing a fruit, using a hand, a stick, or their foot. This, they say, is a symbol of Bali being crushed on his day of defeat. In 'Tapa' village in Vidarbha, Brahmans and other upper-caste villagers engage in a ritual that is even more to the point. Satish, an educated Brahman social worker who returned to Tapa with plans to launch economic development projects, described the ritual as follows:

What I have seen in my village is this: During the two days at the end of the year, and then on the *padva* [the beginning of the Hindu new year], all the upper-caste villagers make an image of Bali out of cow dung and install it by the door of the house. On the padva, then, they explode this image with firecrackers. Then the Dalits go from door to door, saying, 'Bali will return,' and beg for Diwali alms from the upper castes.

Although this focus on Bali is deeply Maharashtrian, the receipt of gifts, sweets, or pay bonuses, which Satish referred to as 'alms', is a central convention of Diwali as celebrated in other parts of India as well. While village possessors of capital—traders, processors, shopkeepers, and sometimes large, labour-employing landowners— view Diwali particularly as a festival for the worship of wealth (that is, the goddess Lakshmi, but also their own acquired wealth), and treat Diwali as the end of their business fiscal year, agricultural labourers, toilers, and rural workers view Diwali largely as an opportunity to claim an annual bonus or small gift from their employers. Satish's comments on the subjective significance of this are echoed by the comments of an informant named Balaram, a thirty-year-old Mahar Dalit from a marginal landholding family in Beed district:

When the labouring people in the village go out to visit the wealthy families, asking for some bonus or something to eat, they do so with an expectation that the strong, the ruling section of society, should show some generosity to the weak. Yes, this is a festival season, but it is the one time of the year the poor are most conscious of their own weakness.

While the practices described above suggest deeply-rooted contests over the meaning of Bali, we need to keep in mind that, in most contexts, these contours of meaning do not represent a strict dichotomy between 'Puranically oriented elites' and 'heterodox subalterns'. In most contexts, folk practices associated with local deities, demons, and spirits enjoy a high degree of compatibility with the dominant Puranic world view. Lower-caste villagers, for example, commonly participate in the major Puranic festivals, and they visit the village temples of Puranic gods such as Maruti (Hanuman) or Shiva. Moreover, they typically have images of the major gods and goddesses in their household shrines—alongside objects or images representing more subaltern deities and demons—and householders can usually narrate stories that establish the identity of the latter as incarnations of the Puranic deities. Thus, within most sections of the village's Hindu community, neither 'orthodox' culture nor heterodox (folk) culture is rejected wholesale. Major elements of both classical and folk religious practices are embraced and patronized throughout the community.

Nonetheless, there are contexts in which subjects consciously recognize the contrast between variant practices and meanings as deliberate oppositions. For example, very few of my lower-caste informants were oblivious to the subtle (and not so subtle) ways that festivals such as Navaratri and Diwali seem to reinforce local social hierarchies and continue the discursive denigration of many of their own religious practices. These active oppositions are particularly apparent in practices associated with Bali—in part because Bali is so widely recognized as a metaphor for actual groups within the community.

While some of the upper-caste practices that reenact the conquest of Bali are conducted in public spaces, lower-caste practices of Bali veneration are far more understated, and are generally confined to the domestic sphere, the near environs of the home, or the family field. And despite reinforcements of social confinement, we have also seen ways in which Shudra and Dalit villagers stealthily project Bali into public space. Burying the ghat in the family field extends Bali's realm beyond the interior confines of the house. Declaring in public that 'Bali will return' and publicly addressing fellow agriculturalists and labourers as 'Bali' verbally assert the validity of Bali in village lanes and public centres. One agrarian practice that achieves this more than any other is the veneration of bulls and bullocks in the festival of Pola. Lower-caste villagers widely describe this practice as a form of 'Bali *puja*'.

Pola (also called Bailpola) is a rural festival celebrated by village agrarian and labouring castes in the lunar month of Shravan (July–August). Nominally, it is a day of compensatory veneration for the bulls and bullocks which, on every other day of the year, labour for their masters' livelihood.[7] On Pola, these 'servants' are treated literally like kings. They are decorated in rich colours with paint and powders. Sometimes they are garlanded with marigold flowers, or their horns are painted gold. They are treated to a day without labour, fed sweets and the finest fodder, and—most importantly—paraded through the village centre for all to see their grandeur, like kings on a royal tour.

On Pola the bull or bullock enjoys a day of hierarchical inversion in which the servant becomes the king. However, there is more going on than this: the animal is treated not just as a king, but also as the king of demons, Bali. Thus, on one level, it is not merely a bull or bullock that enjoys the social inversion and is paraded around the village for all to appreciate; it is Bali. In order to grasp the potential significance of this act, we must recall that the bull or bullock is closely associated with Bali, not merely on Pola but also on every other day of the year when the animal is a servant and, by its very name, a 'helper of Bali' (*balivard*). We must also recall that village agriculturalists and members of lower castes *also* represent Bali, and vice versa. Hence, the veneration of the bull or bullock is simultaneously a veneration of Bali and a veneration of the lower caste and agrarian Self. This is why many informants describe their veneration of bulls and bullocks on Pola not only as 'Bali puja', but also as 'self-puja'.

As opposition, Pola is a relatively subtle practice—far less overt and assertive than the public burning of demon effigies or even the squashing of a fruit under an upper-class man's foot—but these aspects of Pola suggest a widely felt validation of the demon victim.

As with other expressions of Bali veneration, Pola suggests that his invocation within social movements such as the Shetkari Sanghatana is not exclusively a political manipulation of folk culture but also an amplification of existing low-caste and agrarian commentaries on socio-economic and cultural hierarchies in the village community. The more deeply we look at the myth of Bali and its varied practices and implications in Maharashtrian society, the more we recognize him as a vehicle through which these hierarchies are debated, challenged or asserted.

BALI AND THE DIALOGIC OF MAHARASHTRIAN IDENTITY

Although it has not been possible here to offer an exhaustive inquiry into the significance of these cultural expressions, the broad strokes that I have outlined should serve to suggest some of the many ways in which both 'dominant' and 'resistant' meanings of Bali are mutually engaged. Folk practices associated with Bali are not strictly displays of resistance to a dominant, orthodox, or classical ideology. They are also rites of subcultural belonging and expressions of collective selfhood. Nonetheless, there are contexts in which they can be seen to be deliberately opposed to the cultural transcripts of village elites—just as the practices and meanings of village elites may be deliberately opposed to those of their own village Others. These oppositions suggest that the myth of Bali constitutes an important symbolic arena and a site of ongoing negotiations on the terms of cultural identity and social hierarchy in rural Maharashtra.

NOTES

1. Among other Marathi terms associated (through real or folk etymologies) with Bali, some very clearly carry meanings of strength, such as *balishtha* ('potent'), and *bali* ('mighty'). But common Marathi speech includes an almost equal circulation of terms that connote submissiveness. The same word as the proper name (Bali), when used as a non-proper noun, means 'oblation', 'offering', or 'sacrifice'. This is often applied to the actual material given in a religious offering to a deity, such as flowers or items of food, but also refers to donations made to a Brahman. Finally, the term *balidan* (to 'give' bali) refers to either an act of generosity or— somewhere between strength and generosity—'martyrdom'.

2. I have adapted the following from the main elements of the myth as

given in Mani's *Puranic Encyclopedia* (1975). The verses on which this adaptation is based are found in the *Vamana Purana* (Chapters 75–6, 77) and the *Bhagavata Purana* (Book 8).

3. Most major commemorations of demon conquest occur in the same short period of the annual cycle, the tail end of a particularly inauspicious period in the Hindu ritual calendar during which Vishnu is said to have been sleeping for four months. In myth as well as in festival practice, the divine context is that Vishnu has awakened to discover that demonic forces have gathered their strength and extended their power over the Brahmanical world during his slumber. The festivals thus reassert order—not only the divine order that Vishnu is charged with maintaining, but also the village social order of rulers and differentially ranked subjects, which is a microcosm of the cosmic hierarchy (Fuller 1992).

4. This, as with all other proper names of villages or individual informants, is a pseudonym.

5. Ghatasthapana is practiced throughout Maharashtra, but there are many variations on the other village practices that involve Bali on the day of Dasara. As one informant from Sangli district described events in her village:

    After the ghat is buried, the villagers go around exchanging leaves of the *apte* tree, as if they were gold. We make little earthen dolls of Bali and place them outside the home.... Women approach neighbours saying, 'May all evil go away, and may the kingdom of Bali be restored'. But what happens is that, when a Brahman comes along, he takes a long stick and he pokes it into the belly of that Bali doll as he walks past. I don't know how long this has been going on, but that's how it is.

6. The actual duration depends upon the lunar circumstances in each particular year.

7. Although *bail* literally means 'bull' or 'bullock', many low-caste labourers or pastoralists who do not own draught animals commonly celebrate Pola as well, venerating whichever animal performs services for them. Many non-cultivators venerate donkeys on Pola—for example, potters, diggers, or stonebreakers who depend on donkeys for hauling.

REFERENCES

Atre, Trimbak Narayan. 1915. *Gavagada*. Pune: Aryabhushan Press.

Chitrao, M.M. Sidheshwar Shastri. 1964. *Bharatavarshiya Prachin Charitrakosh* (in Marathi). Poona: Bharatiya Charitrakosha Mandal.

Dimmit, Cornelia and J.A.B. van Buitenen. 1978. *Classical Indian Mythology: A Reader in the Sanskrit Puranas*. Philadelphia: Temple University Press.

Feldhaus, Anne. 1995. *Water and Womanhood: Religious Meanings of Rivers in Maharashtra*. New York: Oxford University Press.

Fuller, C.J. 1992. *The Camphor Flame: Popular Hinduism and Society in India*. Princeton: Princeton University Press.

Hale, Wash Edward. 1999 [1986]. *Asura in Early Vedic Religion*. Delhi: Motilal Banarsidass.

Jaiswal, Suvira. 1967. *The Origin and Development of Vaishnavism*. Delhi: Munshiram Manoharlal.

Joshi, Pandit Mahadevashastri. 1962. *Bharatiya Sanskrutikosh* (in Marathi). Pune: Bharatiya Sanskrutikosh Mandal.

Karve, Irawati. 1968. *Maharashtra: Land and Its People* (*Maharashtra State Gazetteer*, General Series). Bombay: Directorate of Government Printing, Stationary and Publications, Maharashtra State.

Kosambi, D.D. 1994 [1962]. *Myth and Reality: Studies in the Formation of Indian Culture*. Bombay: Popular Prakashan.

Mani, Vettam. 1975. *Puranic Encyclopedia*. Delhi: Motilal Banarsidass.

O'Flaherty, Wendy Doniger. 1976. *The Origins of Evil in Hindu Mythology*. Delhi: Motilal Banarsidass.

———. 1988. *Other People's Myths: The Cave of Echos*. New York: Macmillan Publishing Company.

Richman, Paula (ed.). 1991. *Many Ramayanas: The Diversity of a Narrative Tradition in South Asia*. Berkeley: University of California Press.

———. 2000. *Questioning Ramayanas: A South Asian Tradition*. Berkeley: University of California Press.

Shulman, David Dean. 1980. *Tamil Temple Myths: Sacrifice and Divine Marriage in the South Indian Shaiva Tradition*. Princeton: Princeton University Press.

7

'HOW CAN A WIFE SCREECH AND WAIL?'
Respectability and Bengali Women Singers' Lives

Donna M. Wulff

In the Indian subcontinent, as elsewhere, hierarchies are often oppressive, the hierarchy of gender no less than the hierarchy of caste. Eleanor Zelliot's pioneering work on Dalits reaches well beyond her central focus to illuminate multiple forms and degrees of victimization. In the present article I look at two women performers of a semi-dramatic musical form called *padavali kirtan*.[1] Not themselves Dalits, these women have nonetheless suffered because of patriarchal structures and the adverse decisions made by men—in particular, their in-laws—who sought to control them. Despite the formidable roadblocks these men placed in their way, both women ultimately managed to prevail and have successful careers as devotional singers.

The two singers whose lives we shall consider, Binapani Devi and Sukla Hazra, were born thirty years apart in Kolkata. Music played a major role in both their homes. When the girls exhibited great talent from a very young age, as well as an early love of music, their parents provided them with thorough training in classical and devotional vocal music. Thus it seems especially egregious that their in-laws, knowing all this, put a complete stop to their singing right after their marriages. Not only were they prohibited from performing, publicly or in the privacy of their homes, they were even prevented from continuing to study music. As we explore aspects of these women's lives, I shall try to discern some of the reasons underlying these draconian restrictions.[2]

Binapani Devi and Sukla Hazra studied and performed other classical and devotional genres, but it is as singers of padavali kirtan that they have been best known.[3] Padavali kirtan is a religious, dramatic form of storytelling structured around songs with lyrics in medieval Bengali or Brajabuli.[4] Its two broad themes are the love of Radha and Krishna and the life of the ecstatic mystic Chaitanya (1486–1533). By narrating an episode such as 'Mathur', for example, which focuses on Radha's grief and despair at being abandoned by Krishna, and by exemplifying ideal emotional responses toward her especially through the songs that punctuate the story, a skilful kirtan singer is able to draw receptive devotees into the narrative and lead them to experience its emotions, thereby reawakening and enhancing their love for Radha as well as for Krishna.[5]

The usual *male* style of performing padavali kirtan, a style also adopted by some women, is to stand and move around the ritual performance space, employing dramatic gestures and at times dancing to the sharp, intricate rhythms the *khol* players tap out with their highly trained fingers on the two leather heads of their slender, barrel-shaped drums.[6] By contrast, many women *kirtaniya*s, including Binapani Devi and Sukla Hazra, have sung in a sitting posture, many, including Binapani, accompanying themselves on the harmonium.[7] Both these women have been praised for the emotional power and depth of their singing.

This essay is based primarily on interviews I conducted and recorded, most with a research assistant. I have interviewed one of the women, Sukla Hazra, at length on two occasions. For the other, Binapani Devi, who died before I began my project on women kirtaniyas, my research assistant and I interviewed several of her close relatives: the niece who was her constant companion from childhood, her daughter, and her granddaughter and grandson.

BINAPANI DEVI (1914–90)

Binapani Devi was born in 1914 in Kolkata. Her father, an ardent appreciator of music, played the *esraj*, a stringed instrument of classical Hindustani (north Indian)[8] music that has been especially popular in Bengal. Like many early Bengali women singers, Binapani began learning music from an early age. Her father started teaching her songs when she was five, and the next year she took formal initiation into the study of north Indian classical music. From a succession of teachers she learned the major classical vocal forms as well as a body of songs styled *ragpradhan*, a Bengali regional genre based on classical ragas. One of her teachers was the well-known Muslim composer and performer Kazi Nazrul Islam, who was especially famous for his songs on the love of Radha and Krishna. According to her daughter, it was not until much later—in her mid-thirties—that she started learning kirtan.

My chief sources for Binapani's life were her niece, Pusparani Chatterjee, and her daughter, Sandhya Chatterjee.[9] Pusparani, three years older than Binapani, was her constant childhood companion. She and Sandhya spoke to us on separate occasions about Binapani's marriage.

Pusparani's account emphasized Binapani's emotions and the cruelty of her in-laws. She narrated a striking occurrence at the time of the wedding. At some point in the proceedings, Binapani was apparently slow in getting ready. Her new father-in-law refused to wait for her and was on the verge of leaving with his son. Binapani's mother clasped his feet and pleaded with him, but he kept walking, dragging her along with him. Pusparani said it was because of this kind of behaviour that Binapani's parents did not allow her to return to her in-laws once she had been brought back to their home.

According to Pusparani, Binapani's in-laws' cruelty continued at her husband's home. Her mother-in-law withheld food from her, and it was only because of the kindness of her sister-in-law and a brother-in-law, who smuggled food into the cowshed for her, that she was able to eat on those days.

Neither Pusparani nor Sandhya pointed to a single, defining event that precipitated Binapani's departure from her in-laws' house. Pusparani said that after Binapani left his home, she and her husband continued to yearn for each other, but Binapani was afraid to return there because she had been treated so badly by her in-laws. Binapani herself, she said, blamed her youth and immaturity—she was only fifteen or sixteen when she left—for her failure to realize how fortunate she was to have such a good man as her husband. This realization dawned on her only when he married again; when she learned of his second marriage, she wept bitterly from remorse and blamed her parents for not urging her to return to her husband's house.

Both Pusparani and Sandhya spoke of subsequent meetings of Binapani and her husband. Pusparani said her husband and his brother arranged these secret trysts. She spoke of a rendezvous at Kolkata's Eden Gardens during which they both cried incessantly at the way things had turned out for them.

Sandhya's account of the events surrounding Binapani's marriage differs markedly from Pusparani's in some respects. On the other hand, it accords in broad outlines with the story many Bengalis have heard about Binapani, with Sandhya supplying details that are not part of the legend of her famous mother. According to Sandhya, Binapani married at the age of thirteen or fourteen and moved to her husband's home in Srirampur. During our first interview with Sandhya, my research assistant referred to the legend, saying that Binapani wanted to continue singing, and Sandhya implicitly confirmed this account, adding that Binapani's in-laws did not allow her to do so. When asked how Binapani's husband felt about her singing, Sandhya said he was too loyal to his parents, especially his mother, to take a stand in opposition to theirs. Without her husband's support, Binapani's wish to continue singing would have been futile.

Sandhya did not mention the physical cruelty at the hands of the mother-in-law that Pusparani emphasized. However, she alleged instances of mental cruelty, saying that Binapani's in-laws hurt her deeply by denigrating her parents for having educated her in music. Such insults to her parents would have been doubly painful for Binapani because they demeaned her as well. Sandhya said her mother left her in-laws' house in anger.

In Bengal, as across north India, families have often refused to take back a daughter who walks out of her marriage, defying social expectations and abandoning her duties to her husband and his family. Sandhya gave a purely economic explanation for the fact that Binapani's parents took her back into their home when she returned from her in-laws'. She began with a sketch of the family's financial circumstances. Binapani's older brother had died at the age of 21, when Binapani was just twelve, and her sole remaining brother had asthma and other ailments and was never able to take a job. Binapani's returning home would thus provide a solution to her father's dilemma of how to support his family, for he knew Binapani could bring in money through giving private lessons and doing radio programmes. We shall return to this issue in our final section.

SUKLA HAZRA (1944–)

Sukla Hazra was born in 1944, also in Kolkata, into a family of accomplished musicians.[10] Her father, Rathin Ghosh, was one of the most celebrated kirtan singers of his day, and her mother was also a highly trained singer. Sukla was thus exposed to music quite literally from birth, and she began to learn classical music—from some of the best teachers in Kolkata—when she was still a young child. Her father established an atmosphere and a regimen in which music occupied the highest echelon; in her home, exam preparation and other schoolwork were never permitted to take precedence over learning music.

In her teens, Sukla was already an accomplished kirtan singer, with a mastery of an extensive repertoire of kirtan episodes. However, her father, who often took her to assist him in giving radio and television programmes, did not allow her to perform with him in public. He expressed two main concerns. First, he would soon be arranging her marriage, and, as Sukla puts it, he feared that 'people would speak ill of his daughter' if she travelled around with his troupe. Sukla reported that societal norms for the upper and middle classes in Bengal in the early 1960s were strong and unambiguous: it was unacceptable for a respectable woman to travel about with a group of men, even for the purpose of giving devotional performances. She contrasted the situation at that time, when she was in her late teens and early twenties, with the one some thirty years later, at the time of my interviews of her: 'What I am able to do alone today was not possible then'. Referring specifically to her own family situation, she characterized her household as 'much more modern now' than thirty years earlier, when her grandmother was still living and 'people didn't do such things'.

Rathin Ghosh gave a second reason for objecting to Sukla's performing kirtan publicly, and he generalized it to include all women. He argued that a woman performer, especially if she stood in full view of the audience, the way he and other male performers did, would inevitably distract men from the religious meaning of the episode being enacted. Rathin Ghosh's view of a kirtan performance as a religious occasion is a widely shared one; Sukla, for example, emphasized to me its deeply devotional purpose. She characterized her responsibility in singing kirtan as one of 'attracting listeners to a path of devotion to God'.

Although I silently disagreed with the positions her father took, as Sukla represented them, they did not seem wholly unreasonable.

Other Bengalis have also told me that many Indian men would look at a young, attractive woman performer as a sex object rather than a religious interpreter. Rathin Ghosh's restrictions on his daughter may thus be seen as an appropriate response to an intractable societal situation. However, he might also have been exploiting this situation to exert control over his exceptionally talented and accomplished daughter. I was struck by the fact that Sukla never seemed to question her father's dictates; in fact, she typically put forth his views as if they were her own.

Sukla spoke in detail about the visit her prospective in-laws made to her home to meet and interview her. They gave a very good impression by listening to her songs for four hours. Sukla and her parents would thus have had every reason to expect her new husband and his family to be supportive of her musical training. However, after the wedding her husband's family abruptly put an end to her study of music, even preventing her from enrolling for the third and final year of her bachelor's degree in music at Rabindra Bharati University. Such an unanticipated, peremptory act would have been a blow to any aspiring musician, but in Sukla's case it must have been especially devastating. Not only had she been immersed in music, especially kirtan, for her entire life, but because of her great talent and hard work she had stood first in some of the most prestigious music competitions in West Bengal.

Given this history, it was surprising to me that Sukla was so restrained in speaking about the early years of her marriage; I could detect no bitterness or resentment. To my question about how she felt when her husband's family stopped her study of music, she simply responded:

I was very sad when they stopped my studies. Here [in her parents' home] I had grown up in a house of music, and there my music was completely stopped. I did housework all day long; there was no music at all there.

Sukla could not have anticipated the remarkable set of circumstances that would conspire to bring her back into the world of kirtan. Referring to two events that utterly changed the course of her life, she said:

Then God himself changed my situation. There was a financial crisis in my in-laws' house, and we needed money to bring up my sons. At that time [in 1980] my father passed away. So all these changes led me back into the world of kirtan; otherwise everything had been completely stopped in my in-laws' house.

She continued, speaking with perhaps inadvertent irony and providing a rare glimpse into the suffering she had endured in the absence of music:

God made up for this loss [the loss of music] when he brought financial difficulties into my life and made things convenient for me. I've had to fight a lot to bear things in my life; I've had to struggle. But [finally] I was given an opportunity to sing.

Sukla spoke of a third factor. The Birlas, for many years one of India's two leading philanthropist families, revered Rathin Ghosh as their guru and were ardent devotees of his kirtan performances. Heartsick at his premature death, Mr and Mrs B.K. Birla came to Sukla's mother and asked her who would continue singing kirtan the way her husband had done. Sukla's mother replied that his daughters had been trained to sing in that way, but their in-laws would not allow them to sing in public. The Birlas came repeatedly and implored Sukla's mother to persuade Sukla's in-laws to allow her to perform kirtan. They offered to take the in-laws' whole family on a tour of India if they would allow their daughter-in-law to perform. In the end they prevailed, and from that time on Sukla has sung kirtan for audiences. Without the Birlas' intervention, she emphasized, she might never have been able to sing in public.

PERFORMANCE AND RESPECTABILITY

Behind decisions prohibiting women from singing and dancing is the view that such activities are not done by respectable women, especially respectable married women. This view is largely based on the fact that there had been for some time in Bengal and throughout north India a class of prominent women performers called *baijis*, courtesans, and other compromised women. Especially because of their irregular sexual liaisons, these women have come to represent the antithesis of the respectable married woman. Historically members of the royal courts, baijis were highly trained in the arts, especially music and dance.[11] In the popular imagination, however, they have often been conflated with lower-class women, who were seen as lacking in such refinement.

In Kolkata, moreover, many have worked as prostitutes (see Banerjee 1998: 9–12). The resulting stereotype is illustrated by Sandhya's representation of Binapani's in-laws' disdain towards a married woman of a respectable household—*barir bou*—who would engage in singing. My research assistant asked Sandhya whether Binapani's in-laws knew before the wedding that Binapani was a singer. Sandhya replied as follows:

Yes, they knew ... perhaps they thought she would stop singing after the wedding. Now she sings—that's all right—but how can she go on singing after she's married? How can a wife screech and wail?[12]

Sandhya's impersonation struck me as an insightful characterization of certain conservative Bengalis, who have construed a wife's identity as completely incompatible with that of a singer or other performer. The underlying logic of this position appears to be the following:

1. The women who have sung and danced have been baijis.
2. Baijis are disreputable women.
3. If a married woman sang (or worse, danced), she would likewise no longer be respectable, and she would thus bring shame on her husband and his extended family.
4. She must therefore be prevented from engaging in these activities.

Even though Binapani, from early in her marriage, and Sukla, from a later point, both rejected the conventional role of a Bengali wife, they both took pains to establish themselves as respectable performers. As singers, they sought to demonstrate their adherence to the norms of respectability in two chief ways. First, they limited the types of functions and the places in which they would agree to sing. Secondly, they chose a modest posture in which to perform. We shall consider each of these strategies in turn.

Among the most common settings for kirtan performances are *sraddha*s, memorial ceremonies for deceased family members. Binapani consistently declined to sing for such ceremonies. Her daughter said she avoided them because of the manner of payment: at sraddha ceremonies, money, termed *pela*, was commonly given to kirtaniyas on a tray. Sandhya expressed her mother's apprehension in general terms: 'People my mother knew would say, "She is singing in sraddha ceremonies".'

Sukla, by contrast, has regularly sung at sraddha ceremonies, and she gave no indication in my interviews with her that doing so posed any problem for her. However, she drew a general distinction between types of performances in which she would be respected and types in which she would not be given respect, and she asserted firmly that she did not sing in gatherings of the latter sort.[13]

The women's modes of performing and their reflections on performance options constitute another set of clues regarding their concerns about respectability. As we have noted, both women have chosen to sing in a sitting position. However, although both have made use of the traditional accompanying instruments men have used, the elongated barrel-shaped drum (khol) and small brass hand cymbals (kartal), Sukla's troupes, like those of male kirtaniyas, have also included supporting singers (dohars), whereas Binapani has sung entirely without vocal assistance. From the way Sandhya spoke about her mother's policy of not using supporting singers, it was clear that Sandhya, at least, judged that choice to be the more respectable option.

Sandhya's comments contrasting Binapani's mode of singing with other women's use of the characteristic male mode of standing and dancing provide an especially clear window on Sandhya's perceptions of the appropriate boundaries for women performers. She contrasted the simplicity of Binapani's way of singing kirtan with the mode of women who stood and gestured: 'My mother didn't move her arms or her head; she struck no poses—nothing. She would just sing, playing the harmonium.' By way of contrast, she described another woman kirtaniya in decidedly unflattering terms: 'She sings standing, dressed up, her hair loose, constantly moving her arms.' At this point she interrupted herself to interpose, 'I shouldn't be saying such things', and then added, 'Our teachers and my mother didn't do that'.

Sandhya's description of a second early woman singer, the baiji Pannamayi Dasi, also has important bearing on the issue of women's respectability during this early period. Sandhya said Pannamayi Dasi had a booming voice and could perform for huge gatherings without a microphone, and that she danced and whirled around as she sang. She called her 'a very famous kirtaniya' and said that her mother used to listen to recordings of her songs. Entirely absent from Sandhya's comments about Pannamayi Dasi is the judgemental tone she used in speaking of the first woman she described as standing and gesturing. Sandhya's contrasting assessments of these two women singers, both of whom stood and danced, was initially puzzling to me: she had nothing but praise for the baiji Pannamayi Dasi, whereas her view of the first kirtaniya was decidedly critical. The key would seem to lie in the contrasting social status of the two women: like Binapani, the first kirtaniya whose aberrant mode of singing Sandhya characterized was a married woman in society, whereas Pannamayi Dasi, a baiji, was in another realm entirely, one to which ordinary social restrictions were not seen to apply.

Whether consciously or not, then, women kirtaniyas who have chosen to perform in a seated posture rather than standing and dancing—including Binapani and Sukla—have effectively differentiated themselves from the many male kirtaniyas who stood and danced (including Nanda Kishore Das, Panchanan Das, and Rathin Ghosh), as well as from baijis and from the few other women kirtaniyas who have followed the male model.

FACTORS FAVOURING SUCCESS

Several common factors and personal traits contributed to Binapani's and Sukla Hazra's success in becoming professional kirtaniyas. Both women were born into musical families: although Binapani's father was an amateur musician and Sukla's was a professional, both men loved music and inspired a deep love of music in their daughters. Both homes were frequently filled with music. The girls' unusual talent and their eagerness to learn music were evident from their early childhood years, and they studied diligently with the teachers their fathers found for them.

Before Binapani and Sukla could sing kirtan *palas* in public, each had to make a break from her in-laws. These ruptures took place at different stages and to different degrees; for Binapani, the break with her in-laws was more radical and more devastating than for Sukla. Intriguingly, economic hardships were instrumental in making both women's careers possible.

As we have seen, Binapani's break from her in-laws came quite early. The discrepancies between the two accounts of her marriage make it impossible to know with certainty the causes of her leaving or the precise chronology of events. However, the two accounts agree that she left her husband and his family and returned to her parents' home within roughly a year. I have noted that Sandhya's account of the events after Binapani's wedding emphasized economic factors, notably her father's worry about whether he would be able to support his family. Binapani's return to her natal home would solve her family's financial problems. Was her own desire to pursue a career in music enhanced by her awareness of how much her family needed her earnings? Did her parents urge her to stay with them chiefly for financial reasons? We may recall that according to Pusparani, it was Binapani's parents who made the crucial decision not to bring Binapani back to her husband's house, but Pusparani claimed the decision was based on Binapani's father-in-law's behaviour during the wedding, rather than on the family's need of her income.

Despite being wholly deprived of music in her in-laws' house, Sukla lived with her husband and his family for some fifteen years, bearing two sons and carrying out her duties as a barir bou, a respectable woman of the household. Only when a financial crisis developed in her in-laws' family and her own father died prematurely did it seem that there might be a chance for her to become a singer. The third essential factor, as we have seen, was the intervention of the Birlas, who came to Sukla's mother in quest of someone who could sing kirtan the way Sukla's father, Rathin Ghosh, had done. It was at their repeated urging that Sukla's husband's family finally allowed her to perform.

To win the right to sing padavali kirtan, Binapani and Sukla had to endure protracted suffering.[14] Binapani sacrificed her marriage to a man she had grown to love, and she later expressed profound regret for having left him. Sukla lived for some fifteen years with in-laws who prevented her from having any contact with music, her greatest passion. Adapting slightly in relation to Sukla the terminology used for a pervasive, fundamental element in the love of Radha and Krishna, we might say that both women experienced extended periods of biraha (Sanskrit, viraha), love in separation. It may well have been these painful personal experiences that gave them such deep empathy for Radha and the other characters in the kirtan palas, who yearn in one situation after another for an absent Krishna.

Years later, the two women described their experiences of performing in strikingly similar terms, employing expressions reminiscent of those used to represent the highest experiences of yoga as well as the ideal of loving devotion (bhakti). Sandhya related Binapani's reflections as follows: 'When I sing, I forget everything in the world. I have no consciousness [of anything else].' Sukla likewise spoke of transcending earthly concerns while singing kirtan:

I love kirtan supremely much, above all else ... after singing it, I feel joy within me. Whatever sorrows or difficulties there might be in my life, when I sing kirtan I forget everything. I don't remember what I have and what I don't have in my life; I forget all sorrows.... After I finish the kirtan and come home, these [feelings] may return, but for those three or four hours, I experience great joy.

Growing up in the household of Rathin Ghosh, a kirtaniya known for his powerful, inspiring performances, Sukla imbibed a strong sense of the religious importance of performing kirtan palas. We noted earlier that she used religious terms to express her understanding of her mission as a kirtaniya. Her sense of having what in the modern West would be called a religious vocation may have helped give her strength to struggle through the difficulties she had to bear in her in-laws' home.

In Bengal generally, performing kirtan and becoming absorbed in it are both seen as religious acts. More particularly, because a kirtan singer who feels and expresses the devotional emotions at the heart of a pala is able to evoke these emotions in an audience of responsive devotees, kirtan is *ritual* as much as performance. Moreover, because it is these religious emotions, rather than theological propositions or ethical actions, that are understood to be salvific, women kirtaniyas, every bit as much as their male counterparts, perform a priestly function.

Over the course of their long careers, Binapani Devi and Sukla Hazra, by evoking loving emotions in devotees who have come to hear their palas, have subverted to a considerable degree a religious institution, padavali kirtan, that was firmly under male control until the late nineteenth or early twentieth century.[15] Through the inspiration of their singing and their lives, they have further effected social change by helping to establish religious performance as a challenging but rewarding calling or career choice for other Bengali women.

NOTES

1. See below for a description of padavali kirtan. The shorter form, kirtan, has a wider range of meanings in both north and south India. In the

present essay, however, I use the term, as it is often used in Bengal, to stand for padavali kirtan.

2. An informative parallel to these women singers is that of early actresses on the Bengali stage, as illustrated by the autobiographical works of one of the earliest of these, Binodini Dasi (1863–1941). Two of her publications have been translated and interpreted in Bhattacharya's 1998. Although the example of Binodini may be seen as on a continuum with that of Binapani and some of the other early women singers of padavali kirtan, the appalling lack of self-esteem indicated by Binodini's repeated poignant references to herself as 'fallen', 'sinful', 'wretched', and the like goes far beyond the preoccupation with respectability conveyed in Sandhya's account of Binapani's life.

3. Binapani's daughter told us that her mother sang Syama Sangit, songs in praise of Kali, as well as kirtan, and that she gave separate radio programmes on a regular basis for each of these two devotional genres.

4. Brajabuli is a highly mellifluous hybrid language created in the sixteenth century CE by Vaishnava poets in Greater Bengal and employed by them and by subsequent poets over the next centuries to compose Vaishnava lyrics.

5. In the sixteenth century, the theologian and playwright Rupa Gosvami, one of the principal disciples of Chaitanya, expressed in Sanskrit treatises and plays his insight into the religious value of externally enacted as well as internally visualized drama for cultivating devotional emotion. See Wulff 1984: 25–44. Because the musical, narrative form of padavali kirtan has a dramatic structure, Rupa's analysis applies in large measure to kirtan palas as well. See also Haberman 1988.

6. For a somewhat fuller description of this largely male mode of performing kirtan, see Wulff 1996: 124–5.

7. A harmonium is a small organ-like instrument with a keyboard and bellows.

8. There are two distinct forms of classical music in the Indian subcontinent, the Karnatak tradition in the south and the Hindustani tradition in the north. Hindustani music is a blend of indigenous Indian forms with those brought into the subcontinent by Muslim musicians.

9. The two interviews of Sandhya Chatterjee from which the information and quotations in this chapter were taken were conducted on 30 June and 8 July 1993, in Kolkata. The single interview of Pusparani Chatterjee was conducted on 27 November 1998, also in Kolkata.

10. The two interviews of Sukla Hazra from which the information and quotations in this chapter were taken were conducted on 27–8 February 1993, in Kolkata.

11. Veena Talwar Oldenburg (1990) documents the immense cultural,

social and political influence wielded by the courtesans of another major Indian city.

12. With the phrase 'screech and wail' I attempt to approximate the effect of Sandhya's Bengali; she used a repeated verb (cenciye cenciye) that has harsh, nasal sounds.

13. The issue of singing in sraddha ceremonies is a complex one. Sandhya gave another reason for her mother's policy of not singing for these ceremonies: she said the grief expressed on these occasions affected her mother so much that she was not able to sing. More research, including follow-up interviews of Sandhya and Sukla, would be necessary to account for the difference between Binapani's and Sukla's views of the respectability, or lack thereof, of sraddha ceremonies.

14. They have gained the right to perform in practice rather than through official channels. Here, as is commonly the case with religious institutions, there is a considerable discrepancy between official 'rules' or established tradition and what actually exists on the ground.

15. Although the earlier women singers whose names were recorded as having performed kirtan—including Angurbala, Indubala, and Kamala Jharia—were baijis, there may also have been other early women kirtaniyas whose names were never recorded.

REFERENCES

Banerjee, Sumanta. 1998. *Dangerous Outcast: The Prostitute in Nineteenth Century Bengal.* Calcutta: Seagull Books.

Bhattacharya, Rimli. 1998. *Binodini Dasi: My Story and My Life as an Actress.* New Delhi: Kali for Women.

Haberman, David L. 1988. *Acting as a Way of Salvation: A Study of Raganuga Bhakti Sadhana.* New York: Oxford University Press.

Oldenburg, Veena Talwar. 1990. 'Lifestyle as Resistance: The Case of the Courtesans of Lucknow, India'. *Feminist Studies.* vol. 16, no. 2, pp. 259–87.

Wulff, Donna M. 1984. *Drama as a Mode of Religious Realization: The Vidagdhamadhava of Rupa Gosvami.* Chico, California: Scholars Press.

_____. 1996. 'Radha: Consort and Conqueror of Krishna'. In John Stratton Hawley and Donna M. Wulff (eds). *Devi: Goddesses of India.* Berkeley: University of California Press, pp. 109–34.

8

OTHER VOICES, OTHER ROOMS*
The View from the Zenana

Gail Minault

The proverbial view of a woman's life in purdah-observing urban society in north India in the nineteenth century was one of hermetically-sealed respectability: The woman left her father's house only when carried out in a wedding palanquin, and left her husband's house only when carried out on her bier. In reality, however, zenana life was considerably more convivial. Women in urban areas spent a great deal of time on their rooftops, conversing from one house to another. They visited one another frequently within their neighbourhood or circle of relations, and shared food on festival occasions with a whole network of families, bound together by ties of blood or social and economic obligation. A bride returned to her natal family for several visits during the first year of her marriage, then for the birth of her first child, and possibly for later confinements. Sisters remained in close contact, whatever the vicissitudes of their married lives. Women's networks were largely responsible for arranging marriages, even though the formal negotiation of marriage contracts was the prerogative of men.[1]

How is it possible to get an inside view of zenana life in India in the nineteenth century? The historian is handicapped by the fact that

*This is an updated version of an article published in Nita Kumar (ed.). *Women as Subjects: South Asian Histories*. Charlottesville: University Press of Virginia and Calcutta: Stree, 1994, pp. 108–24. © Copyright English language 1994. The University of Virginia Press. Reprinted here by their permission.

most works from the period, whether literary, historical, or religious, are written by men and represent what might be characterized as the 'hegemonic' or 'patriarchal' view of the zenana.[2] Such sources represent outsiders' views of the zenana, and thus to rely upon them is problematic. A critical reading of such works, however, permits one to illuminate their ideological stance, while simultaneously reading between the lines for what they reveal of zenana life.[3]

This discussion will draw extensively upon two texts written by Muslim reformers of the late nineteenth century, the one from the educated middle class associated with the Aligarh movement, and the other from among the ulama associated with the Deoband school.[4] The first text, *Majalis un-Nissa* by Altaf Husain Hali, published in 1874, consists of supposed conversations among women in an urban Muslim household. The purpose of the work is to dramatize the need for women's education in that social milieu, to condemn superstition and useless custom, and to define the ideal Muslim woman (Minault 1986b). The second text is *Bihishti Zewar* by Maulana Ashraf Ali Thanawi, published in 1905 or earlier. The reformist ulama of Deoband sought to improve the quality of Islamic education, to increase personal piety, and to spread the observance of Islamic law more widely among Muslims in India. Their advocacy of a reformed Islam led the Deoband ulama to champion women's education in order to suppress many customary practices and to Islamicize women's religious observances. *Bihishti Zewar* was the major vehicle for this reform, a veritable encyclopedia of religious and family laws, Islamic medicine, and accounts of the lives of pious women. It became a standard guide to religious practice for women in many Muslim homes.[5]

One of the topics that both texts deal with is women's language in Urdu, *begamati zuban*. They do so in order to indicate that it is incorrect, either uninstructed or un-Islamic. Maulana Thanawi particularly notes that women's language goes against religion:

She greets the women of the house ... [M]any do not even take the trouble to speak but simply place their hand to their forehead in greeting. The *hadith* says that this style of greeting is forbidden. Some say ... simply '*salam*'. That too is against the *sunna*. One should say '*As-salamu 'alaikum*' ('Peace be upon you'). Now just look at the responses:

'Keep cool!' ...
'Remain a beloved wife (*suhagan*)!' ...

'May you bathe in milk and enjoy grandsons!' ...
'May your husband live long!'
'May your children live long!'
It is easy to count off the names of the whole family but difficult to say
'As-salamu 'alaikum' ... Always to oppose the *shari 'at* is [a] sin. (Metcalf 1990:
110–11)

Hali's critique of women's language is extensive, and takes the
form of a lesson given by a mother to her son, indicating vocabulary
that he—as a man—must *never* use:

For example: *nauj, dur par, chhain phuin, ab se dur* [all interjections meaning
God forbid; heaven forfend], *chal dur* [get out of here; begone], *sidharna* [to go
away], *muva* [dead], *picchalpai* [demoness, witch], *bodli* [transvestite, whore],
vari, acchi, bua [terms of endearment], *bhayya, bhaina* [younger brother,
younger sister—also terms of endearment used for other women] ... *nikhattu*
[worthless, useless], *nigori* [unfortunate, without support], *bakhtavari* [lucky],
rasna basna [fortunate, one who stays at home] .... Never use these words in
front of anyone! They won't say anything to you, but they will certainly say to
themselves that this boy has started talking like a woman from hanging around
his mother too long (Minault 1986b: 109).

What is going on here? And what can we learn from it? Such
comments show that there is a whole area of idiomatic usage confined
to the segregated world of women from which men are excluded. Their
exclusion may make men feel uncomfortable, but if so, they express
their discomfort in disdainful terms. The idioms of begamati zuban
have to do with the world of the household and with relationships, and
are especially rich in interjections, in terms of endearment and abuse,
and in forebodings of disaster. Other idioms relate to bodily health
and a variety of customs and rituals that reformers also regarded
askance. These are the elements of zenana culture that were under the
control of women, and they developed their own ways of discussing
them. In these matters of the household, women had a special
competence, self-sufficiency, and even power.
        The language of the zenana, according to these and other lexical
and literary sources[6] is earthy, graphic, and colourful. The prevailing
linguistic style is highly colloquial. Even though there are patterns of
deference among women, the flowery phrases of Persianized Urdu do

not come into play. The vocabulary from the language lesson above, when further analysed, reveals a lot about the character of women's lives. An area of rich, varied vocabulary indicates a topic of particular importance—a subject that women feel strongly about and competent to discuss.

To cite a few examples: a woman who did not have to leave her home (*rasna basna*) was deemed very fortunate; but her fortunate state implied family support and domestic responsibilities. A woman without support or companionship was particulary unfortunate (*nigori*). Customs reinforced these ideas. Young girls and women without a full complement of sisters or female relatives would readily 'adopt' female friends as their sisters through customs such as marrying their dolls, exchanging dupattas (*dupatta badalna bahin*), or breaking a chicken wishbone together (*zinakhi ka rishta*). Such vows of fictive sisterhood also survived their marriages and displacements (Hasan 1976: 79–80).

Women's lives were isolated in some respects but not in others. They lived, literally, at the centre of the household, in the courtyard with its manifold activities. Older women managed the household and trained the younger ones in their duties. Women with servants supervised them, checking petty theft and wastage. The amount of domestic work, maintenance, and household production of dishes of food and items of clothing for social occasions was staggering. Their lives may have been claustrophobic, but they were rich in human contact. Comfort was never very far away, but, on the other hand, neither was condemnation. There were always other women around to talk to, defer to, order around, quarrel with, laugh or cry with, or curse.[7]

The nature of women's verbal exchanges gives a clue to their activities, their beliefs, and their values. Begamati zuban is sprinkled with terms of endearment and blessing. Women address each other as bua, *vari* (my dear/dearest), bhaina (younger sister), and *apa* (older sister); but also bhayya (brother), beta (son), and *sahib* (sir). Using male terms for women indicates particular endearment and also respect. For example, when a daughter has done her lessons particularly well, or produced a fine piece of needlework, her mother might call her beta to show special pleasure and admiration. Many blessings take the form not of blessing the woman herself, but of blessing those she holds most dear, such as *kaleja thanda rahe*, or *pet thanda rahe* which mean, literally, 'may your liver/belly keep cool', but figuratively, 'may your children have long lives/be happy/never disappoint you'. Another is *kokh aur mang se thandi rahe*, which means 'may you never become a widow/may your husband live a long time'. Young children may be blessed with *jite raho* or *jam jam jiyo*, 'may you live a long time', but they may also be told *teri ma ka pet thanda rahe*, 'may your mother never lose you/grieve for you' (Nasim 1968: 107–10).

Blessing a woman by wishing her husband and children long lives, or honouring a girl or a woman with a male title, are special characteristics of women's discourse. This is not self-deprecation per se, but rather indicates that one's life is important only in relation to others: the males upon whom the woman is dependent, and the children who are dependent upon her. Maulana Thanawi, however, condemned such expressions as insufficiently Islamic, because to view women as blessed in terms of their relationships to men and children devalues their relationship to God and goes against the tenet that all believers are equal in His sight. Maulana Thanawi thus emphasizes the egalitarian basis of Islam as opposed to custom. Much of the customary usage he so deprecates is a part of patterns of respect and deference deemed necessary for the maintainance of peaceful relations in large, interdependent families. Thanawi, however, would respond that status and honour derive from God (Metcalf 1990: 79–83).

The high value placed upon mutual dependence also comes out in anger. Women have no hesitation in telling other women to drop dead, but they hardly ever would wish their husbands or children dead. To do so might call down the wrath of God upon the speaker herself, whereas the following curses are uttered with seeming impunity: *bhar men jae, chulhe men jae* (into the fire/stove–go to hell); *dar gor, gor khaye, dunya se ure* (into the grave/drop dead); *janhar, marne joga* (worthy of death). Imprecations appear in rich variety in begamati zuban, indicating that women did a lot of quarrelling. In addition to wishing each other dead, they also accused one another of shamelessness and immodesty. Epithets such as bodli, *randi, kasbi, bazaari, ghungru ki sharik* (transvestite, whore, street-walker, dancing girl) were usually reserved for the practitioners of the oldest profession; but not necessarily. Similarly, *picchalpai* and *churel* (demoness, witch) were not always supernatural creatures. Impugning a woman's competence as a housekeeper was a milder form of abuse: *phuar*, *nikhattu, ate ki apa* (incompetent, good-for-nothing, brainless) (Nasim 1968: 100–5).

In women's language, coinage tends to be from regional vernaculars such as Khari Boli, Braj Bhasha, Avadhi, and Dakkani rather than Arabic or Persian. Examples of words from Sanskrit-based local languages in begamati zuban have already been mentioned: nigori, phuar, nikhattu. Others include *surh* (the space of time between children); *sanvarna* (to arrange, prepare, or put right); and *bhag* (fate–instead of *qismat*) (Nasim 1968: 58–9). The reformers took exception to such expressions, finding begamati zuban to be archaic, illiterate, and insufficiently Islamic. Hali and Thanawi, among others, were codifying a modern Urdu idiom as well as a reformed Indian Muslim identity. In so doing, they wanted to purge the vernacular expressions that persisted in women's language and replace them with higher status, classical loan words from Persian and Arabic, thereby reinforcing the identity of Urdu as a Muslim language, whether that was their intention or not.

The influence of local languages on women's speech indicates that one can also expect local influences in household customs and rituals, and a tenuous adherence to the Islamic scriptural tradition. This is most obvious in customs connected with marriage and childbirth, a rich composite of Hindu and Muslim observances which evolved in the zenanas over the centuries. Muslim reformers attacked such customs as being wasteful and un-Islamic, and their advocacy of reform, ironically, provides us with much of our information about these customary observances.[8] Maulana Thanawi here describes marriage customs:

[T]he women of the family gather and confine the girl in a corner .... Etiquette calls for the girl to be seated on a low platform, for ointment to be placed on her right hand, and for her lap to be filled with rice and *batasha* [a crisp sweet made of sugar syrup]. Rice and sweets are also distributed among those present .... This custom involves much foolishness .... Whether it is hot, whether it is stuffy, whether all the doctors and physicians of the world say she will get sick .... This entails the evil of strict adherence to set customs ... then there is the further sin of causing harm to a Muslim .... (Metcalf 1990: 116).

These are popular customs that partake of Indian traditions rather than Islamic ones, and are hence, in the Maulana's view, to be deplored. The cost of the sweets and ointments was a minor issue compared to the non-Islamic nature of the observances. Further:

The women of the families gather at the groom's house to prepare the *bari* [gifts of clothing and so forth] and at the bride's house to prepare the *jahez* [dowry]. In the midst of this, any guest who comes from the other family's house ... has his or her fare paid. This encourages the gathering of women and provides another instance of unnecessary compulsion. To pay for travel whether one wishes it or not ... is done simply for the sake of ostentation and glory.... Such ostentation and compulsion are obviously against the *shari'at* (Metcalf 1990: 118).

The Maulana, in his zeal for Islamic correctness, cannot empathize with women for whom a wedding was one of the few occasions for approved travel and visiting outside their own four walls.

The composite nature of women's culture also becomes clear from the complex of activities designed to cope with evil. Women spent a great deal of time and effort fending off disaster—from the elements, from illness, from uncooperative relatives and children, and from the general tendency of things to break down or wear out. This gave rise to a variety of expressions signifying 'God forbid!' or 'Heaven forfend!': *nauj, dur par, ab se dur, teri jan se dur,* and so on. In addition, women held a variety of beliefs which, as Hali commented, 'you won't find in the Quran or *hadith*'. These beliefs concerned spirits and the evil eye and practices designed to charm them away, cure illness, and generally keep things on an even keel. To the reformers who enumerated them, these superstitions were anathema. Hali nevertheless provides an account of many beliefs and practices that he deemed useless:

If two pieces of metal strike together, it is inauspicious, so when cutting with scissors ... don't strike the two sides together. Nor should you rest your hand on the vessel while drinking water; that too is unlucky .... Don't touch a door frame while you are standing up, but if by chance you should do so, kiss both your hands .... If a broom touches your body, you will become thin as a broomstick. If a ladle touches your body, you will become greedy for food .... Whenever you give children milk, curd, or rice [white things] to eat, give them a slight taste of ashes as well, or else the evil eye will affect them (Minault 1986b: 59–61).

It would be interesting to compare this to a list of popular Hindu beliefs and practices; many of them would doubtless be similar. Reformers were involved in a complex process of cultural critique that, first, judged women's cultural practices as inferior, involving 'superstition' or 'custom', and secondly, defined what was acceptable in terms of scriptural tradition. In so doing, they were delimiting the boundaries of acceptable behaviour in terms of what pious men did, and further defining what it meant to be *either* a Hindu *or* a Muslim.[9]

Many of these superstitions had to do with subjects central to women's lives: housework, food preparation and eating, marriages, children, visits, illnesses, and the good and bad omens associated with them.[10] If in spite of all precautions, illness did occur, then a number of healing rituals could be tried. Hali puts these words into the mouth of a woman instructing her daughter about what *not* to do:

A woman whose children have all died young can try various remedies. In some places, she is covered with ashes, in other places, she is made to bathe. In still others, she is forbidden to cook in a *karhai*, or to eat eggs, fish, *gur*, milk, or curds .... As for women who have never given birth to a child, in some places fairies are invoked for them, in other places, spirits are summoned. *Domnis* come and sing all night before those who are possessed by spirits, and they, in turn, shake their heads wildly and demand whatever they like, as if the spirits were gyrating and speaking within them .... No one ever asks which spirits bring children and points out that it is in God's power alone to grant children or not.[11]

Hali here implies that such rituals are worse than useless, for they waste money, cure nothing, and distract believers from trust in God. Nevertheless, Hali betrays a lack of understanding of the psychological stresses of purdah existence. Non-medical 'cures', belief in the evil eye, and exorcism were all part of an environment in which hostilites often ran high but had to be repressed, and where professional medical help was usually unavailable. *Hakims* or medical doctors were men, and thus could not see their female patients. Feeling a pulse or having symptoms described by a servant did not permit very accurate diagnoses.[12] Ill women, or women with ill children, relied on household remedies or on cures that led to the release of fears and nervous tensions. The summoning of domnis, professional women entertainers and exorcists, did not violate purdah and provided a good evening's entertainment besides. A woman who was 'possessed' could vent her hostilities and frustrations in a socially approved manner and feel better for it.[13] Quite aside from the scriptural or scientific arguments against such all-female ceremonies, these were arenas of ritual life over which men had no control. Such autonomy made reformers like Hali uncomfortable.

Another arena of women's lives in which they were virtually independent of men was their domestic chores. Women did a lot of the cooking, sewing, and mending, even when there were servants. Embroidery was a valuable skill, passed down from mother to daughter. In addition, household maintenance was constant: One had to recover quilts, and restuff them with cotton from time to time in order to keep warm in winter. Clothes had to be aired, cooking pots sent out to be retinned, stoves replastered, roofs checked for leaks, and so on. The literature indicates that women were busy from dawn to dark, and while much of their work was drudgery, it could also be fulfilling when they cooperated. Women helped one another, at least ideally, and the men, though supportive, were not much involved. Men and women were dependent upon one another, but women had their own realm in which they were supreme. It was a world in which practicality and competence counted. Women were dependent upon men economically, but also remarkably self-sufficient. From the women's point of view, their world was central to life, and the outer world of men peripheral.

This sense of competence, self-sufficiency, and importance should not be discounted in assessing zenana life. Women were adept at getting things done tactfully by cooperation among themselves. Here, again in Hali's account, a mother gives her daughter good advice on household consumption:

Now I am going to tell you how to get things from the bazaar day by day, so that [the servants] don't pilfer .... You should ask all those who come to the house from outside (the water carrier, the potter, the miller women, the bangle-seller) what the current market prices are ... [W]hen you detect a discrepancy between the reported price and what you have paid, scold severely the servant who did the shopping .... Vary the person whom you send to do the shopping. That will keep the servants on their toes (Minault 1986b: 71).

A competent housekeeper had to be part spy and part diplomat, able to manage servants and keep the peace among a host of family members. This was the ideal. That reality was not always so is evident from the variety of curse words noted earlier. Hali criticizes women's tendency to quarrel as follows:

[W]hen several [women] get together, they sit around and start complaining. Some complain about their mothers-in-law; others weep about their sisters-in-law. Some pour vitriol on their daughters-in-law; other retail their grievances against their husbands. Some find fault with x's marriage ... the amount of y's dowry, or cast aspersions on z's ancestry. If anyone disagrees with anything another says, they quarrel ... (Minault 1986b: 59).

One might dismiss this as just the standard male complaint that women never talk about anything of substance. Hali's point, however, is that these women, not having a proper education, lack self-control and decorum. If they were educated, they might still talk about children and relationships, and they might discuss matters like good health, child-rearing, or how to bring literacy to the servants. In addition—and this was crucial—women would lead pious lives, control their tempers, and not gratuitously abuse one another, their children, or their servants.

Muslim women may or may not have viewed their isolation as a problem. Indeed, even in its self-containment, zenana life was often very satisfying. For Muslim reformers such as Hali and Thanawi, however, women's realm was problematic, for a number of reasons. Muslim men's preoccupation with the status of women in their community around the turn of the twentieth century is easily explained. As Muslims came to terms with British rule and took up Western education, they found an increasing gap between their public and private lives. Their women, whether educated at home in rudimentary fashion or—more likely—totally uneducated, were the proverbial 'frogs in a well'. The reformers complained that the women were backward, superstitious, and unable to provide intelligent companionship to their husbands or discipline to their sons in an increasingly competitive political and economic environment. What was perhaps worse, the women were ignorant of the basic tenets of their faith, tied to customary rituals and observances that had little to do with scriptural Islam: exorcism, saint worship of the most idolatrous sort, and expensive lifecycle rituals that originated in the surrounding Hindu culture (see also Minault 1998a).

The projected benefits of women's education, in this composite reformist view, were that women would be better companions to their husbands, better mothers to their children, better homemakers, and better Muslims. Muslim social reform was comparable to Hindu social reform in that it was tied to male visions of the need to stem religious and cultural decline, to define culture according to a universally recognizable standard, and to preserve the family through raising the honour and dignity of its women. This was a distinctly patriarchal form of social reform, with women the beneficiaries of male concerns and action, very similar, again, to much Hindu social reform.[14]

In one respect, however, reform was more problematic for Muslims than for Hindus; this involved the custom of purdah. Hindu reformers, whose women also observed a form of purdah, were willing to see the custom scrapped as an artefact of Muslim rule, whether that was a fair characterization or not.[15] To Muslims, the custom had religious sanction and further served as a symbol of the distinctiveness of their culture. There was little or nothing in the writings and plans of Muslim reformers that included tearing down the curtains of purdah. They eloquently criticized the effects of purdah: women's isolation, ignorance, and detachment from externally-imposed standards of behaviour, but not the custom itself. Muslim reformers maintained that women could be educated, competent, free from superstition and backwardness, and still maintain purdah and all the respectability and status-that veiling implied. They wanted to unveil women's minds, in other words, without unveiling their faces.

Within the group of Muslim social and educational reformers, there were men of the western-educated, urban, service, and professional classes, and others who were more traditionally-educated, or ulama. Hali and Maulana Thanawi are only two representative examples. Their views about women's education and legal rights obviously differed. The western-educated tended to emphasize marital companionship and enlightened nurturing as ideal roles for the educated woman. The ulama tended to emphasize scriptural piety. Both contributed elements to the reformist vision of the way Muslim women ought to be. In their reactions to zenana life and its language, however, these differing emphases indicate very different ideological stances.

To the western-educated reformer, the liberal philosophical adage would seem to be axiomatic: That which is separate is inherently unequal, and hence the culture of those that are segregated is necessarily inferior. Indeed, the discourse of inferiority applied by reformist men to their women was parallel to that visited upon the men by the colonial authorities. British rule was frequently justified in terms of the cultural inferiority of Indians, portrayed as passive and effeminate—and thus segregated from positions of power—in contrast to the masculine Anglo-Saxons. To break down their own ideological marginalization, reformers consequently had to break down their women's isolation. To do so involved imposing an externally-determined standard of behaviour, which also involved bringing women more under men's control. The self-sufficiency of the zenana was thus not only a practical difficulty for these men, but a philosophical one as well, and involved their own power relations with their colonial masters.[16]

For the ulama, however, women might inhabit a separate space, but according to the tenets of Islam, they were equal to men—as believers in God. Their inferior status, consequently, was due not to their isolation, but to degenerate custom, falsely identified as religion. The ulama too wanted to impose a patriarchal standard of behaviour upon women, one determined by scripture. But in that scripture—at a certain ideal level at least—women and men were equal. The liberal discourse of separate but inferior and the Islamic discourse of separate but equal were in clear conflict. Ironically, the ideological stance of the ulama had a logical consistency, as well as a source from within their culture, that the liberals' position lacked.

While these debates raged, women could not help being affected by the social and political changes that were taking place. Women in purdah were so used to the security and social prestige that it conferred that their isolation was less a problem for them than it was for the men who were exposed to outside pressures. Women did have to cope with the practical problems posed by purdah: how to shop for vegetables, how to keep the servants from cheating, and so on. But again, these strategies were so much a part of the fabric of their existence, and the status that veiling implied was so valuable, that even these inconveniences did not seem very significant to women.

In seeking education, however, girls had to overcome barriers to going out to school, something that their brothers did as a matter of course. If their families were sufficiently affluent, they might be taught at home by an *ustani* (woman teacher), or by a grey-bearded *maulvi* who would come to the house to teach all the young children to read the Quran. Reading scripture was an honourable accomplishment, but to learn to read Urdu or—harder still—to write it, girls often had to resort to stratagems, such as getting a brother or male cousin to tutor them out of earshot of their elders, or surreptitiously practicing their writing using coal blacking from the stove (Naim 1987: 107–9).

The writing taboo was customary because if a girl learned how to write, there was no telling to whom she might write letters, and this might jeopardize the honour of the family. Reformers in favour of women's education blamed false custom and misplaced notions of prestige for this taboo, but the fact remained that until girls started going out to school, it was virtually impossible for them to get an education in any way equivalent to that of their brothers.

So in practical matters, especially in the matter of education, isolation was a problem for women. Segregation was a barrier to equal education, and separate but equal schooling could take them only so far. The equality of all believers, which supplied the logical consistency in the ulama's reformist stance, was not in evidence when it came to actually achieving a higher education for bright young women, who were in other respects the equals of their brothers.

The women of reformist families followed the lead of their men in championing education for girls without demanding an end to purdah. The prestige of their status and the distinctiveness of Muslim culture were at stake, and in a society where Muslims felt threatened by their minority status, the pressure upon Muslim women not to break ranks with their community was overwhelming. Still, in agreeing with their men, Muslim women were obliged to follow their reasoning, and if women's separate existence was, in fact, inferior, then one possible response to a discourse of inferiority was a discourse of oppression. In order to claim the equality that should be theirs ideally, educated Muslim women could also blame custom for the excesses of the purdah system, and demand a mitigation of its practical effects as a way to the realization of their rights in Islam.

This happened in 1918 in a meeting of Muslim women in Lahore, as reported in the Urdu women's magazine *Tahzib un-Niswan*. The women passed a resolution condemning 'the kind of polygamy practiced by certain sections of the Muslims'—note the qualifying phrase identifying the problem as customary practice—and went on to say that such polygamy was 'against the true spirit of the Quran and of Islam'. They further called upon educated women to 'exercise their influence among their relations to put an end to this practice' (*Tahzib un-Niswan* 1918: 245–9).[17] Some reformist men were scandalized by the fact that women had actually spoken out for their rights, and examples of such outspokenness on the part of Muslim women were rare in the early twentieth century. Still, such a resolution was only echoing what a number of liberal Muslim men had been saying for some time. Aspects of the cultural critique by men, in particular their condemnation of false custom and evocation of the egalitarian nature of Islam, were beginning to make an impression. The men's motivation had been the imposition of a patriarchal standard upon, and some measure of control over, women's customary, 'corrupt', yet autonomous realm—not the liberation of women. And yet, in accepting this discourse of inferiority and an externally-imposed standard of behaviour as the norm, women could in turn blame the oppressiveness of custom and reclaim the egalitarian promise of idealized, scriptural Islam. Liberation from oppression for Muslim women is thus by no means a linear progression from reform, to education, to a realization of rights in the classic liberal pattern, but involves an ongoing dialogue with both male hegemony and the underlying religious authority.

NOTES

1. These generalizations are based on reading the biographies and autobiographies or reminiscences of women from the period, most notably Ahmadi Begam's manuscript biography of her sister, Muhammadi Begam; and Naim 1987.
2. For a fuller discussion of sources, see Minault 1986a and 1998b.
3. Just as the authors in the series *Subaltern Studies* must use government sources and other elite writings for their investigations of non-elites.
4. On Aligarh, see Lelyveld 1978; on Deoband, Metcalf 1982b.
5. Barbara Metcalf has translated parts of it in Metcalf 1990.
6. For a list of sources for the study of begamati zuban, see Minault 1984: 169, n. 4.
7. These generalizations are derived from the texts discussed herein, as well as from Urdu novels such as those of Nazir Ahmad, *Mirat ul-'Arus* and *Taubat un-Nasuh*.
8. Sayyid Ahmad Dehlawi, *Rasum-i-Dehli*; Hali, *Majalis un-Nissa*; and Nazir Ahmad, *Mirat ul-'Arus* are all examples of this kind of literature; see also Metcalf 1982a.
9. Christopher King's work on the Hindi-Urdu controversy makes a similar point, emphasizing their linguistic separation into Sanskritized Hindi and Persianized Urdu, as well as the differentiation of both from the 'surrounding ocean of popular culture'. King 1989: 188.
10. See Shareef 1973: 266–76 for a discussion of auspicious dates and directions.

11. Minault 1986b: 65. A karhai is a cooking vessel, like a wok. Gur is coarse brown sugar. A domni is a professional entertainer (masc. *dom*).
12. Compare the incident of the perforated sheet in Salman Rushdie's *Midnight's Children*.
13. For a psychological inquiry into indigenous healing practices concerning spirit possession, see Kakar 1982: 15–88.
14. It should be noted that Hindu reformers too objected to many such rituals and customs as 'superstitious' and 'decadent'. See Jones 1988.
15. For a discussion of the way that Hindu purdah differs structurally and functionally from that of Muslims, see Vatuk 1982.
16. For a discussion of this point in a different Indian milieu, see O'Hanlon 1991, especially pp. 72–9.
17. For further details see Minault 1998c, pp. 145–6, 283–98.

REFERENCES

Hasan, Muhiyuddin. 1976. *Dilli ki Begamati Zuban*. Delhi: Nayi Awaz.

Jones, Kenneth W. 1988. 'Socio-religious Movements and Changing Gender Relationships Among Hindus of British India'. In James W. Bjorkman (ed.). *Fundamentalism, Revivalists and Violence in South Asia*. New Delhi: Manohar, pp. 40–56.

Kakar, Sudhir. 1982. *Shamans, Mystics, and Doctors*. New Delhi: Oxford University Press.

King, Christopher. 1989. 'Forging a New Linguistic Identity: The Hindi Movement in Banaras, 1868–1914'. In S.B. Freitag (ed.). *Culture and Power in Banaras*. Berkeley: University of California Press, pp. 179–202.

Lelyveld, David. 1978. *Aligarh's First Generation*. Princeton: Princeton University Press.

Metcalf, Barbara. 1982a. 'Islam and Custom in Nineteenth-Century India'. *Contributions to Asian Studies*. vol. 17, pp. 62–78.

———. 1982b. *Islamic Revival in British India: Deoband, 1860–1900*. Princeton: Princeton University Press.

———. 1990. *Perfecting Women: Maulana Ashraf Ali Thanawi's Bihishti Zewar*. Berkeley: University of California Press.

Minault, Gail. 1984. 'Begamati Zuban: Women's Language and Culture in 19th-Century Delhi 2005'. *India International Centre Quarterly*. vol. 11, no. 2, pp. 155–70.

———. 1986a. 'Making Invisible Women Visible: Studying the History of Muslim Women in South Asia'. *South Asia* (Australia). vol. 9, no. 1, pp. 1–13.

———. 1986b. *Voices of Silence: English translation of Hali's Majalis un-Nissa and Chup ki Dad*. Delhi: Chanakya Publications.

_____. 1998a. 'Women, Legal Reform, and Muslim Identity'. *Comparative Studies in South Asia, Africa and the Middle East*. vol. 17, no. 2, pp. 1–10.

_____. 1998b. 'Women's Magazines in Urdu as Sources for Muslim Social History'. *Indian Journal of Gender Studies*. vol. 5, no. 2, pp. 201–14.

_____. 1998c. *Secluded Scholars: Women's Education and Muslim Social Reform in Colonial India*. New Delhi: Oxford University Press.

Naim, C.M. 1987. 'How Bibi Ashraf Learned to Read and Write'. *Annual of Urdu Studies*. vol. 6, pp. 99–115.

Nasim, Wahida. 1968. *Urdu Zuban aur 'Aurat*. Karachi: Intikhab-i-Nau.

O'Hanlon, Rosalind. 1991. 'Issues of Widowhood: Gender and Resistance in Colonial Western India'. In Douglas Haynes and Gyan Prakash (eds). *Contesting Power: Resistance and Everyday Social Relations in South Asia*. Berkeley: University of California Press, pp. 62–104.

Shareef, Jaffur. 1973. *Qanoon-e-Islam or the Customs of the Musulmans of India*. G.A. Herklots (trans.). Reprint, Lahore: Al-Irshad.

Tahzib un-Niswan (Lahore) 1918. vol. 21, 20 April.

Vatuk, Sylvia. 1982. 'Purdah Revisited: A Comparison of Hindu and Muslim Interpretations of the Cultural Meaning of Purdah in South Asia'. In Hanna Papanek and Gail Minault (eds). *Separate Worlds: Studies of Purdah in South Asia*. Delhi: Chanakya Publications, pp. 54–78.

9
DALIT TRANSFORMATION, NARRATIVE, AND VERBAL ART IN THE TAMIL NOVELS OF BAMA

Paula Richman

Twenty years ago, when I asked Eleanor Zelliot for readings on Ambedkar's revival of Buddhism in western India for a course on 'Religions of the Oppressed', it was the first time I had written, out of the blue, to an established scholar for assistance with course materials. In my subsequent two decades of teaching, no one else has ever responded as generously. She mailed me a huge packet of articles, some from Indian journals then unavailable in the United States and others from edited volumes difficult to locate through interlibrary loan. She never cashed the cheque I sent to reimburse her for the costs of photocopying and mailing. Months later, when I asked if she had received the cheque, Eleanor replied that if material on Dalit culture found its way into college syllabi, that would be more than adequate compensation. In honour of Eleanor, this essay analyses two translated novels by Bama (b. 1958), a Dalit woman who writes in Tamil. I focus on three themes crucial to Zelliot's research and Bama's novels: transformations in Dalit lives, narrative representations of Dalit history, and forms of Dalit creativity.

   Zelliot has documented the momentous transformations that took place when many Mahars moved from rural to urban areas, acquired new occupations (in factories, domestic service, and the railroads), gained access to education, and converted to Buddhism.

The scope of the change in Dalit culture over the twentieth century is nearly impossible to grasp if one only reads colonial compendia or ethnographies, which tend to freeze Dalits in the official or anthropological 'present' as if hierarchically-ranked interactions between *jatis* have remained essentially static over the century. Yet census data show that, as early as 1921, 87 per cent of Mahars did not work at jobs that high-caste Hindus traditionally viewed as polluting.[1] In a telling example, Zelliot notes that a Mahar educator named a hostel after Mahar poet Chokamela (d. 1338) in 1914, but just fifteen years later Ambedkar and his followers rejected Chokamela as an ideal because the saint seems to have accepted the notion that he was 'low' and 'polluting' (1981). Furthermore, Zelliot studies Mahars not as a monolithic group but as a complex mix of people whose experiences vary with literacy, gender, and degree of urbanization (1977b; 1978; 1992).

Skilful analysis of Dalit narratives, many of them transmitted orally, has enabled Zelliot to supplement more conventional historical sources, thereby revealing a rich and nuanced view of transformations in Dalit life. Her research on Mahars analyses three categories of stories: origin tales, hero tales, and personal histories (1977a: 536–8, 559). Set in the ancient past, origin stories of those whom high castes view as 'untouchable' present a jati's ancestor as performing, with the most admirable of intentions, an act that nonetheless unjustly condemns his descendents to a defiling occupation. By asserting the essential goodness of Dalits, such stories subvert the Brahmanical view that they are contemptible. Hero stories promote Dalit pride by celebrating their acts of bravery. For example, the narrative of Amrutnak, a Mahar soldier-courtier who saved his Queen, as well as her reputation, bears witness to his courage and sense of honour. Zelliot also interviewed Mahar activists, documenting thereby the agency that has been ubiquitous within local Dalit communities but often unknown outside them.[2] All three kinds of narrative reveal facets of Dalit culture often absent from histories that focus on elites.

Finally, Zelliot has highlighted varied forms of recent Dalit creativity. As early as 1970, she supervised a research project to collect Mahar songs lauding Ambedkar (1977a: 560 n20). She also commented upon distinctive forms of public sculpture emerging from the Ambedkar movement (1977a: 560 n23). Zelliot was among the first writing in English to call scholars' attention to the growing Dalit literary movement; she also collaborates with writers to translate their work into English for a pan-Indian and overseas readership (1978; 1982; 1987) and encourages her students to translate as well (for instance, Hovell 1991). Zelliot's articles were instrumental in spotlighting literary works of Dalit women (for instance, 1992: 104–5). Her focus on Dalit arts counters Brahmanical views that define Dalits almost entirely in terms of polluting duties assigned to them. Indeed, their historical roles as musicians, town criers, and storytellers provided a foundation for current Dalit involvement in musical, visual, and literary arts.

Zelliot has played a major role in changing our understanding of Dalit history from a list of atrocities to an account of how various Dalit groups transformed and have been transformed by social, economic, and political barriers. Her publications analyse Dalit cultural formations from an admirable variety of perspectives drawing on an impressive variety of sources, examining both internal and external effects of pan-Indian adoption of the term 'Dalit' to replace 'Untouchable', 'Harijan', and 'Scheduled Caste'. She has written about both how the Dalit movement helped individuals develop self-respect and how it formed coalitions to combat institutionalized oppression.

The attention given by Tamil writer Bama to transformations, narratives, and creative arts in Dalit culture led me to focus upon her work for this volume of essays. To be sure, Zelliot grew up outside the Dalit community of India and uses the methodology of historical research, while Bama grew up as a Dalit in south India and explores Dalit life as a creative writer. Zelliot's experience in India was rooted in Maharashtra, while Bama's was rooted in Tamil Nadu. Many Dalits whom Zelliot studies converted to Buddhism in the mid-1950s or later, while most Dalits in Bama's village converted to Catholicism at least a generation earlier. Yet, the writings of each enrich our knowledge about Dalit life and letters by highlighting transformation, narrative, and art.

SHARP-EDGED TRANSFORMATION

Bama led a life filled with transformations. Born in 1958 into the Paraya jati in a small Tamil village near the Western Ghats, Bama proved an outstanding student, winning a place in a prestigious Catholic boarding school. Later, she earned a master's degree in education and took monastic vows in a teaching convent, planning to make education of Catholic Paraya girls her highest priority. After more than eight years as a nun, however, Bama left the Order when her dream of bringing about caste equality through work as a Catholic educator was dashed. A selective account of her childhood and early adulthood appears in her first book, *Karukku* (1992).

Karukku's preface emphasizes the pivotal role of suffering in Bama's life. She uses *karukku* (serrated leaves, blades) to articulate the notion that pain need not be an ending point; it can spur realization and new growth, as it did for her. Bama's comments emphasize that pain can generate change:

There are many congruities between the saw-edged palmyra *karukku* and my own life. Not only did I pick up the scattered palmyra *karukku* in the days when I was sent out to gather firewood, scratching and tearing my skin as I played with them; but later they also became the embryo [*karu*] and symbol that grew into this book (1992: xiii).

Bama links the karukku's sharpness to the New Testament passage calling the 'word of God' a two-edged sword (Hebrews 4:10), viewing her experience of caste bigotry as proof that God's word had failed to soften the hard hearts of many so-called Christians. She urges Dalits to 'function as God's word, piercing to the very heart' (1992: xiii), cutting through the hypocrisy of Catholic institutions that ignore the teachings of radical equality which Bama has encountered in the Bible.

Hence, Bama's autobiography combines memories of suffering and joy, humiliation and triumph. Just as Christianity brought Bama both God's word and heartless institutions, her natal village provided her with a landscape of endearing beauty and terrifying violence. She expresses admiration for the ingenuity and perseverance of Paraya women while revealing the contemptible way they are treated by landowners, police officers, and Paraya men, as well as priests and nuns.

A deftly crafted depiction of a child learning what 'untouchable' means exemplifies how *Karukku* highlights moments of transformation. Recalling an event that transpired when she was about eight years old, *Karukku*'s narrator describes sights, sounds, and smells as she slowly wends her way home from school: little stalls selling snacks, performing monkeys, devotees ringing the temple bell, political party members working the crowd, snake charmers, puppet shows, waiters pouring coffee in long streams from one cup to another to cool it, the fragrance of jackfruit in season. Lulled by the meandering sensuous description, the reader is startled when the text turns abruptly to the sight of a Naicka landlord vigilantly overseeing Parayas threshing grain. A respected Paraya elder approaches the landlord, carrying a fried snack from the market wrapped in paper and fastened with a string. Holding it only by its string, he bows obsequiously, contorting his hands so as not to touch the packet, and hands it to the landlord. Bama laughs, amused that such a big man would hold the small packet in such a peculiar way.

Later, when she describes the scene humorously to her brother, he explains that since people believe that Naickas are high caste, Parayas are forbidden to touch them: the Paraya elder held the packet by the string to prevent his hands from polluting the landlord's food. Bama's amusement drains away:

Why should we have to fetch and carry for these people, I wondered. Such an important elder of ours goes off meekly to the shops to fetch snacks and hands them over reverently, bowing and shrinking, to this fellow who just sits there and stuffs them into his mouth (1992: 14).

Earlier, her village had provided a parade of sights in which she immersed herself, but now she realized what she had missed: some people were pure, some impure, and the impure had to abase themselves before the pure. Her once-enchanted world became fraught with hierarchy.

The most searing transformation in *Karukku*, however, revolves around a full-scale police attack on the Parayas of the village, resulting from a long-escalating conflict over the site where Parayas bury their dead. Late one night, there, near the village bus stop, a gang of Chaliyas ambush and kill a lone Paraya man renowned for his courage. In revenge, Parayas storm the Chaliya quarter. When Paraya women throw stones from behind trees and men wield knives, the Chaliyas lock themselves in the school house, confirming their long-standing reputation for cowardice. As animosity escalates, the Chaliyas frame the Parayas, file a criminal complaint, and entice an entire detachment of armed police to a feast of mutton at which they vow to slay all Paraya men in the village. When the Parayas learn of the complaint, they return to the Chaliya quarter but find it utterly deserted. Suddenly, steel-helmeted police emerge from hiding wielding riot gear, beat Paraya men savagely, throw them into huge trucks, and imprison them. Immediately afterwards, the police sweep through the Paraya quarter, enter each house, beating and dragging away every male they find. Wives and daughters weep helplessly.

To escape arrest, the elderly village headman had taken refuge in the storage jar in the back room of Bama's house, but the police soon find him:

Then they kicked the doors open, breaking them apart, burst in, caught hold of the man ... lifted him out by his hair and rained blows upon him. Tears filled my eyes. This was the first time that I had ever seen the police beating up a person they had seized. If one policeman slapped the headman's face, all the rest followed, slapping him in the very same spot (1992: 34).

Before departing, policemen poke their guns into the bodies of Paraya women and tell them that, since their husbands were in prison, the women should be ready to 'entertain' the police that night. The terrified mothers pack up their children, cows, and calves, and go to sleep together in the Catholic churchyard.

Instead of just recounting atrocities, Bama pinpoints several interdependent factors that led to the brutal repression: competition inherent in caste hierarchy encourages middle jatis to maintain downward pressure on those beneath them; police derive their power from the state and their access to the instruments of punishment; patriarchal assumptions about manhood define masculinity in terms of violence; the Catholic hierarchy at the local level is often indifferent to the well-being of Paraya parishioners. Bama describes Paraya men mocking Chaliyas for lack of martial prowess (thus challenging their claims of relatively high status), and Chaliyas feeling tainted by Paraya bodies buried near their neighbourhood. Bama also explains why the police, bribed with the rare treat of freshly cooked meat, take pleasure in teaching Parayas 'to stay in their place'. She shows, as well, how the local priest neither provides refuge to those seeking asylum nor contributes a single rupee for the legal defense of imprisoned Parayas. Bama lays bare the social structures that enable, indeed encourage, such attacks.

Yet the story ends in an unexpected way by drawing attention to how resourceful Paraya women are. She recounts how they arrange legal aid, perform housework, and work in the fields as well, and some secretly supply food to men in hiding while others share resources to feed their children. The police truck them away, hoping to undermine the women's self-reliance, but they simply walk home and begin work anew. A group of women even aids a man in hiding to gaze one last time at the body of his young son, who has just died. Dressing the father in a sari, they smuggle him into their lamentation troupe to weep at the funeral. These acts demonstrate their courage and perseverance.

Karukku's preface describes a third kind of transformation, one that turned Bama into a writer. Bama's convent superiors had demanded submission to church hierarchy; viewing her repeated requests to teach Paraya children, rather than wealthy children, as willful acts of disobedience, they filled her with guilt about her ideals. After leaving the convent, she felt despair at renouncing her monastic vocation. It was only when she met a Jesuit influenced by liberation theology, who urged her to write the story of her life, that she began to record her experiences.[3]

As she wrote, she found herself using in the language of her childhood, the Tamil dialect that Parayas spoke in her natal village. She assumed she would return later and 'correct' it into standardized expository Tamil, the form of Tamil taught in school. Yet the words that first flowed conveyed her experience in ways that standard Tamil never could—it was insufficiently charged to convey the intensity and specificity of what she had experienced. She never 'corrected' the prose; instead, she found her voice as a writer, enabling her to tell not just her story but those of other Paraya women as well.

CLUSTERS OF WOMEN'S NARRATIVE

In her second book, Sangati, Bama moves from recounting a single life to providing an autobiography of a community of Paraya women (1994). The volume's twelve chapters recount stories of female kin, neighbours, and school friends—all but one of them Parayas. At each chapter's end, Bama articulates how constructions of caste and gender influenced the incidents recounted in the chapter. Within a short, accessible, and tightly structured text, Sangati deals with a remarkable variety of Paraya women's experiences. For example, both the pleasures of movement outside of the house (denied to upper-caste women) and the horror of sexual exploitation by upper-caste men find a place in the book. By showing common patterns in a seemingly random variety of women's stories, Bama demythologizes the forces that imprison them and suggests ways to combat those constraints. Each chapter of *Sangati* assembles multiple narratives and interpretation around a single theme, highlighting diversity within Paraya practice.

In Chapter 8, Bama shows the logic and practicality of Paraya wedding customs. Bama's mother, for example, married during a severe famine, so her family dug up anthills, found grass seed that the ants had collected, and cooked the seed into a meal for guests. For similar reasons, five Paraya couples were married simultaneously in the Catholic Church. Yet some Parayas aspiring to higher status have begun instead to demand a dowry from the bride's parents, deviating from the Paraya custom in which the groom's family gives money to the bride's family, and the wedding feast is modest. Bama suggests that this change is not in the best interests of Paraya women:

[W]hatever we do, whatever rituals we copy from other castes, they, for their part, always rate us as beneath them. So what is the point of trying to copy them? Why should we lose all the better customs that are ours, and end up as neither one thing nor the other? (1994: 89).

Bama's experience beyond the village has shown her that dowry demands and grand feasts often drive a bride's family into debt, leading parents to dread the birth of a female child, so she urges Parayas not to imitate high-caste behaviour blindly.

Bama's emphasis on submitting all actions to careful scrutiny also leads her to reject belief in *peys* (ghosts). Many people in Tamil Nadu believe that the spirit of a person who died an unnatural death (by suicide, accident, or murder) haunts isolated sites and preys on young women.[4] Bama recounts in chapter 5 how a girl eloped with a man of the washerman jati and settled in another town, defying her brothers' demand that she marry 'a well-off boy from a good [Paraya] family'. Upon learning that she was pregnant, her brothers pretended to forgive her and, as customary, came to escort her to her natal home for the birth. En route, they murdered her and the child in her womb for ruining the family's honour. She is believed to have turned into a pey who possesses girls until they offer her a cradle and dolls in honour of the child she never brought to term.

Bama systematically interrogates how belief in peys affects Paraya women. She knows that peys will not catch hold of men because men do not fear them, and has been taught that peys attack women when they are alone in isolated places. Upper-caste women hardly ever go out alone to labour in fields or jungles, whereas Paraya women have no choice but to fetch firewood and work in fields in faraway spots. Since Paraya women work at home or in the fields from the moment they wake until the moment they sleep, facing harassment from upper-caste landlords and beatings from their husbands, Bama concludes,

The stronger ones somehow manage to survive all this. The ones who don't have the mental strength ... succumb to mental ill-health and act as if they are possessed by peys (1994: 59).

Reasoning that stories of peys help keep women cowed, she calls upon Paraya women to forget their fears of imaginary peys and join her in living 'resolute lives' that show ardent belief 'in our independence' (ibid.).

Sangati's stories about the strength of Paraya women show that they have the resources to achieve such independence. Bama compares them favourably with upper-caste women imprisoned in the house, who forfeit both exercise and knowledge of the outside world. In contrast, Paraya women's agricultural labour builds physical strength and self-reliance, enabling them to cope far more effectively than high-caste women when widowed or deserted. Bama's eleven-year-old neighbour often cares for six siblings at home while her mother works in the field; the girl also works in a match factory when her mother cannot work. Although Bama laments that the girl misses out on a real childhood, she admires how she supports her family under difficult circumstances.

Bama even examines married life in another jati. The father of Bama's Chakkiliya schoolmate had married her to an alcoholic who beat her regularly and kept a mistress. When the Chakkiliya jati's assembly agrees to end the marriage, the girl's father arranges for her to marry another man, with whom she flourishes. Bama's Catholic mother is shocked because she views wedding vows as eternal promises made before God. Bama disagrees:

It's by calling on all this stuff about God, the promises made to him, our sins and our good deeds, and Heaven and everlasting Hell, that the priests and nuns frighten the life out of us.

Bama concludes, 'God created us so that we can be happy and free. I am sure that God doesn't want us to be living like slaves to the day we die' (1994: 79), refusing to accept beliefs that seem unreasonable. Because Bama provides exegesis of each story by appending a carefully reasoned piece of moral advice, her writing could be said to embody an aesthetic of pedagogy.[5] Thus each chapter has a narrative structure like that of the didactic tales that recur in Indian narrative tradition, from ancient tales of the Buddha's previous births to stories recounted by Hindu holy men today and discourses on New Testament parables presented by Christian preachers in India. Bama has turned the structure of storytelling with a moral into a written form that captures readers' attention and spurs them to think self-critically about their own actions.

RHETORICAL STRATEGIES AND VERBAL ART

While Bama tells stories for pedagogical ends, she does so in ways that put Dalit women and their experience at the centre. In *Sangati*, she makes particularly effective use of several rhetorical strategies. First, she incorporates proverbs into her prose as authoritative 'folk' wisdom in support of her advice. Second, she depicts each story being told to an audience of Paraya women. Finally, she focuses on stories of public shaming as models for fighting caste and gender hierarchy. Her deft use of these strategies enables her to unite literary design, personal experience, and pedagogy.

Unlike classical Sanskrit story collections that use Brahmanical texts as authority, the stories Bama collects in *Sangati* refer to proverbial wisdom. For example, she says:

It's like the proverb that says if a man sees a terrified dog, he is bound to chase it. If we continue to be frightened, everyone will take advantage of us. If we stand up for ourselves without caring whether we die or survive, they'll creep away with their tail between their legs (1994: 66).

The proverb sets the agenda, but Bama's commentary spells out exactly how it applies to men's violence against women. After exhorting women to fight back against abuse, Bama takes the proverb's central image one step further. The scared dog, initially a terrified woman, becomes a would-be male tormenter who encounters a woman who refuses to be intimidated. Bama reverses the proverb's referent, just as she advises women to reverse the central image by refusing to act like a frightened dog.

The proverbs Bama quotes contain practical wisdom that has been transmitted from generation to generation. In her exegesis of a proverb about an onion ('so long as it is hidden in the earth, it claims to be big but when you start peeling it, it's nothing but skin'), Bama explains patriarchy, an abstract sociological term, by likening it to the onion, an item that Paraya women use on a regular basis in their cooking:

Those fellows are just like that—like onions. They'll shout themselves hoarse, making great claims. They'll forbid us to speak a word. They'll seethe like cobras and say that they alone own everything. But why should we hide our own skills and capabilities? We work just as hard as they do. Why, you could even say that we actually work harder .... They'd collapse after a single day of it (1994: 66).

Here, Bama uses the proverb to upend traditional male claims to superiority.

Bama makes use of another rhetorical strategy, using a 'dramatized audience', in a way that foregrounds the experiences of specific Dalit women: a 'dramatized audience' portrays the circumstances under which the story was first told, thereby contextualizing the story and also reporting on the responses of listeners to the story (Richman 1988: 46–52). While most well-known Indian moral tales present stock figures (compassionate king, resourceful merchant's wife, clever fox), Bama's stories feature the women in her neighbourhood where she grew up. Furthermore, her stories deal not with palace intrigue, rich women, or talking animals, but with the quotidian experiences of Dalit women. One of the most effective examples of a dramatized audience appears in the story of Raakamma, who is married to an abusive, violent alcoholic and performs an outrageous act that turns the tables on her tormenter.

Raakamma's story is narrated by a girl who witnessed the incident and also reports how the surrounding crowd responded to it. A raucous quarrel breaks out between Raakamma and her husband one day in the middle of the street, when he calls her a whore and threatens to crush her to pieces. Raakamma retorts:

Disgusting man, only fit to drink a woman's farts! Instead of drinking toddy everyday ... why don't you drink my monthly blood?

and then lifts up her sari in front of the crowd. Her husband walks off, for what can he say in response to such a transgression? When the crowd, scandalized, maligns Raakamma as a shameless shrew, she furiously warns them to shut up and mind their own business: 'If I hadn't shamed him like this, he would surely have split my skull in two, the horrible man,' she shouts (1994: 62). While upper castes use accusations of pollution to stigmatize Dalits, Raakamma converts her body and discourse on pollution into weapons that help protect herself from domestic violence. Her husband believes that his higher rank as a man allows him to humiliate her, so she throws the logic of rank and pollution back in his face. The scale of her transgressive act, performed in the main Paraya street, insures that he is too ashamed and stunned to take revenge.

The dramatized audience also serves to highlight the significance of secret acts of resistance. In Bama's village, since Dalits live in crowded huts with no running water, the women look forward to Saturday night, when they go and bathe in a large step well to purify themselves for attending Sunday mass. One night while bathing, the women hear about Sammuga Kizhavi's act of public shaming. A Brahman landowner erects a barbed-wire fence to keep low-caste people from swimming in, and thereby 'polluting', his well. When he catches Sammuga Kizhavi swimming there, the landlord gets the head of the Paraya council to condemn her action. Soon afterwards, while she is working in the field, she sees the Brahman beating a Paraya child cruelly for touching, by mistake, the landlord's pot of drinking water. In revenge for both acts, Sammuga Kizhavi secretly urinates in his water pot and then broadcasts the deed throughout the village after the Brahman, unknowingly, drinks the polluted water. He will never live down the ignominy.

The dramatized audience of women who hear the story relish their freedom to swim naked each week. They mock upper-caste women, who would not learn to swim, and would never want to be naked: they always remain clothed, 'as if their bodies are somehow different from ours'. One woman jokes about their polluted homes since they perform bodily functions inside their houses: 'In those ladies' houses they've built different ... rooms to bathe, to shit or piss .... So why should they come here?' (1994: 116). Another declares that she would never forfeit her freedom for the opportunity to live in a grand house, and thereby she affirms solidarity among Dalit women.

In these two stories of public shaming, Dalit women use their ingenuity and the limited material circumstances of their situation (menstrual blood, urine) to subvert hierarchies of gender and caste. Raakamma and Sammuga Kizhavi seize the upper hand by turning the logic of subjugation back on their tormenters, refusing to be defeated by the constant abuse to which they are subjected. While the effects of their actions are limited and often provide only temporary respite, their stories spread through the Dalit community as a source of inspiration. Bama's pedagogical design of these stories of shaming presents the news (sangati) of resilience that justifies the book's title.[6]

CONCLUSIONS

Apprehending the extraordinary transformations in Indian life during the last hundred years entails moving Dalit life from the edges to the centre of South Asian history. Rather than viewing changes in Dalit life as 'only' the history of a 'minority' group, Bama suggests that attention to previously marginalized groups reveals much about them but also about the overall picture as well. While focusing upon Paraya women's experience, Bama's books simultaneously reveal a great deal about their relationships with Paraya men, Naicka landlords, rich factory managers, Catholic church authorities, and panchayat elders. Those at the bottom of the social hierarchy often learn a great deal about the cultural traditions of the employers for whom they work as labourers and servants. They need that knowledge in order to survive.

Narratives enable us to plumb the distinct sense of community that characterizes Dalit life and letters. Bama's two books work effectively to recount, amplify, preserve, and transmit Dalit narratives of her natal village to readers outside the village. Some chapters contain 'heroine' stories that disprove Brahmanical evaluations of Dalits as tainted and uncouth. As Bama notes after commenting on the modesty of Paraya weddings, 'So the joke is that other communities assume that all their traditions are good ones and that all our traditions are ugly and uncivilized .... I have to laugh at this' (1994: 75). Just as Amrutnak acted bravely when he valiantly rescued the queen, the heroic Paraya women whom Bama spotlights show extraordinary courage, resourcefulness, and a canny understanding of power relations.

Finally, more attention to Dalit verbal art will also reshape the landscape of Indian literature. By printing and marketing Dalit narratives, publishers do more than simply expand the range and diversity of Indian literature in print. They also showcase the often fresh and artful rhetorical strategies Dalit writers use to achieve their authorial aims. Bama, for example, breaks new literary ground in a number of ways. With a fearless realism lacking in those who recall childhood through the haze of nostalgia, Bama holds up to intense scrutiny the injustices she experienced as a young girl. When the Institute of Development, Education, and Action (henceforth, IDEAS) published *Karukku* by Bama, then an innovative but unknown writer, it allowed readers to enlarge their knowledge about the experiences and perspectives of Paraya women and men. Understanding of Dalit life was further enhanced when IDEAS published *Sangati*, whose memorable voices, canny recollections, and compelling pedagogy set the record straight.

By translating *Karukku* and *Sangati* into English, Lakshmi Holmström has extended the reach of Bama's narratives beyond Tamil readers to the wider arena of pan-Indian English readers, as well as English readers outside of India. Furthermore, Holmström's skilful translation conveys the intelligence and power of the original text without exoticizing or sensationalizing its subject matter. Her care in rendering the intensely local flavour of vocabulary and syntax in her translation helps to make Bama's unique voice heard. By insuring that translations of Bama's books are available across India in a series on Dalit writing from the many regions of India, Oxford's series editor Mini Krishnan facilitates the ability to see Bama's work in light of Dalit writing in Kannada, Marathi, and other regional languages. Translation and distribution, thus, aid in moving Dalit life and letters towards the centre of India's literary canvas as well. Thus, the voices of Dalit women will continue to enrich the literatures of India and demonstrate the truth of what Bama's Paati taught her: 'if the third [child] is a girl to behold, your courtyard will fill with gold' (1994: 13). As Dalit writing from regional South Asian languages becomes more accessible, other talented writers will gain—both in India and beyond—a wide readership enriched by the 'gold' of their writings.

NOTES

1. This statistic is cited in Zelliot (1977a: 560 n31) from *Census of India*, 1921, vol. VIII: *Bombay Presidency*, Part II—Tables, Bombay, 1922: 363. The Mahars are a prominent jati of Dalits in Maharashtra.

2. See for example, Zelliot 1977a: 559 n14. Unlike many anthropologists, Zelliot refers to people she interviews by their proper names, a practice that rejects the assumption that Dalits are 'informants' and therefore may remain unacknowledged as individuals. By including their names, Zelliot also exhibits transparency about her relationship with those about whose voices she is writing, rather than claiming to speak *for* them.
3. Bama's Preface identifies this person as Father M. Jeyaraj of IDEAS.
4. For analysis of Hindu women's possession, see Erndl (1993) and Nabakov (2000).
5. For a wide-ranging analysis of the rhetorical strategies found in Indian religious storytelling, see Narayan (1989).
6. Kanaganayakam discusses several earlier Dalit writers in Sri Lanka (2001: x–xi). In Tamil Nadu, several novels about Dalit culture have also won critical attention: Imayam's *Koveri Kazhudaigal* (1994), Vidivelli's *Kalakkal* (1994), and Sivakami's *Palaiyana Kalitdalum* (1989). For current Tamil Dalit literary and cultural discourse, see debates between Raj Gauthaman (1993) and his conversation partners.

REFERENCES

Bama. 1992. *Karukku*. Madurai. Institute of Development Education, Action and Studies [henceforth, IDEAS]. Lakshmi Holmström (trans.). *Karakku*. Chennai: Macmillan, 2000.
———. 1994. *Sangati* (Tamil). Madurai: IDEAS. Lakshmi Holmstöm (trans.) *Sangati: Events*. New Delhi: Oxford University Press, 2004.
Erndl, Kathleen. 1993. *Victory to the Mother: The Hindu Goddess of Northwest India in Myth, Ritual, and Symbol*. New York: Oxford University Press.
Gauthaman, Raj. 1993. *Dalit Panpaadu*. Puduvai: Gauri Padipakam.
Holmström, Lakshmi. 1998. 'Rebellious Women: Images of Women in the Protest Literature of Tamil Christian Dalits'. K. O'Grady, Ann L. Gilroy, and Janette Gray (eds). *Bodies, Lives, Voices: Gender in Theology*. Sheffield: Sheffield Academic Press, pp. 118–32.
Hovell, Laurie. 1991.'Namdeo Dhasal: Poet and Panther'. *Bulletin of Concerned Asian Scholars*. vol. 23, no. 4, pp. 77–83.
Imayam. 1994. *Koveri Kazhudaiga*. Madras: Cre-A. Lakshmi Holmström (trans.). *Beasts of Burden*. Madras: East-West Books (Manas), 2001.
Kanaganayakam, Chelva (ed.). 2001. *Lutesong and Lament: Tamil Writing from Sri Lanka*. Toronto: TSAR Publications.
Narayan, Kirin. 1989. *Storytellers, Saints, and Scoundrels: Folk Narrative in Hindu Religious Teaching*. Philadelphia: University of Pennsylvania Press.
Nabakov, Isabelle. 2000. *Religion against the Self: An Ethnography of Tamil Rituals*. New York: Oxford University Press.

Richman, Paula. 1988. *Women, Branch Stories, and Religious Rhetoric in a Tamil Buddhist Text*. Syracuse: Syracuse University.

Sivakami. 1989. *Paliayana Kalithalum*. Madras: Tamil Puthakalayam.

Vidivelli. 1994. *Kalakkal*. Madurai: IDEAS.

Zelliot, Eleanor. 1977a. 'The Leadership of Babasaheb Ambedkar'. In B.N. Pandey (ed.). *Leadership in South Asia*. New Delhi: Vikas, pp. 535–62.

_____. 1977b. 'The Psychological Dimension of the Buddhist Movement in India'. In G.A Oddie (ed.). *Religion in South Asia: Religious Conversion and Revival Movements in South Asia in Medieval and Modern Times*. Columbia: South Asia Books, pp. 119–44.

_____. 1978. 'Dalit: New Cultural Context for an Old Marathi Word'. *Contributions to Asian Studies*. vol. 9, pp. 77–97.

_____. 1981. 'Chokhamela and Eknath: Two Bhakti Modes of Legitimacy for Modern Change'. In Jayant Lele (ed.). *Tradition and Modernity in Bhakti Movements*. Leiden: Brill, pp. 135–56.

_____. 1982. 'Introduction to Dalit Poetry'. *Journal of South Asian Literature*. vol. 17, no. 1, pp. 96–101.

_____. 1987. 'Perspectives on the Dalit Cultural Movement'. *South Asia Bulletin*. vol. 7, nos 1 and 2, pp. 68–77.

_____. 1992. 'Buddhist Women of the Contemporary Maharashtrian Conversion Movement'. In Jose Ignacio Cabezon (ed.). *Buddhism, Sexuality, and Gender*. Albany: SUNY Press, pp. 91–107.

_____ and Mulk Raj Anand (eds). 1992. *An Anthology of Dalit Literature: Poems*. New Delhi: Gyan Publishing House.

10

WOMEN'S EMPOWERMENT THROUGH RELIGIOUS CONVERSION[1]

Voices of Buddhists in Nagpur, India

Laura Dudley Jenkins

Only analysis shows that the *ways* in which we believe and expect have a tremendous effect upon what we believe and expect.
—John Dewey (LW 1: 23, quoted in Wolfe 2002: 310)

The psychological impact of Buddhism, the matter of changed identity, cannot be judged by visible signs.
—Eleanor Zelliot (1996: 218)

Although conversion is not a visible process, *listening* to converts reveals the power of this transformation in their lives. The words of Buddhist women convey several forms of empowerment, some evident, others unseen. The women whom I recorded in interviews or group discussion in September 2002 in Nagpur and Delhi had participated in the mass conversions of roughly half a million people to Buddhism in 1956, led by B.R. Ambedkar (Zelliot 1996: 126–7; Omvedt 2003: 246–65). These women do not speak for all such converts but only of their own experiences. Most were poor as children at the time of conversion, but had reached middle-class status by the time they spoke with me. Thus, their enthusiasm about the power of conversion in their lives may not be shared by those who remained in poverty. Nevertheless, their words make two important contributions to the study of conversion. First, refracted through a lens of close to fifty years of subsequent life experiences, these recollections provide views of conversion as both an event and a process. Second, by reflecting on the conversion and its after-effects at a personal level, the women communicate through words the hidden impact of conversion, thereby expanding conventional notions of power.

Lively discussions with elderly Buddhist women illuminate aspects of power that are not entirely captured by major social science approaches to this concept. Wolfe criticizes predominant theories of power for implying 'that any increase in the ability to make a difference depends on enhancing the capacity for domination', and he tries to 'appreciate the variable, complex, and generative character of power relations' (Wolfe 2002: 309). To do this Wolfe draws on the pragmatist approach to power, rooted in John Dewey, who was also a major influence on Ambedkar (Zelliot 1996: 83–4). Dewey wrote, 'Pragmatism ... does not insist on antecedent phenomena but upon consequent phenomena; not upon the precedents but upon the possibilities of action' (LW 2: 12, quoted in Wolfe 2002: 310). For Ambedkar and other converts, apostasy from Hinduism was the ultimate break from antecedents, and conversion to Buddhism was the way to seize the 'possibilities of action'. Dewey was one of Ambedkar's professors at Columbia University, where he studied from 1913 to 1916 (Zelliot 1996: 79). Thus passages from Dewey relating to power as *action, change*, and *understanding* will provide an apt counterpoint to the words of the converts B.R. Ambedkar inspired.

POWER AS (INTER)ACTION

The only power the organism possesses to control its own future ... [is] the way in which its present reactions to things influence the future reactions of things upon it.

        —John Dewey (MW 10: 15, quoted in Wolfe 2002: 311)

Actions, reactions, and interactions at all levels of society generate power relations. Through protests in the years preceding the conversion and then through the conversion itself, women in the Dalit movement acted in response to injustice or atrocities and prominently entered newly opened social spaces. They demonstrated so that other castes would react to Dalits of both sexes with more respect in the future. Kama

Savatkar recalled the 1932 campaign to open the Kala Ram temple in Nasik to Dalits:

The women had taken small children along to join Babasaheb [a loving honourific used for B.R. Ambedkar]. Even on seeing the women and children they threw stones on them and they were injured. Then also they did not have mercy.... Again they did satyagraha [nonviolent resistance, literally 'truth endeavour'] and this time the doors had to be opened, and we were permitted to go inside the temple and worship, but there was nothing for us to see inside. Babasaheb, through satyagraha, wanted to show that we can go inside the temple (group discussion, 8 September 2002).

Savatkar's rendition juxtaposes her initial surprise, as a child, at finally getting into the temple, to see only 'nothing' of particular interest, and her current understanding that this symbolic action would 'show' upper castes and influence their future reactions.

Savatkar recalled another, earlier protest in which Dalits, who had been treated as lower than animals, demanded the right to water at a well in the small town of Mahad in 1927:

The animals and ... caste people were free to drink water. But our people were not permitted to drink water. Then Babasaheb gathered people one by one and thus water became free for everyone to drink. The picture of Babasaheb is still in front of my eyes (group discussion with Savatkar, 8 September 2002).

According to Gail Omvedt, the Mahad incident ended not with access to water but rather with Dalits publicly burning the Hindu laws known as *Manusmriti* (Omvedt 2003: 247). Whatever its outcome, the satyagraha at Mahad sent a message to upper-caste Hindus that Dalits were not going to take oppression any more. In this way, through collective action, even women from a segment of the population that was less respected than animals gained some power. Women had become prepared to challenge society through mass conversion by participating in these earlier protests as well as mass gatherings. The All-India Depressed Classes Political Conference, held at Nagpur in 1942, drew 70,000 people from all over India, one third of them women (Omvedt 1995: 216–17).

Following these protests and meetings, religious conversion was the next step in a series of Dalit reactions to discrimination, and, at least in some cases, conversion positively influenced the future reactions of others to Dalits. Although many converts face continuing discrimination (Omvedt 2003: 264), Hira Nimgade, who moved to New Delhi since her conversion, noted the change in people's reactions to her and her family after conversion. In both the city and the villages, she said, people used to shun them, but 'now we say we are Buddhists', and even her brothers, who still live in small villages, 'are treated nicely'. She said that people who previously might not let them into their courtyard now invite them to weddings. One story from her childhood suggests that this change in people's reactions to her was due to both conversion and education, which she, like many others, saw as closely intertwined. When she was a girl, Nimgade recollected, 'I touched the book of a girl. What are you reading? She got so mad'. Later, said Nimgade, 'I came first in my class' and girls who had shunned her welcomed her (interview with Nimgade, 10 September 2002, New Delhi).

In addition to challenging previous relations between upper and lower castes, Ambedkar's movement, particularly the mass conversions, also influenced interactions between Dalits, offering them a form of unity previously lacking. At the conversions and other gatherings, Dalits came together, sometimes for the first time. Bharat Ratna talked about one such gathering:

I had the privilege of seeing Baba Saheb when I was a child. Phulgaon is a small town in Varda district, and in that small town Baba Saheb had organized a programme. To attend that programme a lot of people from nearby villages had gathered. My father had taken our entire family to attend that programme. I was just studying in eighth standard and I was too small. There was so much of a rush to that programme that the pandal [structure put up for the event] was fully crowded to see Babasaheb. It was even impossible to properly stand in such a crowd. Since I was small, I could not see over the crowd, so I went near the pandal and was peeping inside to see Babasaheb. He was looking so impressive that I memorized him in my eyes (group discussion, 8 September 2002).

The conversion and related gatherings were not only family gatherings, including both women and children, but also inspirational assemblies bringing together Dalits from different villages.

Consider the rhetoric of unity in retired Sanskrit professor Kumud Pawde's account:

It was 14 October 1956 ... I was seventeen years old, so I remember everything. From morning to night we were staying on that ground which I showed to you. And we had taken our tiffins [lunch boxes] with us; we had taken our water with us. And not [only] myself, *all* the basti, not only one basti but *all* of Nagpur, north, east, dakshina [south], southwest, all Nagpur. Not only Nagpur but all villages outside (interview, 6 September 2002).

This early conversion experience had an impact on Pawde's later choices in life, during which she confidently and persistently challenged the status quo.

POWER AS CHANGE

... [E]very experience enacted and undergone modifies the one who acts and undergoes, while this modification affects, whether we wish it or not, the quality of subsequent experiences. For it is a somewhat different person who enters into them.
                              —John Dewey (LW 13: 18, quoted in Wolfe 2002: 311)

Conversion influenced not only the reactions of others to Buddhist Dalits but also their own subsequent actions and experiences, which often challenged static power relations. Kumud Pawde chose a subject, Sanskrit, that women and Dalits were traditionally forbidden to study. After her conversion to Buddhism, she persisted, despite ongoing discrimination, in her plans to study and teach Sanskrit. She remembered,

The conversion of women was taken in his [Ambedkar's] presence and ... lakhs [hundreds of thousands] of women were present ... because he was saying that ... progress in any society depends upon women ... how they are cultured, how they are educated (interview, 6 September 2002).

Pushpa Kakatkar also emphasized the connection between conversion and education, stressing that

People experienced total change in their lives. Much importance then was given for education in our life. Even the poor started preparing to send their children to convents [schools which were considered to provide the best educational opportunities]. They half starved themselves to save money for sending their children. A poor person said he wanted his daughter to take education in Mount Carmel [convent school]—so great is the transformation in the field of education in the villages. People have built their confidence and they felt that they also can achieve something, like other classes of people (group discussion, 8 September 2002).

Not all families immediately treated their daughters and sons equally, but as they could afford it, many sent their girls to school. As Pratibha Ghedamkar put it, 'Such a disciplined life started in our family. The boys and later the girls also took education in our family' (group discussion, 8 September 2002).

Dushantala Uke recalled that her family had to struggle for education, not only due to cost but also due to discrimination in admissions, but they became quite determined:

Babasaheb said the girls should get basic education and later on also they should continue their education, but I was not getting admission in school, so my parents fought for getting me admitted into the school. Babasaheb said that we should study; that is why my father fought with the school authorities for my admission into the school. I got admission in such a school where a majority of the girls were Brahmans (group discussion, 8 September 2002).

Uke noted another change in converts' behaviour, a visible change advocated by Ambedkar, namely dress:

In childhood I used to remain the whole day wearing old clothes. As Babasaheb had said we should always remain neat, clean and properly dressed, my parents taught me always to be neatly dressed and progressive (group discussion, 8 September 2002).

Uke was not the only woman to mention dress. Several women in a discussion on conversion cried but also laughed over their memories, particularly chuckling over the struggle to find enough white saris to wear to the conversion ceremony, white being the uniform of the day.

Uke, like others, saw conversion as so closely linked to related changes in dress, education, and self-respect that she seamlessly included these changes in her discussion of conversion. Due to conversion, she concluded, 'Our life was transformed' (group discussion, 8 September 2002). This holistic conversion of life itself was what Ambedkar aspired to achieve. He had a very comprehensive transformation in mind when he wrote about conversion:

This means a complete change in the fundamental notions of life. It means a complete change in outlook and attitude towards men and things. It means conversion ... it means a new life (Ambedkar 1990 [1936]: 100).

POWER AS UNDERSTANDING

The ... fundamental means of control is not personal but intellectual.... It consists in the habits of understanding.'
                    —John Dewey (MW 9: 38, quoted in Wolfe 2002: 313)

Ambedkar's choice of Buddhism was in large part due to its potential for inducing more positive 'habits of understanding' among converts. He rejected Hinduism two decades before he officially became a Buddhist. Many religious leaders wooed him, and he studied various alternatives before choosing Buddhism. Kumud Pawde recalled,

He studied all religions, Christianity, Islam, Buddhism, Jainism, Sikh[ism].... After study he preferred ... Buddhism .... He said, 'I taught the people to fight for their rights, but I wanted to teach them how to perform duties, how to be in the society, and that is why I have chosen this Buddhism' (interview with Pawde, who was recalling rather than directly quoting Dr Ambedkar, 6 September 2002).

Pawde went on to note that the converts felt Buddhism offered a code of ethics to live by, rather than just replacing one god with another. Pawde contrasted her conversion in 1956 to prior mass conversions in India, describing her new standpoint as a person empowered to ask questions about her previous degradation and to challenge caste through education and literature:

Some people embraced Islam. When British or French came, they embraced Christianity .... They think only of God, but why and how they cannot ask. We asked how and why, and we got answers. After conversion we can write, we can read, we can think rationally about the subject. There was Dalit literature movement (interview, 6 September 2002).

Pawde herself contributed to that movement. An essay by her, 'The Story of My "Sanskrit"', is in a collection of Marathi Dalit literature translated into English (Dangle 1992: 96–106).

The intellectual liberation and new 'habits of understanding' of converts are captured by the recollections of a professor, Nalini Somkuwar (paraphrased):

After conversion, the Dalits got confidence; they left superstition and felt like human beings ... we can understand our position in society. We were not treated as human beings, and that is why we became fighters against a social system that humiliated us more and more. There is equality between men and women. Women work with men as colleagues. We felt our own dignity.... We started thinking over our existence. This is a fundamental change (group discussion, 8 September 2002).

Conversion facilitated a fuller understanding of Dalits' existence and provided the intellectual tools to press for a new kind of life.

Psychological change within the converts is perhaps the most difficult to perceive, as Zelliot points out in the epigraph preceding this essay. Kama Savatkar recalled that her experiences of conversion (*diksha*) not only changed others' perceptions of her but also changed her internally as well:

Before we met him [Dr Ambedkar] we used to feel very uncomfortable. We used to feel all alone and lonely. Nobody is behind us. After taking diksha all our fears vanished and we felt as if some kind of power is behind us, and because of that power behind us we were able to successfully finish all our works (group discussion, 8 September 2002).

Hira Nimgade remembered that after conversion, 'we began to feel we are not less than anyone' and overcame any 'inferiority complex'. Prevailing over the 'intellectual control' discussed by Dewey, she remembered that as a girl she came to believe, 'Now ... we are equal to everybody and due to that we can achieve good marks, even better than them' (interview, 10 September 2002, New Delhi).

Another woman remembered that the mass conversion built on other campaigns to empower Dalits, including the demand to allow Dalits access to drinking water in Mahad, discussed by Savatkar above, by further liberating them through awareness and understanding. After making drinking water available to Dalits,

at that time Babasaheb thought that he would not be able to live in a humanitarian way and with self respect in the Hindu religion. He also realized that as long as the Hindu religious people do not attain awareness, he and his community will not be liberated. Babasaheb then studied all the religions and was impressed more by the principles of Buddhism. He appreciated the concepts of love, equality, and brotherhood in Buddhism. Finally he accepted Buddhism, which did not differentiate people as higher or lower categories in society (comments of Buddhist woman in group discussion, name unknown, 8 September 2002).

Moving beyond such differentiations into a more egalitarian understanding of society had both caste and gender implications. Patriarchal patterns were not eradicated entirely. For example, not all of the women attended the conversion in person; some were converted by association with a father or husband. Bharat Ratna said,

My father accepted diksha for his entire family. After diksha he made us throw out the frames etc. of gods and goddesses. Right from the day of the religious conversion, we started worshipping only Buddha (group discussion with Bharat Ratna, 8 September 2002).

This conversion by proxy, followed by fatherly edicts, does not suggest much agency on the part of the women of the family. Moreover the comment about 'worshipping' Buddha might be contested by Buddhist scholars, and illustrates how many of the women—girls at the time of conversion—lacked formal knowledge of Buddhism. Yet even Ratna was adamant that more positive gender relations flowed directly from the conversion.

Ms Ratna remembered that her father

gave education to all his daughters. It was my batch ... that was the first batch in our village .... My father ventured to give co-education. I can say that the best treatment and respect were given to ladies in our family. Whatever small egos of persons we saw in the families vanished after taking diksha. In this healthy atmosphere we got our education (group discussion with Ratna, 8 September 2002).

She felt that these new habits of understanding stemmed from conversion.

I cannot describe it in detail as I was very small; however I can say that I got the opportunities to be educated. I got a scholarship and studied further. I got a scholarship in college too. All this progress was achieved due to the religious conversion (group discussion with Ratna, 8 September 2002).

CONCLUSION

Our undergoings are experiments in varying the course of events; our active tryings are trials and tests of ourselves.
                    —John Dewey (MW 10: 9, quoted in Wolfe 2002: 318).

One question people may ask is, 'Were Dalits *really* empowered by conversion? Did people no longer treat them as low castes?' The reactions of *others to* Dalit Buddhists have been mixed. Many persist in seeing them as low-caste, even diminishing their status as Buddhists by distinguishing them as 'neo-Buddhists'. While maintaining a distinct identity as Dalit Buddhists has allowed this group to demand and regain, in 1990, their eligibility for affirmative action (Jenkins 2003: 79, 120), the 'neo' label is particularly hurtful to those who consider their conversion a return to a past identity. Zelliot notes that many Dalits 'in need of a myth to explain their Untouchable status' believe Buddhist conversion is really a reconversion for Dalits. Buddhism has given them a new, yet old, identity as returning former Buddhists, who had been 'reduced to a low status for their very loyalty to religion rather than because of sin' (Zelliot 1996: 220). Yet the 'neo' label denies this myth.

      Economic limitations also squelched many Dalits despite the spiritual empowerment of conversion. As Omvedt writes of the 'Buddhist renaissance' in the 1950s,

The Mahars and other Dalits, though self-confident, and with remarkable individuals emerging from them, were overwhelmingly poor and with limited resources. Institution building was slow. The assertion of Buddhism at the level of scholarship and art was slow. For a long time, Buddhism was hardly taken seriously (Omvedt 2003: 264).

Any change in the actions and reactions of upper castes to Dalits after conversion is only one aspect of empowerment, however. Power as change in the attitudes and choices of Dalits is another important aspect, epitomized by the educational empowerment of Dalits. Understanding is yet another form of empowerment, as Dalit Buddhists look back and critically view the past and aspire to a better future.

Empowerment as change and understanding on the part of the Dalits themselves is important precisely because upper-caste attitudes and behaviour in many cases did not change. Dalits' interior changes gave them the determination to persevere in their efforts to better their lives. Thus women who answered an open-ended question about conversion memories spontaneously brought up multiple forms of empowerment and expressed each conversion story as a life-long process and struggle rather than a single, immediate step into a more powerful position. This holistic empowerment is captured in the memories of Pratibha Ghedamkar:

Phulgaon was a small village. They were difficult days. Even drinking water was a separate arrangement for us. Then Babasaheb came to our village and he offered diksha to us. Thereafter the total atmosphere (*vaataavaran*) changed.

This idea that conversion changed the 'total atmosphere' encompasses empowerment as action, change, and understanding and also evokes the difficulty of quantifying this elusive change. Conversion did not solve all the problems of Dalits. It did not solve all the problems of these particular women. It did not give them power in the sense that they could dominate others. Yet, according to Ghedamkar and the other women who spoke with me, conversion transformed their lives.

NOTE

1. I would like to thank Eleanor Zelliot for inspiring my interest in Dalit politics and in B.R. Ambedkar. I would not have been able to do this project without the guidance of her previous work, her advice and contacts in Maharashtra, and the goodwill she has generated in Nagpur. Because I knew Eleanor, I was greeted with enthusiasm, and people were eager to discuss with me something as personal as conversion. I am especially grateful to the amazing Kumud Pawde and her family, who helped me in countless ways. My colleague at the University of Cincinnati, Joel Wolfe, may be surprised that I found his theory of power, which he applies to changing economies in the United Kingdom and European Union, applicable to changes experienced by Dalit women. I am grateful for his expertise on Dewey, which enabled me to draw on his work for this project. When Joel informed me that someone from India contributed to an online Dewey discussion list, it turned out to be a Dalit Buddhist activist I met in Delhi, so the Dalit-Dewey connection is

alive and well. Krishna Manek and her family helped me with excellent transcriptions and translations of many of my taped interviews and discussions, which were carried out in Hindi, Marathi, and English. Finally, I enthusiastically acknowledge a grant from the Charles Phelps Taft Research Center at the University of Cincinnati, which enabled me to meet the extraordinary women featured in this essay.

REFERENCES

Ambedkar, B.R. 1990. 'Annihilation of Caste' (undelivered speech prepared by B.R. Ambedkar for the 1936 Annual conference of the Jat Pat Todak Mandal of Lahore). In Mulk Raj Anand (ed.). New Delhi: Arnold Publishers.

Dangle, Arjun. 1992. *Poisoned Bread: Translations from Modern Marathi Dalit Literature*. Bombay: Orient Longman.

Dewey, John. 1969–72. *The Early Works of John Dewey, 1882–1892* (EW). In J.A. Boydston (ed.). 5 vols. Carbondale: Southern Illinois University Press.

_____. 1976–83. *The Middle Works of John Dewey, 1899–1924* (MW). In J.A. Boydston (ed.). 15 vols. Carbondale: Southern Illinois University Press.

_____. 1981–90. *The Later Works of John Dewey, 1925–1953* (LW). In J.A. Boydston (ed.). 17 vols. Carbondale: Southern Illinois University Press.

Jenkins, Laura Dudley. 2003. *Identity and Identification in India: Defining the Disadvantaged*. London and New York: Routledge Curzon.

Omvedt, Gail. 1995. *Dalits and the Democratic Revolution: Dr Ambedkar and the Dalit Movement in Colonial India*. New Delhi: Sage.

_____. 2003. *Buddhism in India: Challenging Brahmanism and Caste*. New Delhi: Sage.

Wolfe, Joel. 2002. 'Power: A Pragmatist Proposal'. *Studies in Symbolic Interaction*. vol. 25, pp. 303–24.

Zelliot, Eleanor. 1996. *From Untouchable to Dalit: Essays on the Ambedkar Movement*. New Delhi: Manohar.

11

THE BUDDHA AND THE BARBERS
Status, Discipline, and Dissension in Early Buddhism

Guy Welbon

My interpretation puts me at odds with those who see the Buddha as a social reformer. Certainly, in consenting to preach and then in establishing an Order of monks to do likewise, he showed his great compassion and concern for mankind. Moreover, he was supremely kind and understanding towards everyone, so far as we can tell. But his concern was to reform individuals and help them to leave society forever, not to reform the world. Life in the world he regarded as suffering and the problem to which he offered a solution was the otherwise inevitable rebirth into the world. Though it could well be argued that the Buddha made life in the world more worth living, that surely was an unintended consequence of his teaching. To present him as a sort of socialist is a serious anachronism. He never preached against social inequality, only declared its irrelevance to salvation. He neither tried to abolish the caste system nor to do away with slavery (Gombrich 1988: 30).

When Eleanor and I first met—at Deccan College in Pune in October 1963—that pretty much characterized my own attitude about the nature of the Buddha's message. And, largely, it still does. But Eleanor showed me that matters were more complicated and interesting than I had earlier supposed. She introduced me to the broader, actual, and continuing impact of the Buddha's message (as well as to realities of field research more generally) during those mid-autumn weeks. She dragged me among the *navabauddha*, introducing and passing me off as sufficiently knowledgeable and sympathetic that a small contingent of those 'new' and excited Buddhists actually asked me to write a catechism to help them better understand Buddhist teaching. Their request remains as surely one of the greatest compliments I have received, as my declining it stands as one of my most sensible decisions.

I am honoured, too, to have been asked to join the many others felicitating Eleanor. I welcome the opportunity to thank her for her manifold services to South Asia studies, certainly; but, even more profoundly, I thank her for opening my eyes and heart to the living India, for helping me connect texts and histories to vibrant, sometimes recalcitrant actualities. Indeed, it is a pleasure to thank her for the decisive impact she has had on the way I do what I do.

In this little essay, I wander principally through the Pali *Vinayapitaka* (detouring briefly also in the Buddhist Sanskrit *Mahavastu*) searching for traces of a Buddhist hero: Upali, the Sakya barber from Kapilavatthu who, ordained by the Buddha in the early days of his teaching, eventually became the celebrated master and custodian of the *vinaya*, the Pali Buddhist monastic discipline.[1] In the Buddha's phrase, he was *Vinayadharana*: 'Chief among those who know *vinaya* by heart'. Commended as *vinaya agganikkhitto*, Upali was the one called upon by Mahakassapa to recite and elucidate the entire vinaya at the first Buddhist Council (Rajagaha) during the rains, three months after the Buddha's *parinibbana*.[2]

I am concerned here primarily with how Pali Buddhist tradition represents Upali. While tracking this somewhat elusive hero, I encounter occasional clues about the perception and nature of social stratification in the Buddha's time and see something of the attitudes of the Buddha and early Buddhists toward phenomena associated with caste distinctions. So, while it is expressly to the representation of Upali that I direct attention, something more general about early Buddhist social attitudes will feature in my observations.[3] And on this journey I also meet again a couple of villains: the Buddha's cousin Devadatta, so infamous for his relentless efforts to kill the Buddha and to disrupt the Order, and Subhadda, a barber with a grudge.

MAGICAL HAIR? WHO ARE BARBERS AND WHAT'S WRONG WITH THEM?

The Suttavibhanga section of the *Vinayapitaka* calls barbering a 'low craft', classifying it along with the occupations of basket-maker, potter, weaver, and leatherworker.[4] Even the casual student of South Asian society knows that barbers are traditionally regarded as unclean. Among the many designations of 'barber' in Sanskrit and Pali—for instance, *kalpaka* (Sanskrit); *kappaka, nahapita* (Pali)—some expressly identify them as people who live at the margins of the city/village/town (for instance, *antavasayin/antevasayin*). Even today, in villages of Andhra Pradesh and Tamil Nadu, for instance, the barber (Telugu *mangali*; Tamil *ampattan*), who is crucial in the performance of religious rituals like, for instance, *caula* (the hair-cutting *samskara*), may not proceed closer than the outermost margin of the patron's property.

The problems with barbers certainly begin with the way they deal with hair. It is not simply that they cut it, though that is problem enough, for it defines barbers as persons who inescapably deal with— because, in fact, they create—a kind of leftover, remnant, or waste product. And, as growing hair is rich in symbolic power, so is it especially dangerous when its growth is arrested. A more penetrating discussion of the barber's role and predicament than the one intended here would require examining quite closely the perceived nature and qualities of hair. Fortunately, that is an enterprise already well underway.[5]

But barbers do more than cut hair: they wash it. Further, in cleaning hair, they directly address dirt, inevitably get their fingers in it, and necessarily become a kind of receptacle for it as they remove it from their patrons. Moreover, they are traditionally very much involved with bathing activities in general. They prepare baths (hence the designation *snapaka* [Sanskrit], *nahapaka* [Pali]). And they shave their clients, which commonly requires them to deal with body hair as well as head and facial hair. Adding to the complexity of the barber's profile is the fact that he is often seen as surgically adept.

For our present purposes, however, it is enough that barbers are required to deal with waste in cutting hair. We need go no further than that. The *Vinaya* avers that barbers follow a low occupation. It also repeatedly insists that to call a fellow renunciant or a non-renunciant a barber with the intention of shaming him (or even simply in jest) is an offense that must be expiated.[6] While the extensive *Jataka* story told in the *Mahavastu* to account for the propriety of nobles' bowing before the newly ordained Upali states that a sincere act of generosity towards a *paccekabuddha* was a crucial event in one of Upali's previous births,[7] another Buddhist tradition specifically links his being a barber to his having insulted a paccekabuddha in a former birth.[8]

Joining the Order does not immediately—nor even in the long run—make a person's social background irrelevant. Indeed, it is used to make a point. When the Buddha accedes to the request of the Sakyan princes and ordains Upali the barber prior to ordaining them, at least in part there is an affirmation of class distinction and a direct effort to utilize it. The explicit inversion is a reminder of the former status relationship between prince and barber. And later, when Upali's role as master of the discipline (vinaya) is emphasized, some who are constrained by his rulings object vigorously to being forced to follow the decision of a mere washer of hair.

UPALI: FROM SAKYAN BARBER TO MASTER OF VINAYA

The description of Upali emerging from early Buddhist texts is vague and sketchy. Moreover, there clearly seem to be at least three Upali-s. Our Upali—the 'famous' Upali—is usually referred to as Upali *thera*. In addition, there was Upali the householder, a well-informed Jain layperson, who became the Buddha's disciple after a series of encounters narrated in the so-called *Upali Sutta*.[9] Yet another Upali was the pampered son of doting parents who sought to find for him a career that would suit his delicate nature (Malalasekara 1983, vol. I: 410f.).

Ordination: The Backgrounds

For information about Upali the barber before his ordination, we must consult the *Mahavastu*, where we read how Upali's mother introduced him to the Buddha shortly before the famous 'ordination of the Sakyan princes'. It is a rather odd introduction, for Upali is characterized as already formidably accomplished.

Now of these Sakyan young men one was named Upali. He was a barber's assistant, who had acquired the root of virtue under previous Buddhas, had retained the impressions of his former life, had broken his bonds, was not liable to rebirth, enjoyed Aryan status in his last existence and was master of the meditations and the super-knowledges. He had been sent to the Exalted One by his Mother, who said 'He will cut the hair of the Exalted One.' And the Exalted One agreed. So Upali cut the hair of the Exalted One. His mother asked the Exalted One, 'Lord, does Upali cut hair satisfactorily?' The Exalted One replied, 'Yes, but he comes rather too close to the Tathagata.' She then said 'My boy, do not stand so close to the Exalted One.' It was then that Upali entered upon the first meditation.

Thereupon his mother asked ... again, 'Lord, does my boy Upali cut hair satisfactorily?' The Exalted One replied, 'Yes the boy cuts hair satisfactorily, but he oils the razor too much.' So she said, 'My boy, do not oil the razor too much.' And then he entered upon the second meditation.

Upali's mother again asked, ... 'Lord, does my boy Upali cut hair satisfactorily?' 'Yes Upali cuts hair satisfactorily but his breathing annoys the Tathagata.' So she said, 'My boy do not annoy the Exalted One with your breathing.' Then, having passed through the first and second meditations, he entered upon the third and fourth. The Exalted One said to the monks, 'Take the razor from Upali's hand so that it does not fall to the ground.' And the monks took the razor from Upali's hand (Jones 1949–56, vol. III: 175f.; Senart 1897, vol. III: 179f.).

The *Upasampada*

The most familiar account of Upali's becoming a disciple of the Buddha is found in the *Cullavagga* section of the *Vinayapitaka*. This ordination is interesting for more reasons, too: it was the famous occasion on which the Sakyan princes Bhaddiya, Anuruddha, Ananda, Devadatta, Bhaga, and Kimbila were also ordained.

It was about a year after the Buddha's Enlightenment.[10] Bhaddiya had succeeded the Buddha's father, Suddhodana, as Sakya leader.[11] Also among the Sakya nobility were the brothers Mahanama and Anuruddha. The former had urged his younger brother to take the road of renunciation and undertake the quest for release; but Anuruddha resisted and sought counsel from his friend Bhaddiya. Both agreed they should seek ordination together and, after some discussion about when they should do this, finally determined they should do so immediately. So Bhaddiya and Anuruddha prepared to depart to seek the Buddha. They were joined by Ananda and his brother Devadatta, by Bhagu, Kimbila, and, of course, the barber Upali. The setting was the Anupiya grove, on the way to Kapilavatthu, the capital of the Sakyas.

Here, abbreviated at points to eliminate some repetition, is how I.B. Horner continues the translation of this story:

Then Bhaddiya the Sakyan chieftain and Anuraddha and Ananda and Bhagu and Kimbila, and Devadatta with Upali the barber as the seventh, as they had often previously gone out to a ground in a pleasure grove with a fourfold army, so did they (now) go out with a fourfold army. Having gone far, having sent back the army, having passed into other territory, having taken off their ornaments, having tied them up into a bundle with their upper robes, they spoke thus to Upali the barber: 'Come, good Upali, return, this will be enough for your livelihood.' Then it occurred to Upali the barber as he was going back: 'The Sakyans are fierce. Thinking "This one has made the young men come forth" they may even kill me. But if these young Sakyan men will go forth from home to homelessness, why should not I?'

Having loosened the bundle, having hung the goods up on a tree, and having said: 'whoever sees it, it is given (to him), let him take it,' he approached the young Sakyan men. These young Sakyan men saw Upali the barber coming in the distance; having seen him, they spoke thus to Upali the barber: 'Why have you, good Upali, returned?'

'Now it occurred to me, young gentlemen ... the Sakyans ... may well kill me. But if these young men will go forth from home into homelessness, why should not I?'...

'You did well, good Upali. The Sakyans are fierce... they might even have killed you.' Then these young Sakyan men, taking Upali the barber, approached the Lord, greeted him, and spoke thus:

'We, Lord, are Sakyans, we are proud. Lord, this barber, Upali, has been our attendant for a long time. May the Lord let him go forth first. We will greet him, rise up before him, salute him with joined palms, and do the proper duties. Thus will the Sakyan pride be humbled in us Sakyans.' Then the Lord let Upali the barber go forth first, and afterwards these young Sakyan men (Horner 1938–52, vol. V [*Cullavagga*]: 256f. [*Vinaya* II.182]).

How Upali Saved his *Uppajjhaya*

Following his ordination, Upali was assigned Kappitaka as his upajjhaya/*upadhyaya*. Upali's dedication to his discipline master is illustrated in a story which tells of his saving Kappitaka's life and being reviled by a group of nuns as a consequence.

Kappitaka may have been an exemplary *arannavasi* (forest dweller). He was certainly irascible and none too patient (as solitary, meditating sages so often appear in Indian lore). He is said to have lived in a *smasana* (cemetery/cremation yard). On one occasion, six nuns associated with what was apparently an apostate group of ascetics known as *chabbhagiya*[12] brought the ashes of a colleague nun to the cemetery, buried them, erected a stupa, and began weeping and lamenting her passing. Kappitaka, disturbed by the noise, smashed the stupa and scattered the ashes.

The nuns were furious and plotted to kill Kappitaka. But Upali overheard their plan and warned Kappitaka to hide. The nuns finding no one in Kappitaka's shack, destroyed it and celebrated his death. Upon learning that Kappitaka was still alive thanks to Upali's warning, they became angry with him as well. 'Our plan was foiled by Master Upali; [and they reviled him] how can this barber, a shampooing low-caste person, foil our plans?' Learning of this, the Buddha proclaimed that 'whatever nun should revile or should abuse a monk, there is an offence of expiation' (Horner 1938–52, vol. III [*Suttavibhanga*]: 343f. [*Vinaya* IV.307f.]).

UPALI'S DECISIONS ON MATTERS OF RIGHT CONDUCT

Upali's fame traditionally rests not only on his mastery of the entire vinaya and his never breaking a single rule, but also his fair and reasonable decisions when faced with cases of real or apparent misconduct. It is worth noting, too, that questions and appeals were directed to him both by *bhikkhus* and by laypersons, confirming that he was highly regarded outside as well as inside the Order. Three cases illustrate his style:

The Case of Bharukacchaka

The recluse Bharukacchaka dreamed of having sexual intercourse with his former wife. Upali ruled that there was no offense because this had been only a dream (Horner 1938–52, vol. I [*Suttavibhanga*]: 60f. [*Vinaya* III.39]).

The Case of Ajjukka

This monk was asked by a (lay) supporter to grant audience to his nephew, also an *upasaka*. Ajjukka did this, and the man's nephew, who was wealthy, presented a gift to Ajjukka. The man's son then complained to Ananda that Ajjukka had shown favouritism to the nephew. Ananda seemed to agree; but Upali declared that Ajjukka was blameless since he had granted an audience to the man's nephew because of the latter's dedication and faith rather than because of his wealth (ibid.: 111–12 [*Vinaya* III. 66f.]. See also Bailey and Mabbett 2003: 226f.).

The Case of KumaraKassapa

As told in the prologue to *Jataka* 12, the devout and dedicated daughter of a banker in Rajagaha was denied permission to enter the Order by her parents; so she decided to wait until she married. Some time after her wedding, unaware that she was pregnant, the young woman refused to dress and celebrate at a festival. When her husband discovered that she wished to join the Order, he facilitated it. But, near the date of her delivery, the *bhikkhunis*, seeing her condition, reported her to the master of the Order, none other than Devadatta. Fearing that this situation would adversely affect his reputation, Devadatta immediately insisted that she must be expelled. She appealed to the Sisters to take her to the Buddha, who ordered Upali to conduct the 'trial'. Before the four-part assembly, the king and others, Upali ordered that it be determined when the young woman had become pregnant. The examination proved that she had already been pregnant before joining the Order; and Upali pronounced her guiltless. The son she delivered soon after was handed over to the king, who named him Kassapa and raised him as a prince. Hence the child was known as Kassapa the Prince (KumaraKassapa) (Malalasekara 1983, vol. I: 632f.). Eventually both the prince and his mother became *arahants*.

THE RAJAGAHA COUNCIL ... NOT ALL BARBERS ARE HEROES

At the parinibbana of the Buddha, Upali is said to have been sixty years old, an age consistent with the stories that tell us he was ordained by the Buddha about a year after the Enlightenment, when the Buddha would have been 36 or 37 and Upali 16 or 17. According to the *Dipavamsa*, Upali continued as master of *Vinaya* for thirty years following the Buddha's parinibbana and was succeeded by Dasaka, his student/protégé. According to the Pali traditions, the most important event of Upali's career following the parinibbana was his crucial participation in the First Buddhist Council.[13]

Why Convene a Council?

'Now Monks I declare to you: all conditioned things are of a nature to decay—strive on untiringly.' Those were the Buddha's final words. After uttering them he entered the *jhanas* and the spheres and then, leaving the fourth jhana for the final time, he passed away. A week later, just before the cremation of the Buddha's body, amidst the signs and mourning, a voice rose to challenge the mourning and grief and reflection:

Sitting in the group was one Subhadda, who had gone forth late in life, and he said to these monks: 'Enough, friends, do not weep and wail! We are well rid of the Great Ascetic. We were always bothered by his saying: "it is fitting for you to do this, it is not fitting for you to do that!" Now we can do what we like, and not do what we don't like!' (Horner 1938–52, vol. V (*Cullavagga*): 394ff. [*Vinaya, Cullavagga* XI]. Cf. *Digha Nikaya* 16: *Mahaparinibbana Sutta* 6.20).

According to the *Cullavagga* account, it was this comment that alarmed Mahakassapa and inspired him to say,

Come, let us, your reverences, chant *dhamma* and discipline before what is not *dhamma* shines out and *dhamma* is withheld, before what is not discipline shines out and discipline is withheld, before those who speak what is not-*dhamma* become strong and those who speak *dhamma* become feeble, before those who speak what is not discipline become strong, and those who speak discipline become feeble (ibid.).

And so Mahakassapa selected 499 arahant-monks and Ananda to assemble in council under the patronage of King Ajatasattu at Rajagaha during the rains. There, Mahakassapa first questioned Upali about the discipline beginning with the 'first offence involving defeat' and proceeding through the entire *patimokkha* for bhikkhus and for bhikkhunis (ibid.).

Subhadda of Atuma

The person whom Mahakassapa overheard celebrating the Buddha's death was Subhadda of Atuma: *Vuddhapabbajito nahapitapubbo*, 'who had become a novice at an old age, and was formerly a barber.'

We find an explanation for Subhadda's attitude elsewhere in the *Vinayapitaka*.
The Buddha once travelled to Atuma with a large number (1,250) of monks. Living in Atuma was a man named Subhadda, who had renounced at an advanced age. He had two sons, both skilled barbers. Having heard that the Buddha was approaching, Subhadda ordered his sons:

'Go, my dears, and taking a barber's equipment, tour from house to house for *nali* measures of offerings, and collect salt and oil and husked rice and solid food, and when the Lord comes we will make him *kanji*' (Horner 1938–52, vol. VI [*Mahavagga*]: 344f. [*Mahavagga* 37ff.]).

Subhadda's attractive and accomplished sons obeyed their father and returned with substantial amounts of salt, oil, and rice. Late in the night of the Buddha's arrival in Atuma, Subhadda prepared kanji and offered it to the Lord. 'Whence comes this kanji, bhikkhu?' asked the Buddha. When Subhadda told Him, the Buddha

rebuked him, saying: 'It is not suitable, foolish man, it is not fitting, it is not becoming, it is not worthy of a recluse, it is not allowable, it is not to be done. For how can you, foolish man, one who has gone forth, cause others to take what is not allowable.' ... And having rebuked him ... he addressed the monks, saying 'monks, one who has gone forth should not make others take what is not allowable. Whoever should make others take these things, there is an offence of wrong-doing. Nor, monks, should one who was formerly a barber carry about a barber's equipment' (ibid.).

UPALI VS. DEVADATTA: THE BATTLE OVER THE UNITY OF THE ORDER

Of all the oppositions, antagonisms, and controversies described in the *Tipitaka*, none is more striking or instructive than the contrast between Upali and Devadatta. Where the Pali texts portray Devadatta as ceaselessly plotting to disrupt the Order, to dismantle and confuse it, to take it over, even to murder the Buddha, Upali stands for the exact opposite: the clear articulation of the moderate standards of behaviour that structure the Order. John Strong wisely cautions against casually accepting the depiction of Devadatta as a mere villain. He suggests that Devadatta may well have represented a particularly strong ascetic tendency in the Order and have headed a faction that contested the Buddha's because it was insufficiently severe in its lifestyle (Strong 2001: 94f.). But, even allowing that, we can understand how seriously he could have been thought to threaten the Middle Way.

In the *Tipitaka*, Upali is especially heroic in his concern to understand and to defend against schismatic activity, which the Buddha insisted repeatedly was the greatest threat to the Order's survival. Patient, careful, even pedestrian in his slow and meticulous questioning concerning what would constitute schism, Upali focuses upon and elucidates the meaning—hence, the danger—of schism. How, for example, he asks the Buddha, would one distinguish dissension, argument, and appropriate discussion from schismatic assault?

If, Upali, there are four on one side and four on another and a ninth speaks out ... this, Upali, is dissension in an Order as well as schism in an Order. Dissension in an Order, Upali, as well as schism in an Order is (due to there being) nine or more than nine. Upali, a nun does not split an Order even if she goes forward with a schism. Only a regular monk, Upali, belonging to the same communion, staying within the same boundary, splits an Order (Horner 1938–52, vol. V [*Cullavagga*]: 286 [*Cullavagga* VII]).

Upali is not satisfied simply with knowing the number of dissenting monks required for a schism to occur. 'Lord, as to the words: Schism in an Order—to what extent, Lord, can an Order become split?'

As to this, Upali, monks explain non-*dhamma* as dhamma, they explain dhamma as non-dhamma, they explain non-discipline as discipline, they explain discipline as non-discipline. They explain what was not spoken, not uttered by the Truth-finder as spoken, uttered by the Truth-finder .... (ibid.).

CONCLUSION: HEARING UPALI

We reach the end of this cursory exploration of the *Tipitaka* disappointed that we have only learned a little about the life and person of Upali, the barber become arahant. But if he does remain something of a shadow, he is a particularly expressive and instructive shade. Perhaps more clearly and helpfully than any other person celebrated in Buddhist lore, Upali embodies and affirms a teaching central to the Buddha's message and to its power through centuries and in our own time: it is our actions that define us.

That the Buddha was born into a 'pre-caste' environment is not necessarily called into question by the frequent and obvious references to social inequalities and disadvantages in the Pali texts from the beginning. But while it is also not to be denied that Buddhist teachings initially were conveyed most insistently to elite relatives, the Buddha appears always to have responded warmly and positively when approached by the humble and despised.

Among the most charming and engaging passages in early Buddhist literature are the lyrics attributed to distinguished bhikkhus and bhikkhunis who achieved arahatship: the *Theragatha* and the *Therigatha*. In these lyrics, we overhear the personal experiences and the emotional responses of Buddhists of all backgrounds.

Sunita, the sweeper, movingly narrates the circumstances of his entering the Order:

620. I was born in a humble family, poor, having little food;
     my work was lowly—I was a disposer of [withered] flowers.
621. Despised by men, disregarded and reviled, making my mind humble
     I paid homage to many people.
622. Then I saw the enlightened one, revered by the Order of bhikkhus,
     the great hero, entering the supreme city of the Magadhas.
623. Throwing down my carrying pole, I approached to pay homage to him;
     out of sympathy for me the best of men stood still.
624. Having paid homage to the teacher's feet, standing on one side
     I then asked the best of all creatures for admission in the Order.
625. Then the merciful teacher, sympathetic to the whole world, said to me
     'Come Bhikkhu.' That was my ordination (Norman 1969: 62 [Oldenberg
     and Pischel 1999: 63f.]).

Upali, too, speaks to us from the *Theragatha*. We have only three lyrics. Predictably didactic rather than ecstatic, they lack the emotional power of Sunita's recollections. Yet, in them, we can be confident we hear what Upali and Buddhist tradition would regard as his principal instruction and, at the same time, an apt if indirect description of Upali himself:

249. Having departed from the world in faith, a novice newly gone forth should
     associate with good friends who are clean-living, not relaxing.

250. Having departed from the world in faith, a novice newly gone forth, a wise bhikkhu living in the Order should learn the discipline.

251. Having departed from the world in faith, a novice newly gone forth should wander undistracted, skilled in what is proper and not proper (ibid., 29 [Oldenberg and Pischel 1999: 31].

NOTES

1. Other than beginning to assemble information about Upali in a single place, this modest essay claims little originality. Further investigation remains for the future. Comprehensive examination of Vinaya materials from other schools [viz. *Mulasarvastivada, Sarvastivada, Mahisasaka, Dharmaguptaka*, and *Mahasamghika*] is only one of several additional tasks that will be required to inform a properly comprehensive account of the representation of Upali in Buddhist traditions.

2. LaMotte characterizes the several ancient Buddhist traditions concerning the composition of the vinaya as 'multiple, incoherent, and contradictory'. For his overview see LaMotte 1958: 192–7. The *Dipavamsa* seems to suggest that Upali succeeded the Buddha as head of the Order. Its account of the Councils is frequently muddled; but it may be saying that Upali, as master of Vinaya, was indeed the principal authority following the Buddha's parinibbana. See Oldenberg 1879: 134–9 and 143–6. (*Dipavamsa* 4.3, 4.7–8, 4.28–38, 5.7, 5.11–12, and 5.76–103 passim). Bareau (1995b: 449) supports this view, declaring that the *Dipavamsa* affirms 'Upali prend la tête de la Communauté dès la mort de Buddha et la dirige pendant 30 ans.'

3. While all the distinguished scholars listed in the references below have helped me substantially, it is a pleasure to acknowledge how much I have profited in particular from Gail Omvedt's perspectives and insights in her recent *Buddhism in India* (2003).

4. Horner 1938–52. vol. II (*Suttavibhanga*): 176 (*Vinaya* IV.6).

5. Stimulating and informative comments on the meanings of hair in South Asia are found in Olivelle 1998. In the same collection, Alf Hiltebeitel and Barbara Miller's consideration of Buddhist reflections on the sense of hair is imaginative and helpful (1998: 1–9).

6. 'In insulting speech there is an offence of expiation,' Horner 1938–52. vol. II (*Suttavibhanga*): 173–85 (*Vinaya* IV.3–11). This 'abusive language' is the second of 92 offenses (out of a total of 227) in the *bhikkhupatimokkha* that require simple expiation.

7. 'The *jataka* of Gangapala', in Jones 1949–56. vol. III: 178–93.

8. Malalasekara 1983. vol. I: 410, referring to *Apadana* I: 37ff. Interestingly, it

is also said that the anti-hero Subhadda was a barber in this life because he had insulted a paccekabuddha in a previous birth. The fact that Upali, great defender and teacher of the monastic code, should have been accused of insulting a paccekabuddha, a somewhat mysterious figure in Buddhist lore who is characterized by his attainment of enlightenment without the capacity to teach, is also intriguing.

9. Nanamoli and Bodhi 1995: 477–92 (*Majjhima Nikaya* 56). Davis (1931: 398) suggested that it was this Upali, 'the cultured Jain', who became the great authority in vinaya and dismissed as 'mere legend' references to an Upali who was 'former valet or batman of the young Sakyans'.

10. LaMotte (1958: 223) suggests '44 pN'.

11. It does not seem appropriate to call him 'king'.

12. See comments in Malalasekara 1983. vol. I: 524, 927, *et passim*.

13. It would not serve my purposes to discuss here the question of the historicity of the Rajagaha Council. LaMotte (1958: 136–54) helpfully summarizes the long-continuing dispute about the 1st and 2nd Buddhist Councils and concludes that 'il serait imprudent de se prononcer pour ou contre l'historicité des conciles' (1958: 153).

REFERENCES

Bailey, Greg, and Ian Mabbett. 2003. *The Sociology of Early Buddhism*. Cambridge: Cambridge University Press.

Bareau, Andre. 1955. *Les premiers conciles bouddhiques*. Paris: Presses universitaires de France.

———. 1995a [1991]. 'Les agissements de Devadatta selon les chapitres relatifs au schisme dans les divers *Vinayapitaka*'. *Recherches sur la biographie du Buddha dans les Sutrapitaka et les Vinayapitaka anciens*. vol. III. *Articles complementaires*. Paris: EFEO.

———. 1995b [1991]. 'La date du Nirvana'. In *Recherches sur la biographie ...*, vol. III.

Davis, Caroline August Foley Rhys. 1931. *Sakya: or, Buddhist Origins*. London: Kegan Paul, Trench, Trubner & Co., Ltd.

Gombrich, Richard F. 1988. *Theravada Buddhism: A Social History from Ancient Benares to Modern Colombo*. London and New York: Routledge and Kegan Paul.

Hiltebeitel, Alf and Barbara D. Miller (eds). 1998. *Hair: Its Power and Meaning in Asian Cultures*. Albany: State University of New York Press.

Horner, Isaline Blew (trans.). 1938–52. *The Book of the Discipline*. 6 vols. London: Pali Text Society.

Jones, J.J. (trans.). 1949–56. *The Mahavastu*. 3 vols. London: Luzac & Co., Ltd.

LaMotte, Etienne. 1958. *Histoire du bouddhisme indienne: des origines a l'ere Saka*. Bibliotheque du Museon, vol. 43. Louvain: University of Louvain.

Malalasekara, G.P. 1983 [1938]. *Dictionary of Pali Proper Names*. 2 vols. Delhi: Munshiram Manoharlal.

Nakamura, Hajime. 2000 [1969, ca. 1992]. *Gotama Buddha: A Biography Based on the Most Reliable Texts*. vol. I, translated by Gaynor Sekimori (trans.) Second edition. Tokyo: Kosei Publishing Co.

Nanamoli, Bhikkhu, and Bodhi Bhikkhu (trans.). 1995. *The Middle Length Discourses of the Buddha: A New Translation of the Majjhima Nikaya*. Boston: Wisdom Publications.

Norman, K.R. (trans.). 1969. *The Elders' Verses I: Theragatha*. London: Pali Text Society/Luzac and Co. Ltd.

Oldenberg, Hermann (ed.). 1879–83. *The Vinaya Pitakam*. 5 vols. London: Williams and Norgate.

—— (ed. and trans.). 1879. *The Dipavamsa: An Ancient Buddhist Historical Record*. London: Williams and Norgate.

—— and Richard Pischel (eds). 1999. *The Thera- and Therigatha: Stanzas Ascribed to Elders of the Buddhist Order of Recluses*. Second edition, revised by K.R. Norman and L. Alsdorf. Oxford: Pali Text Society.

Olivelle, Patrick. 1998. 'Hair and Society: Social Significance of Hair in South Asian Traditions'. In Hiltebeitel and Miller (eds). *Hair*, pp. 11–49.

Omvedt, Gail. 2003. *Buddhism in India: Challenging Brahmanism and Caste*. New Delhi/Thousand. Oaks/London: Sage Publications.

Przyluski, Jean. 1926–8. *Le concile de Rajagrha*. Paris: Librairie Orientaliste Paul Geuthner.

Senart, Emile (ed.). 1882–97. *Le Mahavastu*. 3 vols. Paris: Imprimerie nationale.

Strong, John S. 2001. *The Buddha: A Short Biography*. Oxford: OneWorld.

12

ART AND IDENTITY*

The Rise of a New Buddhist Imagery

Gary Michael Tartakov

If you want to gain self-respect, change your religion.
If you want to create a cooperating society, change your religion.
If you want power, change your religion.
If you want equality, change your religion.

—B.R. Ambedkar

B.R. Ambedkar was born on 14 April 1891. By the time of his death on 6 December 1956, Maitreya Ambedkar—as he has come to be known by some—succeeded in bringing Buddhism back to the land of its origins. Ambedkar's conversion to Buddhism was largely a response to the oppression of the Brahmanical-caste system. He was born an untouchable Mahar. In the nineteenth-century Mahars were 'village servants', mostly landless labourers, outside the castes acceptable to Hindus. Ambedkar was thus among the one-seventh to one-fifth of India's population condemned to a life of social ostracism, which he later likened to the situation of African-Americans in the United States.[1] His conversion to Buddhism, which disclaimed caste, was a carefully planned remedy for the social distinctions so basic to Hinduism.

*This is an abridged version of an article of the same title that appeared in *Art Journal*, vol. 49 (1990), pp. 409–16. Published by the College Art Association.

On 14 October 1956, a decade after Independence and precisely two decades after his original declaration of his intention to convert, Ambedkar took his Buddhist *diksha* (initiation) at Nagpur. On that day and the next he personally led the conversion of about one-half million who had come for that purpose. By the time of the 1961 census there were 3.25 million Buddhists in India. Millions more have converted since.[2] For Ambedkar and his many associates and followers, the conversion was not merely a practical matter, but one of deep, psychological significance. They were rejecting a system that condemned them, but they were also committing themselves to an ideology that disputed the possibility of karma, transmigration, and a divine hierarchy by birth, embracing instead a faith that stressed the equality of all human beings. In repudiating the power and prestige of the Brahmans and their creed, they were choosing an alternative that promised them progress without limits, that from the beginning rejected the idea of untouchability.[3]

Ambedkar's epithet, Maitreya, carried significance in the movement he founded, for Buddhist tradition held that after the death of the Shakyamuni (the historical Buddha) another Buddha, or Bodhisattva (perfectly enlightened being), called Maitreya would appear on earth to bring a renewed enlightenment. Significantly, Ambedkar's conversion coincided with a worldwide celebration of the Buddha Jayanti, the 2500th anniversary of Shakyamuni's enlightenment.[4] As in this adoption of the epithet Maitreya, the new Buddhists[5] have resurrected and revivified a number of traditional Buddhist concepts and imageries. In the interest of exploring, defining, and legitimizing their Buddhist identity, they have also taken symbols and motifs from Buddhist imagery abroad and invited new imagery to fit their modern situation.

The reuse of Buddhist monuments of the past, with their powerful resonance in pan-Indian elite and popular cultures, has been employed to sanction the new faith by enhancing its identification with established tradition. Beginning in the nineteenth century, British and Indian writers raised a laudatory literary and scholarly appreciation around the rediscovery of India's Buddhist past. The intellectual richness of this tradition and the aesthetic power of its magnificent remains elevated Indian Buddhism in the eyes of the British and of the outside world, and consequently of India's modern elite. In adopting Buddhism, the Mahars and others who followed Ambedkar's lead became heirs to India's vast store of ancient Buddhist imagery. In much the same way that the

Republic of India—also following Ambedkar's lead—found peculiarly Indian, transcommunal symbols in the ancient Ashoka's four-lion standard and wheel, the Buddhists adopted an already established symbolism that expressed not only their aspirations for the future but their connection with a highly honoured Indian past, providing them with a direct link to a significant portion of India's ancient remains. After centuries of denial of entry to temples and of association with the great events and monuments of the past on the basis of caste, they now claimed a great history of their own. Indeed, the Buddhists' monumental temple remains and stone sculpture are even older, and so, by some measure, more prestigious, than those of the Hindus.[6]

Thus in Maharashtra, where most of the new Buddhists are concentrated, they have taken the world-renowned Buddhist monuments and imagery of the west Indian rock-cut temples as their own (Fig. 12.1). Turning their backs on the Hindu temples from which they were for so long denied entrance, they have established a special interest in Karla, Ajanta, Ellora, and numerous other sites of major cultural significance and antiquity. Though they have not been able to take possession of these monuments, most of which are under the control of the Archaeological Survey of India, they have asserted their new identity with them through visits that amount to pilgrimage. In this way they gain the access to a cosmic identification denied to them in many Hindu shrines.[7] One of my most vivid experiences in India was to witness Ellora's Vishvakarma *caitya*—a grey, twelve-century-old aesthetic relic and one of India's best-known historical and tourist monuments—transformed into a living rainbow of actualized faith by a gathering of local Buddhists. Here, the despised descendants of a glorious tradition endowed it with a new legitimacy.

The vast store of ancient Buddhist imagery also serves as a source of emblems and decoration for both public monuments and private homes. In Hindu homes one finds *puja* (worship) rooms and decorative elements filled with deities and pictures of well-known Hindu monuments and in Muslim homes or shops, images of the Kaaba or Taj Mahal; in Buddhist homes one finds replicas of famous Buddhas and photographs of important monuments, such as Sanchi, Sarnath, and Bodhgaya. Already famous and commonly reproduced as India's national treasures, these monuments are once again peculiarly Buddhist. In Mahar homes, and even in some former community temples,

Fig. 12.1 Cave 19, *ca.* 475, Ajanta, Maharashtra

Buddhist images have replaced those of Pandurang and Rakmabai and other Hindu deities formerly honoured, but never so truly available.[8]

It is important to recognize that these Buddhist images are not treated in the same way as the Hindu ones they have replaced. Ambedkar's rationalism goes further than many sorts of Buddhism in flatly denying the existence of gods, and so these images are taken, not as idols for offerings or devotion, but as representations of beings to be respected and emulated (Macy and Zelliot 1980: 146). The garlands placed upon them signify respect, not supplication.

A second source of ready-made imagery is the international Buddhist tradition, which has intensified its involvement in India over the past two centuries, as British colonial interests located important Buddhist sites and made them accessible. When the wealthy Birla family chose to build a Buddhist temple in Bombay in the early 1950s, the Japanese made available images and priests. The Buddhist conversion movement has found similar responses from surrounding Buddhist communities. I have seen Tibetan, Thai, Burmese, Japanese, and Sri Lankan images donated to various new Buddhist temples.[9] A good example of this is the life-size, fibreglass seated Shakyamuni from Sri Lanka in the Shanti Vihara at Nagpur (Fig. 12.2). This imagery too serves strongly in terms of legitimation and identification. It allows the Buddhists to decorate their modest temples with luxurious and impressive images quite beyond their modest means. Whatever the theological viewpoint, this is an important issue for a largely impoverished community. More importantly perhaps, this usage offers a powerless minority community direct connections with a powerful international Buddhist world. As the new Buddhists identify themselves by and with these finely crafted images and the creed for which they stand, they also identify themselves with the international success and power of that world, through the actual possession of these images.[10]

More interesting than these uses of past or imported imagery, however, is the new imagery that serves to express these new Buddhists' particular history and aspirations. This art allows a more direct manifestation of the community's creativity, and harnesses that creativity to one of art's most significant potentials, its ability to explore identity. If the adoption of traditional Buddhist forms allows the community to signal its identification with that tradition and to legitimize itself through this prestigious connection, the creation of new imagery allows

Fig. 12.2 *Shakyamuni Buddha in Meditation, ca.* 1975, fibreglass, donated by the V.A. Sugathadasa and A.B. Gomes Trust, Sri Lanka, to the Shanti Vihara, Shantivana, Nagpur

it to explore its interests and destiny as a modern Indian community struggling for its place in the contemporary world.

Public Buddhist monuments are mostly images of the historical Buddha, Shakyamuni, Ambedkar, and Mahatma Jotirao Phule (the nineteenth-century Maharashtrian leader regarded as Ambedkar's major predecessor). These statues in the new imagery are found at crossroads, public squares, and the entrances to Buddhist neighbourhoods or institutions, in the same kinds of places we are used to seeing other major national figures, such as Mahatma Gandhi, Shivaji, and Subhash Chandra Bose. The Ambedkar statues indicate the presence of the people who have chosen to transform their lives through his teachings.

The style of these monuments varies greatly from a highly perceptual to a more generalized realism, depending upon the nature of the patronage. The monuments in front of the Parliament building in New Delhi and the old Secretariat building in Mumbai are realistic works building in bronze. Those by the roadside in Karnataka and Maharashtra are blander, and often cruder, popular productions in plaster or concrete. Whether the variations in style have more to do with the availability of funds or intentional choice is not yet clear to me. It is possible that there has not yet been enough history to develop the variety of alternatives from which a conscious choice can be made. Nor is there a centralized authority to codify stylistic or iconographic design. As in the past, style is essentially a matter of region, era, and economic support, not of ideology. Most modern Buddhist art shares the same generalized naturalism of bright colours and somewhat stylized features common to other popular imagery in India.

A typical monumental portrait of Ambedkar can be seen at Hasrur, on the highway leading north from Aurangabad to Ajanta (Fig. 12.3). In the spirit of India's traditional religious imagery of the past two thousand years, where such images have much the same style and iconography regardless of where they are located, Ambedkar is presented as a man in a blue business suit, white shirt, and red tie, with a fountain pen in his pocket and a book in his hand. He is bare-headed, his dark hair neatly combed down, and he wears a pair of black-rimmed spectacles. He stands squarely in what the classical iconographic texts called *samabhanga*, or no bends. In the context of Indian religious imagery, this figure makes three points: this is a city man, a man of learning, and *only* a man—not a god.

As a Westerner who first saw this image in the mid-1960s, I found the style immediately called to mind contemporaneous American Pop art, with its use of blandly simplified realism, brightly coloured surfaces, and deadpan expression. But this is how the uninitiated usually respond to things they do not understand, explaining them by distorting them into versions of things they do know. For Buddhists and other people living in Maharashtra, the image is a simple but clear expression of the Mahar's own modest yet cosmic desires and potentiality. Here, those who had been forbidden a public presence announce both their presence and their newly claimed right to a place *at* the centre of creation, by displaying an image of the Bombay statesman who pled their cause before the world and taught them that they were more than the 'children of god', or *Harijan*s, as Gandhi called them. They are the followers of Babasaheb Ambedkar. The garland around the statue's neck is not part of its structure but something added by his respectful followers. Like the image's fresh coat of paint, the garland indicates the community's active presence.

Fig. 12.3 B.R. Ambedkar statue, *ca.* 1960. Facing west on Ajanta Road, north of Aurangabad

The relatively standardized iconography has only existed for a few short decades and has yet to be fixed in a text. Ambedkar's blue business suit is as regular as Shakyamuni Buddha's orange *samghati* robe—I have never seen another garment or colour used[11]—and it is as meaningful. Where the samghati's patchwork of rags stands for Shakyamuni's presence as a wandering beggar, the blue suit indicates a man of modern education and civic status. The book in his hand augments this concept: the enlightened one of the modern era rejects the hierarchies of the past, handed down in canonical texts that the lower castes and outcastes were forbidden to hear, see, or teach. Instead, faith is placed in modern secular learning and civil disputation open to all. When the book is identified, it is the Indian constitution, sometimes it is labelled 'Bharat' (India), but it can also be taken more generally to represent the value Ambedkar and the community place upon education and the secular culture of the cities.

Most often Ambedkar stands with one leg slightly advanced as if walking, his arm raised and index finger extended as if pointing (Fig. 12.4). This particular gesture, which seems to have no narrowly agreed upon definition within the community as yet, does seem to have a generally understood significance. To his followers, Ambedkar's hand gesture stands for oratory or teaching, both activities with which he is popularly associated. Indeed, Ambedkar's *The Buddha and His Dhamma*, the bible of the new movement, has a line drawing of this very hand pose on each page. It is, apparently, the new gesture, or *mudra*, of teaching.[12]

This image of a Bombay lawyer is in striking contrast to the standard Hindu god depicted in the traditional garb of dhoti or sari, with multiple limbs and fantastic attributes. The contemporary Buddhist imagery combines elements of past art with new features, connecting past traditions with a distinctly different present and future. Seeing Ambedkar's image in tandem with the more traditional one of Shakyamuni, as they are regularly shown, emphasizes just this juxtaposition (Figs 12.4, 12.5, and 12.10). Following the rationalism of Ambedkar's interpretation of Buddhist doctrine, his portraits emphasize his humanity. In this vision, we return to one of the earliest attitudes of Buddhist theology, which claims that the Buddha is not a god but an enlightened man. Pictorializing the issue proclaims it.

In the Ambedkar image's formal pose, and in the repetition of the pose and iconography, we see a construction of the formal identity

Fig. 12.4 B.R. Ambedkar and Shakyamuni Buddha statues at the entrance to
the Tarodi Settlement, Nagpur

of Indian traditional art. Thus the Ambedkar image is not only
identifiable but comparable with the icons of the hegemonic traditions.
Variations in its form have been elaborated to explore its meaning.
One Ambedkar image in Aurangabad, for instance, has beneath it a
wheel flanked by seated deer, a familiar composition from ancient art
of nearby Ajanta, symbolizing the wheel of the law put into motion
by Shakyamuni's first teaching in the deer park at Sarnath. Though
the intent here seems to be projection of Ambedkar as a teacher, it
also likens him to Shakyamuni.

The least expensive and so most popular of all religious images
in India are the ubiquitous chromolithographs made by the Sharmas
and their competitors, which include images of every sect and popular
hero.[13] Among these images, which are created for Buddhists by artists
who are not themselves Buddhists, we find Buddha, Ambedkar (Fig.
12.5), and Phule. Ambedkar is here shown in a sympathetic bust portrait,
an ethereal vision of Shakyamuni Buddha with one hand raised in the
abhaya gesture for dispelling fear floating behind him.

A poster using Ambedkar's photograph to call a mass civil rights
rally in downtown Mumbai also has images of an ancient Bodhisattva
and a black panther (Fig. 12.6). It links the contemporary Buddhist

Fig. 12.5 B.G. Sharma, *Sri Ambedkar, ca.* 1960, chromolithograph

Fig. 12.6 Dalit Panther poster, December 1988, Mumbai

movement to its international history through the eighth-century Bodhisattva from Thailand[14] and to an international civil rights movement through the 1960s and 1970s iconography of the American Black Panther party.[15] The Dalit Panthers, who sponsored the rally, are a politicized movement of the Left, composed largely of Buddhists. This combination of images indicates the Buddhists' exploration of their identity and potential. While some more conservative Buddhists might reject the panther symbolism, some Marxist Dalits might reject the Bodhisattva. In this poster, the polarities of the community are embraced. This is more than just quotation and combination of ancient and contemporary imagery; it is conscious exploration of the Buddhist community's identity and of the meaning of the Buddhism it is developing.

The site of Ambedkar's funeral pyre, or *samadhi*, on the beach at Dadar, in Mumbai, is marked by a domed memorial in a small garden. Pilgrimage is common and a particularly large *darshan*, or witness, is held each year on 6 December, the anniversary of his 'death' (Fig. 12.7). The Ambedkar Memorial Shrine, which amounts to what in Buddhist terminology is called a *chaitya* or stupa, combines traditional and modern elements. The most striking traditional elements are the half-round dome rising from a square platform, and the *torana* gateway

Fig. 12.7 Ambedkar Memorial Shrine, Sivaji Park, Dadar, Mumbai

(arches) on the south and north of the platform. The relatively squat proportions of the wall supporting the dome possibly relate to the relief imagery of ancient stupas in central India (Zimmer 1955: vol. 2, plate 18), and the square platform may refer to the stupas of ancient India's northwest (for instance, Huntington and Huntington 1985: plate 8.8). The gateways, on the other hand, are similar to those depicted in reliefs from both central and southern regions of ancient India.[16] The design is, in any case, not a copy of older imagery but a new synthesis.

Beyond these general forms and proportions, similarities with past structures cease. The body of this stupa, like many, if not most, religious structures built in India today, is constructed in reinforced concrete, rather than the traditional brick or stone. This new and structurally liberating medium has allowed the creation of a stupa type largely unknown to historians of Indian art.[17] Unlike the ancient stupas, which are nearly all solid masses, the Ambedkar chaitya is a hollow, inhabitable shell, containing chambers with figurative imagery as well as a portion of Ambedkar's ashes, which can be seen through openings in the dome and base and approached directly.

The other great site of the new Buddhist geography, the location of Ambedkar's conversion and the first mass conversion, is the Diksha Bhumi (conversion ground) at Nagpur, where a great stupa hall has been constructed.[18] Perhaps it would be more useful to see this as a hall containing a stupa. There is a model of the structure, designed by the architect Sheo Dan Mal, at the site (Fig. 12.8). Its extremely low base, upper walkway, and flatter profile resemble the ancient stupas of Sanchi (Fig. 12.9) and Amaravati. It also has northern style toranas and a number of rather new features such as an embanked, grassy platform and corner fountains.

This is a great stupa-shaped auditorium for mass community gatherings. While the old stupas are sites commemorating the great events of the Buddha's life, relics of the faith, or, most often, the Buddha's passing, these new stupas are sites for staging the new Buddhists' future. At Nagpur, the hall's basement contains living spaces for bhikkhus (members of the monastic brotherhood) and smaller meeting rooms, which are marked on the exterior by the windows lining the embanked basement. Although the arched form of the windows refers to the traditional past, the very presence of windows indicates the transformation of the stupa's content. At the centre of the structure at basement level, a small stupa marks the spot of the great conversion, another connection

Fig. 12.8 Model of Babasaheb Ambedkar Memorial Complex, designed by Sheo Dan Mal. Diksha Bhumi, Nagpur (begun 1982)

Fig. 12.9 Great Stupa, first century BCE–CE, Sanchi

with the past. The current needs and interests of the Buddhists, however, are represented by new forms that shape a different future. Commemorating the original conversion, Diksha Bhumi Day, one of the community's four great annual observances, has its major ceremony here.

Another kind of building constructed by the community are meeting halls, which it calls *viharas*. While the term viharas traditionally referred to monastic dormitories, and bhikkhus still sometimes stay in them, this is not their main function today. Nor are viharas temples, which they resemble with their images of deities at one end and even towers over these deities. The common Marathi terms for temple, *mandir* and *deul*, are carefully avoided when speaking of viharas (Macy and Zelliot 1980: 146). The new viharas differ significantly from the Buddhist temples built by the Mahabodhi Society at Sarnath or the Birla family at Mumbai, which resemble the temples of the ancient past. Indeed, these viharas have a different purpose altogether.

Like the Diksha Bhumi hall, viharas are gathering places that contain commemorative imagery. The images placed at the end of the hall resemble the sanctum images of the Hindu temple, but here they are part of the human space, not separated in a chamber for ritual purity, with attending priests. People do not pray or make vows to these images; they are memorials, not icons. Some may have rooms for bhikkhus, but the bhikkhus' purpose is to instruct and lead the community, not to attend to the images.

Viharas present a visual imagery that requires care to read. Though not worship halls, they take a form that is only slightly different, encompassing altarlike platforms and images. The apparent contradictions seem heightened when we witness a scene approximating worship, such as the one shown in Triratna Buddha Vihara in Mumbai (Fig. 12.10). Here is a community in the process of transformation. The common Indian form of the temple hall, altar, and worshipper have been altered only slightly, but the change is highly significant. In a Tibetan context, the Tibetan Buddha image on this altar would be worshipped with devotional faith; in another era, the bhikkhu would be a priest or a worshipper and the woman holding the incense would be praying. But in this context, where the ideology of devotion is explicitly rejected and an ideology of rationalized action is proclaimed, the woman standing between the ancient imagery of the Buddha on one side and

Fig. 12.10 Interior. Triratna Buddha Vihara, Hanuman Nagar Government Colony, Mumbai

the modern imagery of Ambedkar before Parliament on the other is offering homage, not worship. Old forms are transformed by new meanings.

The viharas are used for community meetings and functions of all sorts, from Buddhist education and political action to pre-school. The Buddhist teachings offered there, called *wandana*, are memorial services centred on the Pali texts of the Theravada canon. Since they are not worship services, they are never called by common terms like puja, used to designate worship. For the most part, they are led by lay people, men and women. Discussions begin with an honouring of the Buddha and Ambedkar, but not a call for their blessings.

The Shanti Vihara, at Shantivana, on the outskirts of Nagpur, shows the same contradictions (Fig. 12.11). A modest brick structure finished in brightly painted plaster, it has a gathering hall with one image at the far end (Fig. 12.2), surrounded by rooms for the bhikkhus and others who may reside or meet there. Unlike most viharas, it has the tower that marks the traditional Indian temple, here assuming the form of a small stupa. And indeed it is intended to house relics of Ambedkar, which have been donated to the Shantivana complex. The forms are thus not so unlike those of a Hindu temple. It is clearly a

Fig. 12.11 Shanti Vihara, designed by W.M. Godbole, Shantivana, Nagpur

religious structure, with which all Indians are familiar.[19] But the use
of the building is to link the messages of Ambedkar and the Buddha,
and to transform former habits of supplication into those of social
action. W.M. Godbole, a long-time associate of Ambedkar's and
organizer of the great diksha, is the vihara's designer. It is part of an as
yet unfinished seminary complex for training bhikkhus in the
evangelical work of spreading Ambedkar's message, in which social
transformation takes a religious form.

Finally, an aspect of the new Buddhist art we need to consider is
the work of individual artists and designers. Ram Tirpude, a local Nagpur
artist and perhaps the first new Buddhist artist, began the community's
aesthetic activity by giving already existing imagery a new Buddhist
use. Tirpude designed the stage at the Diksha Bhumi for the original
conversion with materials at hand to fashion a miniature of the Sanchi
stupa as a canopy over the heads of Ambedkar and his associates.

The common situation of Buddhist artists today is seen in the
work of P.B. Ramteke. The most popular Buddhist works are portraits
of Ambedkar, either taken from the original or based on surviving
likenesses in photographs. Ramteke's *Babasaheb Ambedkar* of 1987
falls into the latter category. An oil painting based on a photograph, it
shows the familiar bespectacled face, with only parts of the coat and tie.

More personal than some images, intensely human, it is unquestionably a successful attempt to bring out the acutely penetrating, yet compassionate gaze of the young man who would become a Maitreya for his community and modern India. The original oil was done as the basis for a widely available, inexpensive colour lithograph (Fig. 12.12).

This community-oriented, inspirational art is the equivalent of the traditional art of solidarity and identity found in most religions or political movements in the world. Artists may express themselves either personally or impersonally in this vein; indeed, the B.G. Sharma

Fig. 12.12 P.B. Ramteke, *Babasaheb Ambedkar*, 1988, photo offset reproduction of original oil painting, 15 × 17 inches. Private collection

lithograph (Fig. 12.5) and other commercial works, as we have seen, may be by artists who are not themselves Buddhists. The primary point of these works is what they say, not how or who says it. This is an art of community, of emblems of identification with group ideals. It stands in distinct contrast to the individualist art of the gallery world of the bourgeois cities.

In the case of Ramteke, we have an academically trained artist with a gallery career quite separate from his religious art. In his gallery art Ramteke may occasionally, but only subtly, reveal elements of his Buddhist orientation. While his Buddhist art is naturalistic and communal, his gallery art is essentially abstract and personal in both form and content.

Ramteke sees his gallery work as having developed in stages over the years from a colourful diagrammatic style in the surrealistic vein of Paul Klee or Joan Miró—both of whose influences he cites with alacrity—to increasingly abstract formulations. The stage he reached in 1988 and 1989, he feels, expresses his independence from models and his most particular vision. Of the three dozen works of his I have seen, only *Joy of Unity* (Fig. 12.13) of 1987 has an identifiable Buddhist content. An essentially abstract design of colourful insect, reptile, and bird-like shapes flickering about a reticulated plane of grays and whites, the work on closer inspection reveals a statement on the harmony of India's religions. The dark rectangle at the bottom represents a structure decked with motifs symbolizing India's different faiths: a trident for Shaivism, a cross for Christianity, and a half-moon for Islam. These forms are contained within a curving grey form recognizable as the outline of a Buddhist stupa that unites the other religions. In India, as everywhere in the modern bourgeois world, gallery art is essentially personal and decorative. To succeed in that world, religious artists must leave their social interests relatively obscured.

The study of this new Buddhist art offers a variety of useful insights, not the least of which help us to understand earlier Buddhist art. Since ancient India's Buddhist tradition came to an end without leaving a literature explaining its beliefs, it is difficult to interpret a great deal of the symbolism and instrumentality of the remains. The presence of this new Buddhist tradition suggests alternative readings for many items about which we now can only speculate. It can offer expressive interpretations for objects and texts whose functional

Fig. 12.13 P.B. Ramteke, *Joy of Unity*, 1987, oil on canvas, 30 × 36 inches. Private collection

context we have lost. More important, it can provide evidence of a fluidity of possible meanings in contrast to the limited ones offered by a literal reading of texts.

Finally, and most significantly, the new Buddhist imagery gives us a genuine revolutionary art. In a discipline that spends much of its effort considering whether or not selected imagery is 'revolutionary', or emblematic of change, or even a facilitator of change, here is an art that is an instrument of social change of the most vital kind. India's new Buddhists are a community in the process of a profound revolutionary change, which is using visual imagery as a major means to accomplish that transformation.

Normally, when we speak of revolutionary artistic forms in western art criticism or history we refer to normal novelty. Art that has a technically unusual surface form—a new decorative style, more often than not—we term revolutionary. The changes involved are significant only in the world of aesthetic decoration and elite cultural discourse. Most likely they involve no development in meaning and certainly none in the social or material reality of their producers and consumers— their creators and buyers, if you will. This use of the concept of a revolutionary art is largely a matter of inflated rhetoric.

The art of these new Buddhists is different in two ways. First, it is an art stylistically and pictorially conventional in the extreme. There is no formal novelty. Changes from the past are essentially matters of content. Second, it is an art of social and material transformation, a significant tool in the transformation of Indian culture and society. The identities it portrays are precisely those being used by the Buddhist community to reshape its psychology and reorient its social and material life. To the degree that it recognizes the Buddhist personality and focuses energy on new and different statuses and material possibilities via education, election, and conversion, the new Buddhist art is a materially powerful and socially significant instrument for change.

This may not be the usual way to speak of revolutionary art, but we have so thoroughly lost track of our basic meanings, and taken the analogy of Pablo Picasso's and Jackson Pollock's 'revolutionary' transformations of decorative vocabulary so seriously, that it is refreshing to have a genuine revolutionary imagery to remind us of the difference between the analogy and the real thing and to point out how much time we spend on the trivial imagery, which our wealthy compete to possess, and how little time on the imagery that defines our living reality.

NOTES

1. Ambedkar lived on the edge of Harlem while attending Columbia University. His writings include numerous comparisons of India's

untouchables and American Blacks. The most comprehensive biography of Ambedkar is Keer 1962.

2. Since the 1990 Parliament has readmitted those converting to Buddhism to eligibility for the Scheduled Caste reservations in education, government jobs, etc., that they had previously lost upon conversion, this number is expected to double; see *The Times of India*, 8 May 1990.

3. Ambedkar's interpretation of Buddhism is supremely rational and relatively distinct from the many other schools and sects now in existence. Its prime text is his posthumously published *The Buddha and His Dhamma* (Ambedkar 1974). Ambedkar's interpretations are compared with others in Macy and Zelliot 1980: 133–53 and in Goyal 1987: 412–23.

4. The international Buddha Jayanti, marking 2500 years after Shakyamuni's enlightenment (or his birth or *nirvana*, depending on your source), was celebrated in India, Sri Lanka, and around the world in 1956. Since the Buddhist calendar and its dates, like the Christian, are disputed, all Buddhists do not agree precisely on the same dates for these events. Nor do all new Buddhists feel comfortable with the title Maitreya for Ambedkar, some seeing this as a Mahayana concept, which does not fit their more Theravada vision.

5. Some have called them new Buddhists or neo-Buddhists, but many among them resent the implication that they are less authentic than other Buddhist sects. Keer reports Ambedkar telling reporters on the evening before his conversion that what he was initiating was a 'neo-Buddhism or Navayan[a]' (Keer 1962: 495).

6. One of the most interesting facts of Indian art history is the early avoidance of permanent materials by the Brahmanical worshippers. There exists Buddhist art in significant amounts from the third century BCE, but little Brahmanical art in stone before the third century CE.

7. Though the practice of untouchability was outlawed soon after Independence, and entrance to public temples guaranteed to all and enforced by civil authorities, there is still in actuality a good amount of discrimination. Seventy-one per cent of villages bar former Untouchables from local Hindu temples, according to the 1978–9 *Report of the Commissioner for Scheduled Castes and Scheduled Tribes*. In the numerous private temples, civil codes do not require openness.

8. This includes even deities such as Matamaya, the Mahar smallpox goddess, which belonged to the untouchable community rather than to the Brahmans and to which there was never a bar.

9. A Tibetan image occupies the central place at the Triratna Buddha Vihara, Bandra East, Mumbai (Fig. 12.10). There is a life-size Thai bronze image

in Nagpur's Indra Buddha Vihar. A Burmese image sits on a small altar at the Shantivana, next to the reliquary with Ambedkar's relics, Nagpur. A Japanese image can be found in Nagpur's Ananda Vihara.

10. As in the Shanti Vihara image, there is commonly a dedicatory inscription giving the name of the donor.

11. The recent dedication of a portrait in the Lok Sabha (Lower House of the Indian Parliament in New Delhi) showing Ambedkar in the long caftan often worn by Jawaharlal Nehru, India's first prime minister, was met with instant criticism by his followers. It was not because of lack of proof that he had on occasion worn such a garment in his days as a cabinet minister—photographs of him dressed in a caftan were, in fact, the basis for the painting—but because this was not the way the Buddhists want him memorialized. See *The Times of India*, 19 and 28 April (with picture), 1990.

12. The Japanese bhikku at Ananda Vihara in Nagpur calls it *Prajna Tarowar*, or sword of knowledge. Eleanor Zelliot's phrase 'pointing toward enlightenment' fits what I have heard many Buddhists say.

13. It is not at all uncommon in India to have one community create images for another.

14. The fact that it is a specifically Thai image seems to carry no significance. Its presence refers more to Buddhism's ancient and international history.

15. The Dalit (literally, oppressed) Panthers took part of their name from the Black Panther Party for Self-Defene. The Black Panther Party for Self-Defense was founded in Oakland, California in the late 1960s and was active in the larger American cities of the late 1960s and the 1970s. The Panther Party was a radical (they called themselves 'revolutionary') organization of African-Americans known in particular for their use of firearms to protect the African-American community from police harassment and for their alliances with white Communists and Liberals, stimulated in part by writing such as Eldridge Cleaver's memoir, *Soul on Ice*. See Contursi 1989.

16. Such images from Sanchi and Amaravati can be seen in Zimmer 1955: volume 2, plates 10 and 91.

17. The form, which is not as rare as modern historians tend to assume, has essentially not been discussed in modern studies, however. For a comparable image of a Buddhist temple in a Gandharan relief in the Lahore Museum, see Franz 1965: plate 209.

18. Stupas are raised to enshrine three sorts of relics: bits of scriptures, the remains of those who have achieved enlightenment (such as Ambedkar), and great sites of the faith, such as this one.

19. The Christian theological seminary at Tumkur makes similar use of a
towered-temple form for its chapel, with the same purpose of displaying
an appropriate shape for an Indian religious structure.

REFERENCES   /

Ambedkar, B.R. 1974. *The Buddha and His Dhamma*. Second edition. Bombay:
    Siddharth Publications.
Contursi, Janet. 1989. 'Militant Hindus and Buddhist Dalits: Hegemony
    and Resistance in an Indian Slum'. *American Ethnologist*. vol. 16, no. 3,
    pp. 441–57.
Franz, Heinrich Gerhard. 1965. *Buddhistische Kunst Indiens*. Leipzig:
    E.A. Seemann.
Goyal, S.R. 1987. *A History of Indian Buddhism*. Meerut: Kusumanjali
    Prakashan.
Huntington, Susan and John Huntington. 1985. *The Art of Ancient India*. New
    York: Weatherhill.
Keer, Dhananjay. 1962. *Dr Ambedkar: Life and Mission*. Second edition.
    Bombay: Popular Prakashan.
Macy, Joanna Rogers and Eleanor Zelliot. 1980. 'Tradition and Innovation in
    Contemporary Indian Buddhism'. In A.K. Narain (ed.). *Studies in the
    History of Buddhism*. Delhi: B.R. Publishing Company.
Zimmer, Heinrich. 1955. *The Arts of Indian Asia*. New York: Pantheon.

13
UNDERSTANDING MULTIPLE IMAGES
OF B.R. AMBEDKAR*

Gopal Guru

Today, B.R. Ambedkar is the only national, or at least pan-Indian hero that we have. Patel is admired in his native Gujarat, Bose hardly remembered except in his native Bengal. Muslim and non-Muslim forget Azad. Nehru is vilified by Left and Right. While Gandhi is still admired and is still followed by some brave social activists, in the wider popular consciousness he has no serious impact any more.[1]

B.R. Ambedkar has undoubtedly reached everywhere in India, though in different forms. Not only is his iconographic image ubiquitous, but his posthumous political importance is obvious to any observer of the Indian scene. Politicians of all varieties, ranging from extreme Left to extreme Right, compete to claim the name if not the intellectual legacy of Ambedkar. Needless to say, this love for Ambedkar is very recent, and is motivated by various kinds of political compulsions. For example, the Left want to invoke Ambedkar to keep the Dalits away from the Hindutva forces, so the Left have become a little more hospitable to Ambedkar, no longer condemning him as

*Editor's Note: This chapter is intended as an essay expressing the author's own views, based not on a particular current research project but on a lifetime of scholarly inquiry and reflection.

the stooge of British Imperialism. Even the Congress, once very sceptical of him, now finds Ambedkar's nationalism of the same sterling quality as that of Jawaharlal Nehru and Mahatma Gandhi. In fact, Gandhi himself gave Ambedkar this certificate during his lifetime. The Hindutva forces want to celebrate Ambedkar with the sole intention of enlisting Dalit support to create a Hindu majority. As a result, each Hindutva group is attempting to associate itself with Ambedkar, even though they once were absolutely wary of him. Sawarkar condemned Ambedkar's Buddhism as a feminine (*bayakay* in Marathi) kind of religion, lacking masculinity because it believes in extreme non-violence. Yet most academic scholarship, except that undertaken with an explicit commitment to Dalit politics, considers Ambedkar an untouchable rather than a Buddhist. Modern Indian anthropology, historiography, and even political science maintain a stunning silence in this respect. In a Derridian sense Ambedkar has been reaffirmed through absence rather than presence.

In recent years, however, there has been a growing interest in Ambedkar in both academic circles and formal politics. Ambedkar has received the attention of well-known scholars both in India and abroad. It is also quite satisfying to see the increasing efforts to institutionalize Ambedkar's memory. It is in the realm of formal politics, however, that Ambedkar has become most competitive. The fact that several mainstream political parties no longer find it inconvenient to invoke the name of Ambedkar is mainly due to the collapse of the Congress system and the consequent political uncertainty articulated in the form of coalition politics. The belated hospitable attitude towards Ambedkar, motivated by the need to make inroads into a Dalit constituency, means that these parties have to reconcile themselves with him at least rhetorically. They do not want to lose out on Ambedkar.

Thus, except for those who still treat him as the false god of the Dalits, Ambedkar is no longer an object of hatred. Even the Shiv Sainiks of Maharashtra, once known for their outright and vocal condemnation of Ambedkar, have now decided to be much more hospitable to him. Their love too, however, seems not to flow from conviction but to trickle from electoral compulsion. One does not know what will happen to the other, competing Dalit groups, such as some Matangs and Chambars from Maharashtra, who joined the Shiv Sena for exactly the opposite reason, because of its relentless criticism of Ambedkar. Recent developments in Maharashtra suggest that the Shiv Sena would like to maintain a low profile as far as Ambedkar is concerned. The move is to bring Shiv Shakti and Bhim Shakti together for electoral purposes.

Ambedkar's growing political and cultural importance is quite spectacular; however, we need to know how Ambedkar has been received by Dalits themselves. In what form has he reached these groups? The present essay will map the cultural image of Ambedkar. This effort is to be located in the research tradition that has been handed down to us by Eleanor Zelliot, whose work on Ambedkar shows that cultural understanding has been the core of her engagement with him. Although Dalits seem to have revered Ambedkar, there are different images of him even within the Dalit community itself. This differential perception can be understood in terms of the internal differentiation that has taken place in this community during the last fifty years.

In this article I will argue that there are at least three images of Ambedkar that Dalits have constructed: Ambedkar as Maha Manav (a Great Man), as messiah, and as a perfect modernist. The modernist image of Ambedkar, in particular, is overdetermined in the cultural landscape of Dalits, who articulate this image through iconography, narratives, and folk literature. There are also three different sections of the Dalit community: the Dalit masses, the lower middle class, and the Dalit middle class. The three images belong to all three sections, but the idioms and metaphors differ according to their social location in the Dalit community. Let us see how the three social layers relate to Ambedkar in the cultural realm.

AMBEDKAR AS *MAHA MANAV*

The Maha Manav image is an abstraction drawn from the mass of the common people and made to belong to a different order and universe. As it is perceived by Dalits, Ambedkar possessed extraordinary qualities, both moral and intellectual, that are not found among ordinary people. This cultural construction thus entails a dichotomy between the ordinary and the extraordinary. Dalits suggest that Ambedkar had an unmatchable moral capacity to seek complete distancing from anything that would have subverted his moral self. They argue that he had an unusual moral capacity to make supreme sacrifices for the Dalit cause. He endured pain, both personal and familial, for achieving the emancipatory goals of Dalits in particular and Dalit-*bahujans* (masses) in general. He is called Maha Manav not because he possessed any supernatural qualities but because he showed extraordinary intellectual and political capacity to deal with mighty opposition from the Hindu social order, on the one hand, and political opponents both within and outside, on the other. It is suggested that he had the power to change the course of history in favour of Dalits.

There is another reason why Ambedkar is a *Maha Manav* for the Dalit masses. This image is not an empty one for them, but is loaded with an enormous intellectual power that Ambedkar deployed for demolishing adversaries. These Dalits believe that Ambedkar's acquisition of a star-studded array of academic degrees was possible only for a super-human, and would not be possible for an ordinary human being. This image of a super-human being gets its validity in a society where the intellectual achievement of Ambedkar is something beyond the reach of almost everyone else. In this regard, one has to understand that although most Dalits have not read or even seen the huge corpus of Ambedkar's writings, the symbolic presentation of his achievement in the form of his degrees easily makes him a Maha Manav. This Maha Manav image is best summarized in the Marathi ditty *asa jhalac nahi kuni ani honar nahi kuni dinaca dhani ga*, suggesting that no one like Ambedkar can be found in history or in the future either. Thus, this cultural construction suggests that Ambedkar exists outside the limits of history. He has acquired an essence that is timeless. The image suggests the empowerment of Dalits at the cultural level.

Dalits have constructed this Maha Manav image for polemical reasons as well. The Dalits feel forced to elevate the image of Ambedkar to the level of a super-human being because they feel that he has not received his due recognition from non-Dalit society. Compared to Ambedkar, other national leaders, though intellectually much inferior, have received a disproportionate share of popularity in India. On the contrary, Dalits argue, non-Dalits have made repeated attempts to reduce Ambedkar to a ghettoized intellectual universe, and some decimate him further to the miniscule figure of a leader representing only the Mahar community, a sub-caste of Dalits from Maharashtra. Such attempts have been made by both Gandhian and Hindutva groups. Some prominent Muslim intellectuals now are recognizing Ambedkar and his universal qualities, and, as already mentioned, Congress leaders are also being forced to recognize Ambedkar's sterling qualities—noteworthy, after the worshiping-false-god diatribes of the past. Dalits feel especially annoyed at attempts to ghettoize Ambedkar when Gandhi enjoys the unquestionable status of Mahatma. They attempt to remove this cultural discrepancy between the Mahatma and the ghettoized Ambedkar by elevating Ambedkar from the status of 'Bharat Ratna' to 'Vishwa Ratna' ('Universal Gem' and not just 'Indian Diamond'). Thus, Dalit cultural perception attributes a universal status to Ambedkar.

But the sensibility of the Dalit masses is not amenable to such intellectual challenges and alternative readings. What is important for most of the Dalit masses is that no Dalit or non-Dalit could match Ambedkar's moral qualities: his confidence, his determination, and his dream of a bright future for the Dalits. To them, Ambedkar appears as a messiah who has come to relieve their pain, thus replacing the gods that previously worked as the relievers of pain for the Dalit masses.

AMBEDKAR AS MESSIAH

Ambedkar has been seen as a messiah who has come once again and brought solace and relief to Dalits. This invocation of Ambedkar suggests two things. First, it shows complete frustration with the contemporary Dalit movement and its leadership. Secondly, it suggests a complete disappointment with the mainstream political parties. The Dalit masses have replaced the Hindu gods with the Buddha and Ambedkar as a new spiritual force that can work to relieve their pain. Ambedkar is made to join the Hindu pantheon. This is evident from cultural practices in northern Karnataka and Maharashtra. On the first day of Diwali, Dalits from these regions worship Ambedkar along with Laxmi, the goddess of wealth. The distinction they draw between the two is that Ambedkar represents spiritual/intellectual wealth while Laxmi signifies material wealth. For them intellectual wealth is much more important than material wealth.

At another level, it is very interesting to note that some Dalit women invoke Ambedkar as the messiah for saving them from exploitation by their dreadful mothers-in-law. This summoning of the messiah is evident in folk songs sung by Dalit women from rural parts of Maharashtra. These women seek security from Ambedkar at the spiritual level and treat him as a super-power with a healing touch.

However, this image is not common among Dalits. In fact, more Dalits, particularly those from a lower-middle-class background, see in Ambedkar a perfect modernist. For the most part, however, this reading of Ambedkar is limited to the cultural sphere.

AMBEDKAR AS MODERNIST

In Maharashtra and even in India at large, the Dalit masses discover in Ambedkar a perfect modernist. Dalits, it seems, use a narrative mode that involves the construction of an enlightened image of Ambedkar. In this mode the narrator also deploys a certain kind of negative dialectic, creating an opposite reference point and then building up Ambedkar's image through narrative demolition of the opponents. Let us see how this happens in a narrative from Maharashtra. The narrative is developed around three major figures in Indian politics: Gandhi, Jinnah, and Ambedkar. The occasion for telling the narrative is usually the birth anniversary of Ambedkar, when a Dalit activist at the local level shares it with local Dalits. The narrative also has another party, a team of British journalists visiting India on the eve of Independence. The narrative begins with Gandhi: the team goes to visit him at 9 p.m., and Gandhi refuses to see them because he has already gone to sleep. Then they visit Jinnah, at about 11 p.m., and also find him sleeping. Ultimately they go to Ambedkar at 2 a.m. and find him still working at his desk. The narrative suggests, first, that Ambedkar was a thinker who was completely devoted to both scholarship and a social cause, and, secondly, that he had incomparable moral stamina, because his devotion was driven more by social commitment than by individual triumphalism. Moreover, this modernist narrative is constructed with the intention of motivating young people and orienting Dalit children toward Ambedkar.

The impact of such a narrative on the Dalit masses is so profound that they do not feel it necessary to question the narrator about the evidence for or authenticity of the journalists' meeting with the three leaders. The narrative is constructed in an imaginary time frame outside of normal time. Dalits are convinced that there is an essential link between Ambedkar's burning the midnight oil and Dalit emancipation. This link between their emancipation and Ambedkar's Herculean efforts can be found in the Indian Constitution, which he wrote almost by himself. This consciousness is generated more through practical reason than as a theoretical construct. Dalits endorse the narrative and immerse themselves in it because it creates aspirations for a secure future. Thus, Dalits everywhere are empowered through the narratives of Ambedkar.

The several volumes of Ambedkar's collected works that the Government of Maharashtra has brought out (about twenty-one volumes to date) further strengthen this modernist narrative about him. It would, however, be quite interesting to find out the relationship between these volumes and the Dalit masses. Our experience of Dalits from different parts of the country makes it clear that they have given hermeneutic responsibility to specialists from their community. Thus, they seem to have reified Ambedkar. Most Dalits would quote the cultural capital (the extraordinary list of academic degrees that he obtained from foreign universities) that Ambedkar so labouriously acquired to those who deny such capital to them. They adopt this as an everyday form of polemic with members of the upper castes, and use the moral quality of Ambedkar's writings in order to score points against upper-caste adversaries. These Dalits hold onto voluminous books written by Ambedkar or even Marx, and treat the books as necessary for their own emancipation, either externally through education or through the iconography of Ambedkar. Dalits have found the mode of iconography to be the surest and safest route to Ambedkar. They see the essence of his philosophy in the statues and other monuments that have been created as community resources over the past decades.

For Dalits involved in struggles all over the country, the bust of Ambedkar is very important. For Dalits from Tamil Nadu, he can save their Panchama land from both the local high caste and the state. In urban areas he helps Dalits to save their little shanty huts from the local authorities. For Dalit women, he is the one who relieves their pain and exploitation. The life-size statue with a book in his hand and the finger of the right hand pointing towards the sky symbolically suggests to these Dalits two modernist challenges. The book indicates his scholarship and the finger suggests that the sky is the limit for efforts to change. Thus, the statue plays a very important role in the cultural and political life of the Dalits, as it helps them establish easy contact with Ambedkar's dream. Some Dalits from Maharashtra seems to have devised novel ways to collect funds for constructing busts of Ambedkar.

For example, Shankar Sakpal, a Dalit from Lohari village in Akola District of Maharashtra, collected flour and sold it, until he had enough money to buy statues of Ambedkar and the Buddha.

Such efforts are praiseworthy when there is no support coming either from the state or from Dalit leaders. But there is also a certain moral problem involved in these efforts: Is it morally correct to collect even a small portion of flour from a starving Dalit family? Is it morally correct to erect a statue of Ambedkar out of it? Would Ambedkar allow this kind of bhakti? The answer is, categorically, no, because Ambedkar disallowed any kind of iconography. It did not fit into his rational thinking.

Yet, on another level, Ambedkar appeared on the one-rupee coin that the V.P. Singh government issued during the Ambedkar centenary year, 1991. This gesture of commemorating Ambedkar was well received by Dalits for two reasons. First, Ambedkar was given space in an arena that is otherwise completely occupied by Gandhi—Gandhi appears on every denomination of Indian currency. Secondly, the one-rupee coin on which the image of Ambedkar is embossed is a very subaltern coin that can reach even the poorest of the poor in the country. It is quite ironical that Gandhi appears on thousand-rupee notes, while his 'Daridri Narayan' ('common poor person') finds it quite difficult to earn even one rupee. Ambedkar's one-rupee coin certainly prompted some Dalits to appreciate this gesture by V.P. Singh; they composed a song about the coin that goes like this:

V.P. Singh mazya shipaya,
Tu kadhala Baba Sahebancha bandha rupaya!

This folk song voices gratitude to V.P. Singh, the then Prime Minister of India, for having issued the one-rupee coin with Ambedkar's little icon on it. This coin is called *bandha rupiya*. '*Bandha*' has a very definite meaning in Marathi, suggesting the high quality of the coin and ultimately of the person portrayed on it. Like 22-carat gold, this coin also has the virtue of making a sonorous sound if dropped on the floor.

The folk song suggests many things. First, it suggests that Ambedkar has absolute moral integrity and hence is reliable and of great value. A 'bandha' is normally juxtaposed to a fake coin. This imagery of the bandha rupiya suggests that, as compared to other Dalit and non-Dalit leaders in the contemporary period, Ambedkar had enormous moral stamina in staying with the cause of Dalits. It also suggests that Ambedkar was never vulnerable to the everyday forms of petty politcs that seem to be so rampant among Dalits. The song thus implies that contemporary Dalit leadership is vulnerable to all kinds of pressure and can be sold to anybody, including Hindutva forces, for petty gains. The bandha rupiya coin sets high moral standards that are normally non-negotiable in today's politics of bargaining, and hence it is difficult to fragment this complete *rupaya* in the market. The metaphor of the rupiya becomes especially meaningful because the contemporary leadership has become absolutely opportunistic and is available for sale in the market of electoral politics. The metaphor of bandha rupiya also suggests that Ambedkar's theoretical and ideological framework is tightly organized around emancipatory values. Of course, this imagery flies in the face of those scholars who would dissolve Ambedkar in a post-modernist fashion by saying that he does not have any framework.

One problem with the Ambedkar coins was that some Dalits would hoard them, not spending them even for essentials or for a small pack of *bidis*. Would Ambedkar have allowed such austerity? The answer is no: he cared for human beings, and not for the accumulation of money.

Busts and life-size statues of Ambedkar are being put up all over India. Who among the Dalits requires them, and why? These are important questions that need to be answered. It can be easily observed that the Dalits who require this iconography are the masses, the workers, and the lower middle class. Lower-middle-class Dalits who work in smaller offices want it because they know they cannot handle their tormentors in academic language. They realize that they do not have language powerful enough to confront their adversaries, both those within and those on the outside. The icon can provide them some energy to fight. They also believe that hiding behind Ambedkar is the best bet in the urban situation. At least in certain parts of the country, it is a risk for opponents to touch him. Such Dalits would like to graft Ambedkar's image in public places like government offices, especially the welfare department, post offices, and railway offices. Government colonies (railways and corporation) provide an opportunity for lower-middle-class Dalits to install icons of Ambedkar. These colonies also openly celebrate Ambedkar's birth anniversary.

Thus, this section is very high-profile and vocal in its open commitment to and association with Ambedkar. Because of this, they are the ones who suffer most from upper-caste atrocities against Dalits, whether the occasion is the Ambedkar statue in Ramabai Nagar in Mumbai or the question of renaming Marathwada University in Aurangabad after Ambedkar. These Dalits are the ones who came out into the streets in the millions to defend Ambedkar's book on the Rama-Krishna riddles when it was questioned by the Shiv Sena in Maharashtra in 1987. They do not feel embarrassed to greet each other by referring to Ambedkar's name publicly. In a little corner at a leather-ball factory in the city of Meerut in Uttar Pradesh, Dalits have written Ambedkar's name quite prominently, in bold letters, without fearing what the non-Dalit owner of the workshop will think. When a movie on Ambedkar made by a leading progressive filmmaker, Jabbar Patel, was released in Maharashtra, a number of Dalits from a lower-middle-class background went to see this movie clad in three-piece suits that must have cost them almost a month's salary. In Mumbai and Nagpur, some of the more enthusiastic even garlanded the cinema poster of Ambedkar.

During Ambedkar's centenary year, 1991, many Dalits from the lower middle class bought and wore watches bearing a little icon of Ambekar on the dial. These watches were made by Hindustan Machine Tools, a public-sector firm in India. These Dalits did not have any problems in associating with Ambedkar publicly. But wearing the watch was also very ironical in some cases: many Dalits who wore the watch did not keep pace with time, which was always moving forward. If one deploys the watch and its dynamism in accord with Ambedkar's philosophy, one finds that for some Dalits the intellectual clock has almost stopped, or in some cases it is working in reverse. Some of them, for example, did not show any hesitation in joining Hindutva parties. While they were wearing the watch with Ambedkar's icon, they somehow lost touch with his ideological dynamism. Unlike Ambedkar, these Dalits forgot that success comes from gaining speed. Gaining speed is important in terms of scoring points over members of the upper castes who do not care for the Dalits. But its logic also creates a distance for those who cannot catch up with the fast-moving Dalits. Thus modernity becomes a kind of frustration, like sand slipping all the time from the hands of the Dalits. It is this modernity that involves speed that has created the gap between the Dalit masses and the modernizing Dalits, a gap that will become clear in the following section. The watch is a symbol of modernity, but those Dalits who wear the Ambedkar watch relate to the notion of modernity only at the symbolic level.

This reading of Ambedkar by the majority of Dalits flies in the face of scholars who try to depict Ambedkar as a post-modernist. This kind of construction might be useful for achieving success in the war of semantics. However, the question that needs to be asked is whether Ambedkar endorsed this kind of image building. Let us examine this in the following section. Babasaheb himself is not responsible for the kind of supra-historical images that are imposed on him.

AMBEDKAR'S CRITIQUE OF THE MAHA MANAV IMAGE

As is clear from the writing and speeches of Ambedkar, he held a completely different view, one running contrary to all three of the popular Dalit images of him. First, Ambedkar argued that all images are historically constructed. In other words, they become possible historically and hence cannot be imagined outside known, lived history. His use of history as pedagogy sufficiently proves this point. During the Dalit mobilization, Ambedkar distinctly used the radical history of Dalits as a motivational point. Unlike a super-human being, he did require history as a resource of mobilization. Ambedkar did not claim that his personal abilities were his own creation and thus without any bearing on the enduring social and political struggle of the common masses. On the contrary, as his intellectual practices show, he believed in the transformative energies of common men and women. Second, Ambedkar borrowed his cultural and intellectual resources from both western and eastern intellectual traditions. His was the tradition of association. He identified with the Buddha, Kabir, Tukaram, and Phule and a host of western thinkers as well, most notably John Dewey, Seligman, and others. Third, Ambedkar followed Buddhist intellectual traditions, which do not believe in creating Maha Manav images. Buddhist tradition suggests, *'atta dippo bhav'*, ('Be your own guide'). It certainly is the tradition of enlightenment. Fourth, Ambedkar's tradition was very self-reflective, suggesting that a person is a common human being and not a super-human being. Hence no person can be completely perfect and incapable of making a mistake. Ambedkar represented rationalist strands in his thinking and practice. His tradition was not one that preached devotion and blind dedication to an image. Moreover, once Ambedkar is transformed into a Maha Manav, this image, with its completely spiritual profile, denies Ambedkar other significant descriptions, such as those of his aesthetics, self, friends, colleagues, or comrades. Was Ambedkar without all these? The Maha Manav image, which invalidates other descriptions, also does not allow even radical accommodations of other images. Babasaheb himself is not responsible for such supra-historical images that are imposed on him. It is his 'followers' who are the sole beneficiaries of such convenient constructions.

For middle-class Dalits, Ambedkar is not an asset but rather an object of terrible embarrassment. Their commitment to Ambedkar as a cultural symbol is very much shaken. They refuse to refer to Ambedkar in greeting each other. 'Good Morning' has become quite handy to this community of smart Hindus. They avoid associating themselves directly with Ambedkar and refuse to oblige those Dalits who expect these 'sahibs' to use Dalit protocols. They avoid putting up an Ambedkar portrait on the wall of their drawing room, as they are worried that it would reveal their caste to their upper-caste neighbours. These Dalits prefer to put up an image of Michael Jackson or Lord Ganesh, depending on the locality in which they reside. If they are in a mixed locality they put up Michael Jackson, and if their neighbourhood is Hindu-dominated they put up Ganesh. They would even turn off the TV programme focused on Ambedkar that is telecast once a year on 14 April. They do not want upper-caste people to catch them watching this programme.

Some Dalit activists, aware of the unhappy consciousness that these Dalits suffer from, choose to further embarrass them. These activists make a phone call, for example, to a Dalit officer in his high-profile office. If he is alone then he may use the Dalit protocols, reciprocating with 'Jai Bhim'. But if the officer is surrounded by members of upper castes when he receives the call, he is really in a fix. He finds a trick and hides in a code language. The code is 'JB', meaning 'Jai Bhim'. This language confuses the upper-caste people in the room and amuses the Dalit activist at the other end of the line. Although officers like these want to avoid associating with Ambedkar at the cultural level, it is also true that in Dalit-dominated colleges members of the upper castes do not mind saying 'Jai Bhim' loudly—also out of compulsion. This is what I mean by the 'unhappy consciousness' of the Dalit: he wants to maintain the protocol and yet, due to the upper-caste gaze, cannot do so.

For some middle-class Dalits, the Ambedkar celebration provides an opportunity to build up their community exclusively on the basis of class background. They find Ambedkar relevant in building up the community, because they are not assimilated into the upper-caste community and they find it difficult to adapt to the cultural segment of which Michael Jackson is naturally a part. In such a predicament they have to fall back on Ambedkar and his Buddhism. They celebrate Ambedkar not for any ideological or intellectual exchange but simply in order to have some fun. But, to give the celebration a certain seriousness, they arrange a talk by some Dalit professor and use their children as the audience that serves as the shock absorber for the Dalit talk, while they themselves look forward to the cultural programme, which ranges from Lawani to modern orchestra. The Dalit middle class also uses these occasions for arranging matrimonial alliances. Because the Dalits do not have Brahmanical institutions to perform this job, of late some bhikkhus have been doing it.

Thus, there seem to be two images of Ambedkar in the Dalit middle class. For some, Ambedkar has become a source of embarrassment, while others have a very pragmatic relationship with him. This suggests that Ambedkar has not been accepted by the upper caste as the hero of the whole society. He continues to be the hero of the untouchables, or of the Dalits. Due to lack of confidence, middle-class Dalits find it difficult to associate with Ambedkar in any situation without feeling pressure from members of the upper castes.

Exactly the opposite is the case with the class of Dalit social activists and politicians. For them, Ambedkar is not an embarrassment. On the contrary, they find him a source of encouragement. For Dalit politicians the statues and monuments of Ambedkar have become so important that they even fight among themselves for control of them. In the early 1980s, some such fights were conducted openly. Tension built up around the Nagpur Diksha Bhumi, the place where Ambedkar embraced Buddhism along with his followers. Since 1956, this has become the most important Dalit pilgrimage place in the country. On 14 October every year, lakhs of people gather here from different parts of the country. However, such places do not remain immune to Dalit politics. In 1984, Dalit leaders fought over control of this place. When a member of Ambedkar's family tried to claim it, the well-established, seasoned Dalit leader who had been controlling the place for the last several decades resisted the claim. The fight turned dirty. After failing to gain control of the Nagpur site, the family member then claimed another site, the Chaitya Bhumi. This is the place in Mumbai where Ambedkar was cremated, another important pilgrimage place for Dalits from all over the country.

After this leader took over the Chaitya Bhumi, other Dalit leaders were left without cultural resources of this kind. These leaders have invented new places for Dalits. One of the newly discovered places is Koregaon (Bhima), 30 km east of Pune. For the last few years, educated Dalits have started gathering here on 1 January to commemorate the valiant Dalits who defeated Brahmanical forces in a battle here in 1818. The historical significance of this place is that the Dalits were able to defeat the most pernicious Brahman rulers, who had reduced the life of Dalits to dirt. Dalit leaders now seem to be cashing in very well on this historical memory. Another place being claimed for the first time by Dalit leaders from Maharashtra is the Chawdar tank at Mahad in the coastal region of Maharashtra: this tank is now being converted into a Dalit pilgrimage place. Dalits converge in large numbers at the Chawdar tank in March, the month during which Ambedkar conducted his first struggle for Dalit independence here in 1927.

Dalit politics in Uttar Pradesh (UP) does not lag behind. The Bahujan Samaj Party (BSP) in fact once objected to such cultural politics on the part of the Dalit masses. This party went on record as opposed to renaming Marathwada University after Ambedkar. They were very critical of such politics. But now they are practicing cultural politics in UP. BSP leaders are creating new centres of Ambedkar worship throughout UP. They have already created a big 'Pariwartan Park' ('Conversion Park') in Lucknow. These new monuments are different from the ones in Maharashtra in the sense that, with the creation of the Pariwartan Park, the deification of Ambedkar in UP is complete. In fact, this place of worship seems to be modelled on mainstream religious places in UP. As reported in the media, the UP government, led by a Dalit Chief Minister, has named the river near the Ambedkar park at Lucknow 'Bhim Ganga', replicating the original Ganga. Dalits who recently gathered at the park also took a bath in this holy Bhim Ganga.

The question that needs to be asked is why the common people on the one hand and Dalit politicians on the other have a stake in creating such places that eventually turn into religious places. In the first case the answer is very simple: the common people find a kind of cultural empowerment in such places. But why do the leaders find these places important? Both the establishment and the Dalit leaders get benefits from such monuments and the events that are held at these venues. The establishment funds the monuments by giving donations for their maintenance. In addition, the Central government arranges for free trains from different places to Bombay on 6 December and to Nagpur on 14 October every year. In turn, the government gets support from the Dalits for its alleged generosity. The Dalit leaders also get various benefits from the state, such as a seat as a Member of the Legislative Council or the position of Deputy Speaker of the Vidhan Sabha. In addition to these tangible benefits, there is also a sort of a trade-off, an expectation that the established party will get the votes of the people who gather at these places and that the Dalit leaders will ensure these people's support in the election. In reality, it is always difficult to prove that such cultural power can be converted into political power. Dalit voters do not follow the dictates of their leaders: they are autonomous and do not seem to mix the cultural with the political.

These new efforts to portray Ambedkar in iconography also have some serious implications for Dalit modernity. A photograph or a statue can cause discomfort from the modernist point of view because it halts movement: it spatializes time, locating its characters in a single scene in which Ambedkar is addressing a mob or writing the Indian Constitution. The fact that Ambedkar stands still for so long is quite alarming. It suggests a kind of intellectual stillness in him. He is not moving at all; he has stopped for many years. A photograph or statue represents the anti-modernist thinking of the masses. Why do Dalit modernists not want to summon the past in their memory? The dark-blue colour of Ambedkar's coat does not accommodate other colours. It does not allow the Dalits to go separate ways.

It would be interesting to learn how non-Dalits look at the portrait and bust of Ambedkar. If only there were a machine or some scientific mechanism to measure what Hindutva leaders think when they offer garlands to the portrait of Ambedkar in the Parliament! Although we do not have access to the inner self of Hindutva leaders, we can be sure that they too suffer from a kind of unhappy consciousness: they deeply dislike Ambedkar in their heart of hearts, and yet they have to garland his portrait. In the high offices, particularly in the social welfare departments, Ambedkar does find a prominent place. But even here the non-Dalit high-level officials deeply dislike him. They garland his images out of electoral compulsion. It is this same compulsion that is bringing Shiv Shakti and Bhim Shakti close to each other and that is found in some Dalit NGOs that would not have heard of resurrecting Ambedkar a few years ago. They too are taking an increasing interest in Ambedkar, though only at the level of rhetoric. At one level, it is desirable that in some places, such as in Punjab, Haryana, and Rajasthan, there be a political party, and hence the Dalit NGOs are popularizing Ambedkar, though only at the symbolic level. One hopes that the Dalit masses can come to elevate Ambedkar not in terms of static statues but as an organic statue, one that through his philosophy can move, both intellectually and politically. This is the real challenge before Dalit politics: to fight the spurious appropriation of Ambedkar by various forces, including by Dalits themselves.

NOTES

1. This quote is from one of India's leading public intellectuals, Ramchandra Guha. I cite it only to show how Ambedkar has lately been attracting scholars across the board.

14

CONTEMPLATING THE DIVINE*

Syed Akbar Hyder

In spite of their profound effect on South Asian devotional traditions, the literary merits of the *qawwali* genre have gone critically unnoticed. The word qawwali derives from the Arabic word *qawl*, which in general means 'saying', but more specifically refers to the sayings of the Prophet Muhammad—though the qawwali texts take stock of works of literature beyond those ascribed to the Prophet. In fact, it is through the qawwali tradition that many classic mystical texts are routed for mass consumption in South Asia. Qawwalis are instructional as well as entertaining. They frequently provide a significant counterweight to discourses generated from other sites of religious knowledge production, such as mosques and madrasas, thereby leading their audiences into an alternative world in which the gender divide is not as rigid, where ideological differences pertaining to an understanding of God and religion are accommodated, and where a circumvention of a hyper-theosophical and scholastic discourse is possible through simple, heartfelt sentiments.

The poetic strands that tie together many qawwali narratives through the technique of *girah bandi* (knot-tying) range from classical works of Sufism, such as the *Masnavi* of Jalaluddin Rumi and the ghazals

*First published as 'Allah Hu! (God, Just He!)', *The Annual of Urdu Studies*. vol. 21, 2006, pp. 273–7.

of Amir Khusrau, to verses composed by local poets. Girah bandi allows *qawwals* (qawwali singers) to embed invigorating variations on a single theme by interpolating poetry from disparate sources in order to create a coherent narrative.

The three qawwalis that are translated here were made popular by the acclaimed Hyderabadi qawwal, Aziz Ahmad Khan Warsi.

QAWWALI 1

The first stanza of the qawwali is a quatrain composed by Hyderabad's most renowned Sufi poet, Amjad Hyderabadi (d. 1961), and the second stanza is a quatrain of the greatest Urdu elegist, Mir Anis (d. 1872). This qawwali impresses complex ideals on its audience by adopting finely wrought parables: the first (Stanza 3) is a translation of a section of Rumi's *Masnavi*, and the second and third (Stanzas 5 and 6) are the exegeses of the ideas of *wahdat al-wujud* (unity of being), closely tied to Muhiuddin Ibn al-'Arabi, the grand master of theosophical Sufism. The translators of these parables, Bedam Warsi (d. 1936) and Zamin Ali (d. 1855), are Urdu poets known for their lucid expressions of complex Sufi ideas.

The main locus of the first parable valourizes devotion as an intimately personal experience that is beyond even a prophet's comprehension. Also threaded into this parable is a devotional allusion to Lord Krishna, a manifestation of the divine who at times appears as an adorable youth in his cradle. The second and third parables help the audience understand the idea that all appearances are a manifestation of the One Real Being. The pivot of Muslim devotional life, the Kaba in Mecca, is itself invoked in the symbolic language of Laila's veil, as God compares Himself to this dark-skinned, moon-like sweetheart of Islamic literature who drove mad her lover Qais (Majnun). The mystical cadences that lace this qawwali come to life most notably through the tension-laden elision and reinforcement of differences in the relationship between God and His creation: Moses must recognize that his devotional path is different from that of the shepherd and Majnun must come to terms with his Laila by accepting her as God's splendorous manifestation, a variation of Himself.

God, Just He (*Allah Hu*)

Stanza 1
From within my body's abode I called,
'Who dwells within this house?'

From the heart's threshold was heard a cry,
'God, there is none else but God!'
God, just He
God, just He
God, just He
God, just He

You, the One, ever lavishing mercy
Amjad, the one adrift on the path
habituated to transgressions
You, accustomed to clemency
Let us see who can exceed the other

Stanza 2
In the rose garden the zephyr yearns for You
From the nightingale's lips Your talk springs
In every hue Your majesty shines
From every flower, Your fragrance emanates
Neither will the roses last in the garden
Nor their perfumes dwell there
All these will perish for Your sake
You alone will stay

God, just He
God, just He
God, just He
God, just He

Stanza 3
Once upon a time, a shepherd lived in a forest
Like a full moon, eclipsed by clouds
Always drunk with the memory of his master
The canopy of heaven, lying low on his earth
Entangled in His remembrance, he grew weary one day
In agony he cried out in dismay:
'Why do You not come to my small hut?
Does not my wilderness hold some charm?
Come, come down from Your heavenly throne to my home
I'll quench my thirst by washing Your feet
Waking up in the morning, I'll cleanse Your face

Night and day I'll rock Your cradle
Begging door to door, I'll gather goods for You
Only after feeding You will I eat my fill'
Such were his cries and rants
When the honourable Moses passed his home
Then with an anger-ridden voice roared this God's Prophet:
'Watch the words you recklessly utter
Imprisoned you hold this limitless light
How wretched you are, O silly fool!
Is God a mere human just like you?
Certainly, you'll reap the wrath of this breach
By the rage of the Truth, you'll turn to ashes'
Just when Moses racked his heart through
God's revelation echoed:
'What have you done Moses, what have you done
From the master you have sundered his slave
You were sent to mend hearts
You exist not to break hearts
O you! Prescribed for the clever is their own path,
A different way designed for the smoldering hearts'

God, just He
God, just He
God, just He
God, just He

Stanza 4
One night, turning to the Truth, Majnun said:
'My Master, Lord of all directions
My pitiful state deserves clemency
Have mercy on me, my Sustainer
The cloak of my heart is sullied by infidelity
Your slave has become Laila's lover
Why did You make me Laila's lover
Why did You disgrace me in Your eyes'
Suddenly, a voice from the invisible issued:
'My Majnun, do not bewail with such hurt
If Laila's love fills you with anguish,
Grieve not, for your Lord is with you
It is love's calling to make Majnuns,

It is my disclosure named Laila'
Hidden behind that curtain is the Laila of both worlds
Oh Bedam, there is a reason the Kaba dons the black cloak

God, just He
God, just He
God, just He
God, just He

Stanza 5
The moon-faced Laila asked Qais one day:
'Whom do you pursue besides this dark one?'
Enraptured, Qais rendered into words:
'T'is but a secret, listen O Moon-lit one
I am not Majnun, neither are you Laila
I am not mad, neither are you black

God, just He
God, just He
God, just He
God, just He

Stanza 6
There is no quarrel over the 'I'—
This matter, free of qualms
Those vanished in You alone gain honour
Your presence looms at every turn
No Other subsists, You and only You

God, just He
God, just He
God, just He
God, just He

Zamin Ali, annihilated in remembering
God, just He
God, just He

QAWWALI 2

According to the lore of the Hyderabadi qawwali tradition, Amjad
wrote 'A Three-Coloured Picture' after the death of his young daughter,

as a cathartic consolation for the young girl's mother. In the first stanza, Amjad celebrates the arrival of his daughter. He invokes the tradition attributed to the Prophet Muhammad that the salutations of God, Muhammad, and the archangel Gabriel will be sent upon whichever house is blessed by a daughter. Amjad speaks of his daughter's arrival as though it were surreal and dream-like.

Amjad speaks in a feminine voice while praising his child in a masculine langue. This discourse is intertextually bound to the discourse of the bhakti tradition in which the lover speaks in a feminine Radha-like voice. John Stratton Hawley clarifies this:

But when they [Hindu devotional/bhakti poets] speak of lovesickness, they project themselves almost exclusively into the voice of one of the women who wait for Krishna—before love-making or, even more likely, afterwards. And although there is plenty of humor, there is a deep sense of longing and lament. This lament is echoed in the narrative line, for according to most versions, this love story has no happy ending: Krishna never really returns to the women he leaves behind. Whether one conceives it in the secular or religious sense (and these are not entirely separable), longing has a definite gender: it is feminine (Hawley, 2000: 240).

There is also a tradition of Urdu poetry known as *rekhti* in which male poets speak in a female voice. But as Carla Petievich and others have pointed out, much of this literature is a parody-laden, wishful male imagination, with no charge of a serious discourse (see Petievich 2001). In Urdu literary circles of the late nineteenth-century, shaped very much by colonial aesthetics, a discourse in the feminine voice was not seen as legitimate in terms of its literary merits, or in terms of its Sufi stature. So these qawwalis are very much a reflection of how Urdu poets like Amjad cast their devotion, not only in a transcommunal language, but also in a transmasculine idiom, hence resisting the hegemony of the Urdu canon-guardians. Again, we can see clearly why qawwalis have not been studied as serious literary artefacts: they never met the standards of male literary or religious sentries.

In the second stanza, the daughter is spoken of as the beloved, jealously guarded by her lover. The lover hopes that she will never depart from his sight. But, alas, fate has decreed something else: in the third stanza, as the lover/father blinks in his dream-like state, his beloved vanishes. The poet, without risking neat celebratory or elegiac effects, employs the bhakti/Sufi language of eros to relay a state of mind for which he has no name at all, attesting to the mysteries of debuts and departures, meditating on the transience of joy and the open-endedness of grief. It is perhaps the likeness of this state of mind that occasions the double-bindedness of Jacques Derrida's idea of mourning:

One should not develop a taste for mourning, and yet mourn we *must*. We *must*, but we must not like it—mourning, that is, mourning *itself*, if such a thing exists: not to like or love through one's own tear but only through the other, and every tear is from the other, the friend, the living, as long as we ourselves are living, reminding us, in holding life, to hold on to it (Derrida 2001: 110).

A Three-Coloured Picture (*Sah Rangi Tasvir*)

Hear my tale, dear [girl] friend,
Last night I slumbered, alone
A perfume scent wafted down to me
Someone's breath touched my soul
A cloud of mercy covered my mind
With eyes closed, a lightning force glimmered
Favours rained from the highest lord
The heavenly-one descended to my place

Struck by the vision—my beloved's cheeks
Do I dream, do I wake?
Envy-ridden rival, may she burn in fire
While I cling to my sweetheart's garb, tight
Never to grant his leave
Never to grant his vision of my other
In sorrow's abode, spreads splendid joy
Day and night I hold him in sight

In this very rapture, I swayed
Kissing passion, my fate's lips
In the instant my eye blinked
lightning sorrow struck, a roaring sound
Alas, fate changed its colours
I saw then: I'll never see him again
Why display his splendour to me
Why come to depart

Without reason he burnt my heart
Why alight then vanish
I am not the same, nor my mate
Alas, in so much, there's nothing left

QAWWALI 3

This next qawwali, 'Where's my Ram', is an extrapolation of the idea of *hama ust* (Everything is He), which is tied to Ibn al-'Arabi and Muhammad Ashraf Simnani. Amjad uses the image of a female lover-devotee in the process of discovering her beloved; when she does, she realizes that he's within herself. The beloved of this qawwali is Ram, who like Krishna is an avatara (manifestation) of Lord Vishnu. The geographical motifs (the Ganges, the rain clouds) of this poem are clearly meant to engage theosophical ideas of Sufi and bhakti traditions that valourize the 'Oneness of Being'. Not only is the lover in this poem thirsting for her beloved just like the devotees of Krishna do, but she also identifies with the Biblical-Koranic Prophet Jacob, who loses his vision because of his incessant searching and weeping for his son Joseph. Amjad, writing in the early twentieth century, is exerting a hermeneutics closely tied to Kabir and Guru Nanak as well as to the Arabic and Persian Sufi discourses that often speak of the lover-seeker as Jacob and the object of their search as Joseph, frequently referred to as the 'Moon of Canaan'. Apart from the Hindu/bhakti traditions, the supreme lord is identified as Parameshwar even in the Sikh devotional literature. Toward the end, the qawwali also contains a type of wordplay quite frequently employed in bhakti poetry: Har, from Sanskrit, is an epithet of Lord Shiva; and *har* in Persian and several Indian linguistic traditions means 'every'.

Where's my Ram? (*Mera Ram kahan hai*)

At night while all slumbered
Silently, I stood on the shores of Ganga
The river's water churned waves
The stream's youth flowing full with passion
Fallen reflection, the moon in water—
Mother Ganga's bosomy youth
I laid eyes on this alluring sight
and with a pang of pain so sharp, I cried out:

Injured is my soul, half-dead my life
I am here, but where's my Ram?

Those clouds that roam the spheres,
Those clouds that kiss the moon,
Your reach, to the sky
My worth, only dust
Your glances land on a heavenly throne
My pained head, on the spread of dust
Point me towards the long-lost Joseph
Seek him for me, and tell me this:
Oh moon, in which sphere does he hide?
I am here, but where's my Ram?

Watch how lightning roars
Terrified, my soul flutters in my heart
Drops pour down on the mouth of this parched soil
The sky has bowed to earth's presence
How the black clouds spread themselves
fearful moon in hiding
My heart, too, restless with fear
In whose protection shall I seek my shelter
Alas, where is my darling mate
I am here, but where's my Ram?

Nowhere does the destitute find his guide
Not a single soul favours me
A thousand times I cried out
to the whole world, lost in utter stupor
When the dew of despair rained on my heart
Thunder, roaring, replied, a cry:
Look, the Parameshwar is in me, and in you
Ram is, in you and in me
Ram is, in soul and in body
Ram in flowing streams, Ram in forests
Ram's remembrance graces every name
All is in Ram and Ram is in all
His splendour, in the good and in the bad
Har's majesty shines from every single (*har*) form
Why then are these cries and tumults raised:
'I am here, but where's my Ram?'

CONCLUSION

The qawwali tradition has retained a subaltern gravitas kindred in spirit to the resistive lyricism of Chokhamela and Eknath that Zelliot introduced eloquently into the arena of South Asian cultural studies. Coruscating throughout South Asia for more than seven centuries, the musically-staged qawwalis provide rejoinder to the patronizingly exclusivist truth claims: the story of Moses and the shepherd rejects sharply attempts to privilege a prophetic discourse over the subaltern one; the scintillatingly Eros-laden complaint from 'A Three-Coloured Picture' enables the readers and listeners to visualize the ambivalently gendered personified fate; 'Where's my Ram' attests to the composite religious traditions of South Asia by seeking a shared devotional idiom among the spiritual traditions of Sufis, Sikhs, and Bhaktas. All three of these qawwalis foreground the devotee's intimate relationship with the divine and rework rigid gender, nationalist, and communal hierarchies. This indomitable tradition makes those who wish to safeguard neat and text-centric cultural and religious divides more inured to alternative existential modes: the primary (and most legitimate) epistemic basis of devotion in these qawwalis is the sincere heart and not any written text. Zelliot's writings and the qawwalis discussed in this essay celebrate intertextual and interdisciplinary humanism in the broadest sense and forge a spirit of solidarity across the abodes of literature, religion, history, gender studies, and anthropology.

REFERENCES

Derrida, Jacques. 2001. *The Work of Mourning*. Pascale-Anne Brault and Michael Naas (eds). Chicago: University of Chicago Press.

Hawley, John Stratton. 2000. 'Krishna and the Gender of Longing'. Joseph Runzo and Nancy Martin (eds). *Love, Sex and Gender in the World Religions*. Oxford: Oneworld, pp. 239–56.

Hyder, Syed Akbar. 2007. *Reliving Karbala: Martyrdom in South Asian Memory*. New York: Oxford University Press.

Petievich, Carla. 2001. '*Rekhti*: Impersonating the Feminine in Urdu Poetry'. *South Asia*. vol. 24, pp. 75–90.

APPENDIX
Published Writings of Eleanor Zelliot
[as of May 2008]

'Buddhism and Politics in Maharashtra'. In Donald E. Smith (ed.). *South Asian Politics and Religion*. Princeton: Princeton University Press, 1966. Paperback edition, 1969.

'Background of the Mahar Buddhist Conversion'. In Robert Sakai (ed.). *Studies on Asia, 1966*. Lincoln: University of Nebraska, 1966.

'The Revival of Buddhism in India'. *Asia*. vol. 10, 1968.

'Gujarat'. *Encyclopedia Americana*. International edition, 1975.

'Learning the Use of Political Means: The Mahars of Maharashtra'. In Rajni Kothari (ed.). *Caste in Indian Politics*. New Delhi: Allied Publishers, 1970. Reprinted 1973, 1985, 1991 (Orient Longman).

'The Nineteenth Century Background of Mahar and Non-Brahman Movements in Maharashtra'. *Indian Economic and Social History Review*. vol. 7, no. 3, 1970.

'Literary Images of the Indian City'. In Richard G. Fox (ed.). *Urban India: Society, Space and Image*. Durham: Duke University Press, 1971.

'Gandhi and Ambedkar: A Study in Leadership' and 'Bibliography on Untouchability'. In J. Michael Mahar (ed.). *The Untouchables in Contemporary India*. Tucson: University of Arizona Press, 1972. Reprinted as a pamphlet by Triratna Grantha Mala, Pune, 1983.

'Dr Ambedkar and the Mahars'. *Illustrated Weekly*. vol. 92, no. 14, 2 April 1972.

'The Medieval Bhakti Movement in History: An Essay on the Literature in English'. In Bardwell L. Smith (ed.). *Hinduism: New Essays in the History of Religions*. Leiden: E.J. Brill, 1976 (Numen Series). Reprinted in 1982.

'Dalit Sahitya: The Historical Background' together with a translation (with Vidyut Bhagwat) of Baburao Bagul, *Maran Swast Hot Ahe* ('Death is Getting Cheaper'), from Marathi. *Vagartha*. vol. 12, 1976.

'The Psychological Dimension of the Buddhist Movement in India'. In G.A. Oddie (ed.). *Religion in South Asia: Religious Conversion and Revival Movements in Medieval and Modern Times*. Second edition. New Delhi: Manohar, 1991 (first edition, 1977).

'The Leadership of Babasaheb Ambedkar'. In B.N. Pandey (ed.). *Leadership in South Asia* (University of London symposium). New Delhi: Vikas, 1977. Translated into Marathi as 'Dr Ambedkarance Netrutva' by Vasant Moon. Pune: Sugawa Prakashan, 1986.

'The American Experience of Dr B.R. Ambedkar'. In R.D. Suman (ed.). *Dr Ambedkar: Pioneer of Human Rights*. New Delhi: Bodhisattva Publications, Ambedkar Institute of Buddhist Studies, 1977.

'Dalit: New Cultural Context of an Old Marathi Word'. In Clarence Maloney (ed.). *Language and Civilization Change in South Asia*. (*Contributions to Asian Studies*. vol. 11). Leiden: E.J. Brill, 1978. Reprinted in *Contemporary India* (Professor Sirsikar Felicitation Volume). Pune: Continental Prakashan, 1982.

'Introduction to Dalit Poems' (with Gail Omvedt). *Bulletin of Concerned Asian Scholars*. vol. 10, no. 3, 1978.

Maps and texts for the following plates in Joseph E. Schwartzberg (ed.). *A Historical Atlas of South Asia*. Chicago: University of Chicago Press, 1978: Revolt of 1857, Political Events of the Nationalist Period, the Indian National Congress, the Muslim League and other Political Parties, Fiction depicting South Asian Life, the Daily Press, Religious Revival and Reform, the Growth of Lahore and Calcutta.

'Religion and Legitimization in the Mahar Movement'. In Bardwell L. Smith (ed.). *Religion and Legitimization in South Asia*. Leiden: E.J. Brill, 1978.

'The Indian Rediscovery of Buddhism, 1855–1956'. In A.K. Narain (ed.). *Studies in Pali and Buddhism* (Jagdish Kashyap Memorial Volume). New Delhi: D.K. Publishers, 1978, 2006.

'Journals of Indian History for the Scholar, the Student and the Limited Library'. *South Asia Library Notes and Queries* (December 1978).

'Dalit Poetry'. *Illustrated Weekly*. vol. 100, no. 33, 1979.

'Tradition and Innovation in the Contemporary Buddhist Movement in India' (with Joanna Macy). In A.K. Narain (ed.). *Studies in the History of Buddhism*. Delhi: B.R. Publication Corporation, 1980.

'British Nostalgia: The Long Look Back at Empire' (annotated bibliography). *South Asia Library Notes and Queries* (March 1980).

'Chokhamela and Eknath: Two Bhakti Modes of Legitimacy for Modern Change'. *Journal of Asian and African Studies*. vol. 15, 1980. Reprinted in Jayant Lele (ed.). *Tradition and Modernity in Bhakti Movements*. Leiden: E.J. Brill, 1981. Reprinted in Aloka Parasher-Sen (ed.). *Subordinate and Marginal Groups in Early India*. New Delhi: Oxford University Press, 2004.

'An Historical View of the Maharashtrian Intellectual and Social Change'. In Yogendra K. Malik (ed.). *South Asian Intellectuals and Social Change: A Study of the Role of Vernacular-Speaking Intellectuals*. Columbia, Mo.: South Asia Books/New Delhi: Heritage Publishers, 1982.

'A Marathi Sampler: Varied Voices in Contemporary Marathi Short Stories and Poetry'. Eleanor Zelliot and Philip Engblom (eds). *Journal of South Asian Literature*. vol. 17, no.1, 1982.

'A Medieval Encounter between Hindu and Muslim: Eknath's Drama-poem *Hindu-turk samvad*'. In Fred Clothey (ed.). *Images of Man: Religion and Historical Process in South Asia*. Madras: New Era, 1982. Reprinted in Richard M. Eaton (ed.). *India's Islamic Traditions, 711– 1750*. New Delhi: Oxford University Press, 2003.

'Gupta History and Literature: A Bibliographic Essay'(with the assistance of Ann Whitfield). In Bardwell Smith (ed.). *Essays on Gupta Culture*. Delhi: Motilal Banarsidass, 1983.

'The World of Gundam Raul'. In Anne Feldhaus. *The Deeds of God in Ṛddhipur*. New York: Oxford University Press, 1984.

'Buddhist Sects in Contemporary India: Identity and Organization'. In Peter Gaeffke and David A. Utz (eds). *Identity and Division in Cults and Sects in South Asia*. Proceedings of the South Asia Seminar, University of Pennsylvania, I: 1980–1. Philadelphia: South Asia Regional Studies, 1984.

Translation of Vijay Tendulkar's *Ghashiram Kotwal*. Calcutta:

Seagull Books, 1984. (New York production by Pan Asian Repertory Theater, 1985.) Second edition 1999, reprinted 2002.

Consultant on Maharashtrian figure on the 'Peoples of South Asia' map. *National Geographic Magazine*. December 1984.

'The Buddhist Literature of Modern Maharashtra'. In Hugh van Skyhawk (ed.). *Minorities: On Themselves. South Asia Digest of Regional Writing*. vol. 11, 1985. Heidelberg: South Asia Institute, University of Heidelberg, 1986.

'The Political Thought of Dr B.R. Ambedkar'. In Thomas Pantham and Kenneth L. Deutsch (eds). *Contemporary Indian Political Thought*. Delhi: Sage Publications, 1986.

'Dr B.R. Ambedkar' and (with Anne Feldhaus) 'Marathi Religions'. In Mircea Eliade (ed.). *Encyclopedia of Religion*. New York: Macmillan, 1986. Newly edited version, in press.

'Eknath's Barude: The *Sant* as Link Between Cultures'. In Karine Schomer and W.H. McLeod (eds). *The Sants: Studies in a Devotional Tradition of India*. Berkeley: Religious Studies Series; Delhi: Motilal Banarsidass, 1987.

'Four Radical Saints of Maharashtra'. In Milton Israel and N. K. Wagle (eds). *Religion and Society in Maharashtra*. Toronto: Centre for South Asian Studies, University of Toronto, 1987.

Introduction to *Palkhi*, by D.B. Mokashi, translated by Philip Engblom. Albany: State University of New York Press, 1987. Reprinted by Orient Longman, Hyderabad, 1990.

'Untouchability'. In Ainslee Embree *et al.* (eds). *Encyclopedia of Asian History*. N.Y.: Charles Scribners Sons, 1988. Shorter entries: 'Dr B.R. Ambedkar', 'Poona Sarvajanik Sabha', 'Republican Party'.

Selections from the writings of Dr B.R. Ambedkar and comment for the revised edition of Stephen Hay (ed.). *Sources of Indian Tradition*. vol. II. *Modern India and Pakistan*. New York: Columbia University Press, 1988.

The Experience of Hinduism: Essays on Religion in Maharashtra. Eleanor Zelliot and Maxine Berntsen (eds). Albany: State University of New York Press, 1988. Reprint, Delhi: Sri Satguru Publications, 1992.

'Congress and the Untouchables'. In Stanley Wolpert and Richard Sisson (eds). *Congress and Indian Nationalism*. Berkeley: University of California Press, 1988.

'Dalit: New Perspectives on India's Untouchables'. In Philip Oldenburg (ed.). *India Briefing: 1991*. Boulder: Westview Press, 1991.

From Untouchable to Dalit: Essays on the Ambedkar Movement. New Delhi: Manohar, 1992. Second edition with new introduction, 1996. Reprinted 1998. Third edition 2001.

'Buddhist Women of the Contemporary Maharashtrian Conversion Movement'. In José Cabezón (ed.). *Buddhism, Sexuality and Gender*. Albany: State University of New York Press, 1992.

An Anthology of Dalit Literature (Poetry). Mulk Raj Anand and Eleanor Zelliot (eds). New Delhi: Gyan Publishing House, 1992.

'Mahar' and 'Chitpavan Brahman'. In Paul Hockings (ed.). *Encyclopedia of World Cultures*. vol. III (South Asia). Boston: G.K. Hall, 1992.

'Dr Ambedkar through Western Eyes'. In K.N. Kadam (ed.). *Dr B.R. Ambedkar: The Emancipator of the Oppressed*. Bombay: Popular Prakashan, 1993.

'New Voices of the Buddhists of India'. In A.K. Narain and D.C. Ahir (eds). *Dr Ambedkar, Buddhism and Social Change*. Delhi: B.R. Publishing Corporation, 1994.

'Daya Pawar's "The Buddha"'. Translated by Eleanor Zelliot. In *Oxford Anthology of Modern Indian Poetry*. New Delhi: Oxford University Press, 1994.

'Should We Study Caste in Order to Abolish it?'. In Sandeep Pendse (ed.). *Dalit Movement Today*. Bombay: Vikas Adhyayan Kendra, 1994.

'The Folklore of Pride: Three Components of Contemporary Dalit Belief'. In Gunther D. Sontheimer (ed.). *Folk Culture, Folk Religion and Oral Traditions as a Component in Maharashtrian Culture*. New Delhi: Manohar, 1995.

'Cokhamela: Piety and Protest'. In David Lorenzen (ed.). *Bhakti Religion in North India: Community, Identity and Political Action*. Albany: State University of New York Press, 1995.

'The Householder Saints of Maharashtra'. In Alan W. Entwistle, Carol Salomon *et al.* (eds). *Studies in Early Modern Indo-Aryan Languages, Literature and Culture*. New Delhi: Manohar, 1999.

'The Dalit Movement'. In John Webster (ed.). *Dalit International Newsletter*. vol. 1, no. 1, February 1996.

'Stri Dalit Sahitya: The New Voice of Women Poets'. In Anne Feldhaus (ed.). *Images of Women in Maharashtrian Literature and Religion*. Albany: State University of New York Press, 1996.

'The Poetry of Dalit Women'. In Saral K. Chatterji and Hunter P. Mabry (eds). *Culture, Religion and Society: Essays in Honour of*

Richard W. Taylor. Published for the Christian Institute for the Study of Religion and Society, Bangalore by ISPCK, Delhi, 1996.
    'A Bibliographic Essay on Women in Maharashtra'. In Anne Feldhaus (ed.). *Images of Women in Maharashtrian Society.* Albany: State University of New York Press, 1998.
    'Dalit Literature: Twenty-five years of Protest? of Progress?' (with Veena Deo). *Journal of South Asian Literature.* vol. 29, no. 2, 1994.
    'The Religious Imagination of Maharashtrian Women Bhaktas'. In Shrikant Paranjpe, Raja Dixit, and C.R. Das (eds). *Western India: History, Society and Culture.* (Dr Arvind Deshpande Felicitation Volume). Kolhapur: Itihas Shikshak Mahamandal, 1997.
    'Ovi' and 'Tamasha'. In Margaret A. Mills, Peter J. Claus, and Sarah Diamond (eds). *South Asian Folklore: An Encyclopedia.* New York/ London: Routledge, 2003.
    'Fifty Years of Dalit Politics'. In Yogendra Malik and Ashok Kapur (eds). *India: Fifty Years of Independence: Assessment and Prospects.* New Delhi: APH Publishing Corporation, 1998.
    'Bhimrao Ramji Ambedkar'. In Henry Scholberg (ed.). *The Biographical Dictionary of Greater India.* New Delhi: Promilla and Co., 1998.
    'Religious Leadership among Maharashtrian Buddhist Women'. In Ellison Banks Findly (ed.). *Women's Buddhism; Buddhism's Women.* Sumerville, MA: Wisdom Publications, 2000.
    'Ordination'(with Ingrid Klass) and 'Buddhism: Modern Movements'. In Serenity Young (ed.). *Encyclopedia of Women and World Religion,* New York: Macmillan Reference, 1998.
    'Roots of Dalit Consciousness'. In Harsh Sethi and Tejbir Singh (eds). *Seminar.* no. 471, November 1998.
    'Women in the Homes of the Saints'. In Irina Glushkova and Rajendra Vora (eds). *Home, Family and Kinship in Maharashtra.* New Delhi: Oxford University Press, 1999.
    'Dr Ambedkar Speaks to Government' and 'The American Experience of Dr B.R. Ambedkar'. In Verinder Grover (ed.). *Bhimrao Ramji Ambedkar: A Biography of His Vision and Ideas.* New Delhi: Deep and Deep, 1998.
    'New Books on Dalits'. *Dalit International Newsletter.* vol. 4, no. 2, June 1999; vol. 6, no. 2, June 2001; vol. 8, no. 2, June 2003; and vol. 10, no. 2, June 2005.

'The Untouchable Women Saint-poets of Maharashtra'. In Mariola Offredi (ed.). *The Banyan Tree: Essays on Early Literature in New Indo-Aryan Languages*. New Delhi: Manohar, 2000.

'Sant Sahitya and Dalit Movements'. In Meera Kosambi (ed.). *Intersections: Socio-cultural Trends in Maharashtra*. Hyderabad: Orient Longman, 2000.

'Women Saints in Medieval Maharashtra'. In Mandakranta Bose (ed.). *Faces of the Feminine in Ancient, Medieval, and Modern India*. New York: Oxford University Press, 2000.

'Dr Ambedkar and the Empowerment of Women'. In Anupama Rao (ed.). *Gender and Caste*. New Delhi: Kali for Women, 2004.

'B.R. Ambedkar and the Search for a Meaningful Buddhism'. In Surendra Jondhale and Johannes Beltz (eds). *Reconstructing the World: B.R. Ambedkar and Buddhism in India*. New Delhi: Oxford University Press, 2004.

'The Meaning of Ambedkar'. In Ghanshyam Shah (ed.). *Dalit Identity and Politics*. Delhi/Thousand Oaks: Sage, 2001.

'Experiments in Dalit Education (Pre-Independence)'. In S. Bhattacharya (ed.). *Education and the Disprivileged*. Hyderabad: Orient Longman, 2002.

'Dalit Tradition and Dalit Consciousness'. In Niraja Gopal Jayal and Sudha Pai (eds). *Democratic Government in India: Challenges of Poverty, Development and Identity*. New Delhi: Sage, 2001.

'Dalit Samaj' for *Shahar Pune: Ekā Sāmskritik Samchitācā Māgovā....*, Aroon Tikekar (ed.). vol. 1. Pune: Nilubhāū Limaye Foundation, 2000. In English: 'The History of Dalits in Pune'. *The Journal of the Asiatic Society of Bombay*. N.S. vol. 74, 1999.

'Untouchables, Purity and Pollution' for the Eighth International Conference on Maharashtra Studies, held in Sydney, Australia in 1999, to be edited by Jim Masselos.

'Introduction', 'Glossary', and 'Biographical Notes'. In Vasant Moon. *Growing up Untouchable in India: A Dalit Autobiography*, translated from the Marathi by Gail Omvedt. Lanham, Maryland: Rowman and Littlefield, 2001. New Delhi: Sage, 2002.

'Kipling's *Kim* in the Classroom'. In *Asianetwork Exchange*. vol. 8, no.1, Fall 2000.

'Self Critical Honesty: The Writing of Urmilla Pawar'. *Manushi*. no. 122 (January–February 2001). Introduction to *Chauti Bhint* ('The Fourth Wall') by Urmilla Pawar.

'Ahilyabai Holkar'. *Manushi*. no. 124.

'Dr Ambedkar and the Constitution'. *Journal of the Asiatic Society of Bombay*. vols 77, 78, 2002–3.

Translation (with Vimal Thorat) of 'Whirlwind' by Datta Bhagat, in G.P. Deshpande (ed.). *An Anthology of Modern Indian Drama*. New Delhi: Sahitya Akademi, 2000.

'Bombay/Mumbai and the Ambedkar Movement: Past and Present'. In Sujata Patel *et al.* (eds). *Thinking Social Science in India: Essays in Honour of Alice Thorner*. New Delhi: Sage, 2002.

'The Search for Cokhamela'. *The Dalit*. March–April 2002.

'Immortalizing Babasaheb' (an interview with Meena Kandasamy), *The Dalit*. May–June 2002.

Foreword and Comments for Detlef Kantowsky, *Buddhists in India Today*, translated from the German by Hans-Georg Tuerstig. New Delhi: Manohar, 2003.

Sant Cokhamela: Vividh Darshan, edited with V. L. Manjul. Pune: Sugawa Prakashan, 2002, including Marathi translations of three articles by Zelliot: 'Cokhamelayaca shodh', 'Cokhamela ani Eknath', and 'Soyrabai ani Nirmala'.

'Ashok Kelkar and Dalit Literature'. *The Bulletin of Deccan College Postgraduate and Research Institute*. vols 62 and 63 (2002 and 2003). Professor Ashok R. Kelkar Felicitation Volume (published in 2004).

'A Maharashtrian Buddhist Family: The Kambles of Pune'. In P. K. Roy (ed.). *Family Diversity in India: Patterns, Practices and Ethos*. New Delhi: Gyan Publishing House, 2003.

'Relating to the Voices of India's Untouchables'. *AsiaNetwork Exchange*. vol. 11, no. 3, Spring 2004.

'A Note on Bhakti Poetry'. In Molly Daniels-Ramanujan (ed.). *The Oxford India Ramanujan*. New Delhi: Oxford University Press, 2004.

'Caste in Contemporary India'. In Robin Rinehart (ed.). *Contemporary Hinduism: Ritual, Culture and Practice*. Oxford: ABC-CLIO, 2004.

'Untouchability'. In *New Dictionary of the History of Ideas*. New York: Charles Scribner's Sons, 2004.

'Bhimrao Ramji Ambedkar'. In *Oxford Dictionary of National Biography*. Oxford: Oxford University Press, 2004.

'Untouchables (Dalits)'. In *Encyclopedia of the Developing World*. Chicago: Fitzroy Dearborn Publishers, 2004.

Untouchable Saints: An Indian Phenomenon, edited with Rohini Mokashi-Punekar. New Delhi: Manohar, 2005.

Dr Babasaheb Ambedkar and the Untouchable Movement. New Delhi: Blumoon Books, 2004.

'Ambedkar Abroad'. Sixth Dr Ambedkar Memorial Annual Lecture. Jawaharlal Nehru University, New Delhi, 2004.

'The Importance of Ambedkar's World View to India's Social Progress'. Fourth Manchester Ambedkar Memorial Lecture, Manchester, UK, 10 October 2005.

'Dr Ambedkar's Path to Buddhism: A Marg to Navayana?' In M. Naito, I. Shima, and H. Kotani (eds). *Marga: Ways of Liberation, Empowerment and Social Change in Maharashtra*. New Delhi: Manohar, 2007.

'The Early Voices of Untouchables: The Bhakti Saints'. In Mikael Aktor and Robert Deliège (eds). *Untouchables—Scheduled Castes—Dalits: Identity and Power in Early and Modern Expressions of Untouchability in India* (E-book). Copenhagen: Museum Tusculanum Press, forthcoming.

'Dalit', in John H. Moore (ed.). *Encyclopedia of Race and Racism*. New York: Macmillan Reference USA, 2007.

'Understanding Dr B.R. Ambedkar'. *Religion Compass*. Online Resource from Blackwell Publishing, 2008.

'Dalit Literature'. In Braj Kachru and S.N. Sridhar (eds). *Language in South Asia*. Cambridge: Cambridge University Press, 2008.

CONTRIBUTORS

MANU BHAGAVAN is Assistant Professor in the Department of History at Hunter College-The City University of New York (CUNY).

JEFFREY M. BRACKETT is Assistant Professor of Religious Studies at Ball State University.

JANET M. DAVIS is Associate Professor of American Studies and History and Chair of the Department of American Studies at the University of Texas at Austin.

ANNE FELDHAUS is Foundation Professor of Religious Studies at Arizona State University.

ANN GRODZINS GOLD is Professor of Religion and Anthropology at Syracuse University.

GOPAL GURU is Professor at the Centre for Political Studies, School of Social Sciences at Jawaharlal Nehru University.

SYED AKBAR HYDER is Associate Professor of Asian Studies and Chair of Islamic Studies at the University of Texas at Austin.

LAURA DUDLEY JENKINS is Associate Professor of Political Science at the University of Cincinnati.

GAIL MINAULT is Professor of History at the University of Texas at Austin.

CHRISTIAN LEE NOVETZKE is Assistant Professor in the South Asia Program and Comparative Religion Program in the Jackson School of International Studies at the University of Washington.

GAIL OMVEDT has been a Senior Fellow at the Nehru Memorial Museum and Library in New Delhi, and is currently Visiting Professor at the School of Social Justice, University of Pune.

PAULA RICHMAN, William H. Danforth Professor of South Asian Religions at Oberlin College.

GARY MICHAEL TARTAKOV is Professor Emeritus of Art and Design History at Iowa State University.

GUY WELBON is Associate Professor of Religious Studies and South Asia Studies and Chairman of the Graduate Group in Religious Studies at the University of Pennsylvania.

DONNA M. WULFF is Associate Professor of Religious Studies at Brown University.

MICHAEL YOUNGBLOOD is a cultural anthropologist based in New York.